Dear Reader:

The book you are about to read is the latest bestseller from the St. Martin's True Crime Library, the imprint the *New York Times* calls "the leader in true crime!" Each month, we offer you a fascinating account of the latest, most sensational crime that has captured national attention. St. Martin's is the publisher of perennial best-selling true crime author Jack Olsen, whose SALT OF THE EARTH is the true story of one woman's triumph over life-shattering violence; Joseph Wambaugh called it "powerful and absorbing." Fannie Weinstein and Melinda Wilson tell the story of a beautiful honors student who was lured into the dark world of sex for hire in THE COED CALL GIRL MURDER. St. Martin's is also proud to publish critically acclaimed author Carlton Stowers, whose Edgar Award-winning TO THE LAST BREATH recounts a two-year-old girl's mysterious death and the dogged investigation that led loved ones to the most unlikely murderer: her own father. In the book you now hold, TO DIE FOR, Kathy Braidhill examines the criminal career of a rare kind of murderer—a female serial killer who used extreme violence to subdue her victims.

St. Martin's True Crime Library gives you the stories *behind* the headlines. Our authors take you right to the scene of the crime and into the minds of the most notorious murderers to show you what really makes them tick. St. Martin's True Crime Library paperbacks are better than the most terrifying thriller, because it's all true! The next time you want a crackling good read, make sure it's got the St. Martin's True Crime Library logo on the spine—you'll be up all night!

Charles E. Spicer, Jr.
Executive Editor, St. Martin's True Crime Library

WHAT DANA DID . . .

- June Roberts, 66, was strapped to a chair in her home, strangled with a telephone cord, and bludgeoned in the face with a wine bottle. As Dana Sue Gray went about her business, her boyfriend's five-year-old son waited in the front seat of her Cadillac parked out front.

- Dorinda Hawkins, 57, was strangled and left for dead in the antique store where she worked—but Hawkins survived to tell of her blonde, female attacker. According to Dana Sue Gray, Hawkins was being condescending to her. Said Gray, "I felt sick to my stomach. I wanted to vomit. I wanted her to die."

- Eighty-seven-year-old Dora Beebe opened her door to a stranger asking for directions. That stranger was Dana Sue Gray, who proceeded to strangle her with a phone cord and bash her so hard with an iron that it dented. Gray claimed to have been angered when Beebe opened her door and allegedly complained, "I don't have time for this."

TO DIE FOR

Kathy Braidhill

St. Martin's Paperbacks

TO DIE FOR

Copyright © 2000 by Kathy Braidhill.

Cover photograph © Marcos Lujam.

ISBN: 0-312-97416-7

Printed in the United States of America

St. Martin's Paperbacks edition / September 2000

10 9 8 7 6 5 4

This book is dedicated to my mother.

ACKNOWLEDGMENTS

I would like to wholeheartedly thank the men and women of the Riverside County Sheriff's Department, District Attorney's Office and state Department of Justice who investigate, track and try perpetrators of horrifyingly senseless murders. I thank Riverside County Sheriff's Department Det. Joe Greco for his investigative skills and soul-searching candor in putting a human face on the daunting prospect of finding a most unusual serial killer; former Riverside County Sheriff's Department Det. Chris Antoniadas for his selfless dedication to police work, his impressive investigative expertise and true grit; Riverside County Deputy District Attorney Rich Bentley for his lawyerly expertise; Riverside County Sheriff's Department Inv. Andre O'Harra for his expertise on jail life. I also thank Riverside County Sheriff's Department Det. James McElvain, Det. Rene Rodriguez and Officer Wyatt McElvain for their hard work. I would like to express my undying appreciation for Riverside County District Attorney Inv. George Hudson for his assistance and support on this project. I thank criminalists Marianne Stam, Ric Cooksie and photographer Jim Potts.

I thank and appreciate my "6 a.m. Happy Hour" workout buddies for keeping our souls and spirits balanced and our heart rates soaring; my West Coast Swing dance buddies for understanding when I disappeared during the last months' final push; ballet teachers Gilma Bustillo, Charles and Phillip Fuller of Le Studio for their kind and thoughtful guidance; and ballet instructor Joseph Nugent of the Pasadena Dance Academy and Theater, for his unique blend of humor and barre work.

Most of all, I thank my friends and family for their moral support and loving enthusiasm.

ACKNOWLEDGMENTS

AUTHOR'S NOTE

To Die For is a work of nonfiction. The events depicted in this book are true. Much of the dialogue has been reconstructed from personal interviews, police records, and courts documents. Additionally, some scenes have been dramatically recreated in order to portray most effectively the personalities of the individuals involved in this story and the atmosphere surrounding the events depicted in this book. The names of the following individuals are pseudonyms: Tom, Darlene, Joanie Fulton, Jason Wilkins, Jim Wilkins, Kellie Jacobs, Jean Smothers, Charles Van Owen, Linda Dorsey, Julie Bennett, Lisa Thompkins, Laureen Johanson, Sharon Callendar, Rhonda, Carrie Ann, Michael Carpenter, Yvonne, Rob Beaudry, Chris Dodson, Evan Campbell, Cindy Anderson and Marion Snyder.

TO DIE FOR

PROLOGUE

Dana Sue Gray is a rarity, even among the small sorority of female serial killers dwarfed by dime-a-dozen male serial killers. There are 36 documented female serial killers whose murderous careers spanned the late 19th and 20th centuries. A serial killer is defined by the FBI as one who commits a murder in one location followed by a period of time where they live a relatively normal life without criminal activity, followed by another murder in another location and another crime-free period. This kind of killer is distinguishable from from someone who commits multiple murder or mass murder in a single event or in a killing spree, which include multiple incidents over a more compressed period of time.

Female serial killers typically kill their partners, children, or people under their care, and the overwhelming majority do so at a distance, with poison or guns. Dana is highly unusual by her choice of victim and the gruesomely intimate *in-your-face* method of ending their lives by using her hands and a phone cord to strangle, then a handy tool to bludgeon. There are only two known serial killers who chose strangulation as a primary means to dispatch their victims: one of them killed her own children for profit, and the other killed other people's children. According to *Murder Most Rare* (Kelleher), there are no known cases in which a woman strangled her victims both with a ligature and manually, then finished them off by bludgeoning.

The other unique aspect of Gray's crimes is her choice of victims. Kelleher categorized serial killers by motive, such as black widows, killers who murder for profit, angels of death and those who are clearly mentally disturbed. Women overwhelmingly kill their husbands or boyfriends, their children, other people's children or people for whom they are caring. Once they have a pattern, or a modus operandi, they don't typically digress. There are no other known young serial killers who target elderly women. In the lexicon of serial murder, Dana was a switch-hitter. Two of her victims were those with whom she had a remote family bond, and the other two were complete strangers.

What makes Dana rare is her method of killing—using far more force than was necessary to end the lives of frail and elderly victims in two cases, and a woman 30 years older than her in another. Dr. Patricia Kirby, a psychologist, once a homicide detective for the Baltimore police and a former FBI profiler, said that if Dana truly wanted credit cards, she would have found a way to obtain them without harming anyone. Kirby suggests that it was the act of killing and, in particular, the act of struggling with her victims that was her goal. Dana sought lethal excitement much the same way she sought excitement by leaping out of airplanes, wind-surfing and other thrill sports. Lunch, beauty-shop pampering and shopping afterward was the celebration of the kill.

Given the extreme violence that Dana exhibited in murdering her victims, Kirby and others have wondered when Dana's killing spree truly began and question the relationship of the loss of her nursing job with the start of her killing spree. Hospital authorities for each of the institutions that employed Dana insist there were no "unusual" deaths during the time that Dana was employed there.

CHAPTER ONE

WEDNESDAY, FEBRUARY 16, 1994, 9 A.M.

The phone was ringing. No one knew Norma was dead. But there she sat, upright in her comfy gold armchair for two days, an oversized, wood-handled utility knife buried to the hilt in her neck, the matching fillet knife in her chest. Other than one broken, pearly pink fingernail on her right hand, gracefully draped over the arm rest, she bore no other marks. Norma Davis, in a fleeting glance, looked no more sinister than an 86-year-old heart patient napping in front of the television, head sagging to one side, with a brown, fringed afghan covering the flowered-print blue slipper she wore on her foot. The coagulated pool of blood had seeped up around the wounds, darkening the animal designs on her black sweater.

It was obvious that Norma had been murdered in her chair, her roost, the place she curled up to watch TV, read her beloved books, knit, open mail and perhaps entertain visitors, including her last. The nubby gold armchair holding Norma's body belonged to a matching set of two, both of which sat in the second-floor den of her condo. The chairs faced a wood console-style TV set that she'd decorated with family photos and ceramic animal figures. A bag of golf clubs was propped against the TV. Both chairs backed up to the wrought-iron railing overlooking the first floor. Surrounding the chair, and on the dark, Mediterranean-style, carved-wood side table, were all the necessities for someone who, once they settled into their favorite chair, didn't want to be bothered getting up again: the TV remote-control, a small flashlight, two needlework bags, a romance novel and reading glasses, a pink pitcher and glass, a blue plastic pill-box, a fabric-and-lace photo album and a small fencing-style letter opener. On the other side of her chair was a wastebasket. The discarded mail was dotted with blood.

The phone had gone silent. There was a tentative tapping at the front door. Unlocked, it swung open.

"Norma?"

It was 9:15 a.m. Alice Williams knew Norma was usually up by 6. She'd tried calling twice yesterday and once this morning. When there was no answer, she thought she'd come by and check on her. They were both 86 and had been like sisters ever since Norma moved to Canyon Lake five years ago. It was time for a trip to the beauty salon and they usually went together. It was Norma's habit to leave the front door open when she was expecting someone. Since she was hard of hearing, Alice yelled as loud as she could.

"Norma!"

Alice's voice wasn't as strong as it used to be. But something was wrong. Norma usually had the television turned up to an ear-splitting pitch. It was silent. Maybe she had gone out. Norma had been so excited last week because she had passed her driver's test. She hated being confined to the house.

"Norma!"

Alice slowly made her way through the spotless living room and into the gleaming kitchen. Everything looked orderly. No, Norma hadn't gone out. Her brown patchwork purse was in its usual place by the refrigerator. Alice looked at the plastic seven-day pillbox on the counter, but nothing registered. She peeked into the downstairs den, where the mirrored bar showcased gleaming glasses and an array of golf trophies. As she made her way into Norma's bedroom, Alice's mind raced to the last time she had seen Norma. It was Monday, Valentine's Day. That was just two days ago. They had gone to the bank to cash Norma's Medicare check. She got $148 in cash. Then Alice drove her to the hardware store, where Norma had two keys made. They made their round of errands early in the day, as usual. She dropped Norma off by about 11 a.m. Had Norma been expecting a visitor? She couldn't remember.

Norma's bed was unmade, a closet door stood open and a pile of purses rested on the floor. On the chair was an open, empty vanity case, its mirrored lid agape. In one of the guest rooms, a drawer in the otherwise empty chest stood open.

Norma was not downstairs. Alice was getting worried. Going up stairs was hard at her age. She pursed her lips, grabbed the handrail and steadily put one foot in front of the other. At the landing, she paused and leaned against a white-upholstered chair. She did not see the smear of blood on the seat. She continued up the stairs. A few feet from the top, Alice looked left into the second-floor den and her gaze rested on her best friend's body in the chair. She tried to scream, but could only gasp as her knees started to buckle.

No matter where you live in Canyon Lake, it's a nice, easy walk to either the golf course or the dock. But most residents of the private community just drive their golf carts. The massive development, ringed by 12-foot wall, and with 24-hour security posted at its three gates, was constructed around a meandering golf course and a man-made lake resembling a runny inkblot with dozens of fjords carved from the desert to give every homeowner a cul-de-sac *and* their choice of fronting either the lake or a chunk of the golf course. An equine wing of the development rambled along some low hills on its westernmost edge. A scattering of larger homes, tucked into the foothills off the main drive, would fetch upwards of a million dollars. Unlike most planned developments, where the only picturesque scenery exists in the minds of the builders who christen the streets, Canyon Lake supplied more than a vicarious whiff of boating, golf and horseback riding. The recreation-friendly scheme furnished planners with an abundant argot from which to choose street names and enhance the cheerful, theme-park feel of the development. Even the more moderately priced homes accessible from the main street boasted driveways brimming with boats, fully equipped RVs, tasteful off-road vehicles, sport utility vehicles and luxury cars.

Although residents were a mix of retirees, empty-nesters on the brink of retirement, and some young families, the most mature residents were the most visible. On streets pleasantly named Big Tee, Skipper's Way, Early Round

Drive and Silver Saddle Court, white-haired women in helmeted coifs piloted late-model Cadillacs and Buicks, outnumbered only by deeply tanned, knobby-kneed men in shorts and caps scooting around in golf carts. This secure community, in the desert heat of California's Riverside County, gave upscale retirees the comfort of enjoying their sunset years in leisure.

Outside the gates of the resort community, life fell short of exquisite. But on a modest income, a good life in Riverside County could be had cheaply. Seventy-five miles from the greater Los Angeles basin, the area featured bargain real estate and a remote desert landscape that was linked to the city by Southern California's veinous freeway system. For the price of a hellish commute, families with entry-level incomes could afford comfortable homes. A latter-day gold rush in constructional had created boom towns out of sparsely populated patches, strung together by highways that sliced through miles of desert brush, spectacular spires of yucca blossoms, and sage. Huge developments sprung up from the hardscrabble desert floor, peppering the landscape with lookalike homes that queued up along preternaturally smooth blacktopped streets and displayed "Model House" banners. Strip malls, chain discount stores and fast-food joints galloped right behind the residential developers to service new homeowners. Homely towns anchored by dusty trailer parks, which never caught the eye of developers, slouched in the shadow of the gleaming new developments, their deeply rutted dirt roads—without street lights, curbs or even signs—leading to run-down grocery stores and well-used bars.

The unending parade of construction made the Inland Empire, which encompasses Riverside and neighboring San Bernardino Counties, among the fastest-growing regions in the country. But the influx of ex-suburbanites seeking mortgage relief upset the eco-system of native desert-dwellers—bikers, the poor, naturalists, retirees and criminals. To the FBI and the DEA, the Inland Empire houses the most active and dangerous of the nation's manufacturers and distributors of methamphetamine, a powerful, illegal stimulant that rivals cocaine in popularity. The desert's seclusion offered lawbreakers a unique opportunity to establish an underground industry of meth labs, whose distinctive chemical odor make them easy to sniff out in heavily populated areas. Along with the meth labs came a supporting cast of unsavory types that Canyon Lake builders had in mind when they put a wall around the private, monitored and guarded enclave.

11:45 A.M.

Inside job.

The minute he saw the gates to the private community, Deputy District Attorney Richard Bentley figured the killer knew how to get inside this place. Bentley paused his county cruiser at the guard shack long enough to flash his badge and get waved through. At 47, the ex-schoolteacher had a thick wave of strawberry blonde hair and a gap-toothed smile that gave him a boyish look. Bentley drove slowly through the development looking for the address on Continental Way.

Canyon Lake. He'd heard of it, but had never been inside. He knew it was an upscale neighborhood of mostly elderly residents. Not uber-rich, just a nice part of the world next to some not-so-nice areas. It made sense that they'd want gates around it. He assumed the other two entrances also had gates and 24-hour guards.

Turning the corner, he saw the familiar yellow tape and a clump of black-and-whites. A team of criminalists in a Department of Justice van pulled up as he parked. Bentley recognized Ricci Cooksey, a senior criminalist, as he hopped out and removed his field kit from the van, his ever-present flashlight crooked under his arm, but he didn't recognize the woman with Cooksey. The Riverside County ID techs had also just arrived in a county truck. The coroner's van was already there. Not the meat truck, which would come later, but the tech van. Inside the yellow tape was a tiny white-haired woman, her head bowed, being comforted by friends. That must be either a relative or the person who found the body, Bentley thought. He didn't see any gawking neighbors standing in clusters, the way they did at most scenes, just some gardeners working across the street, occasionally glancing at the police activity. Bentley caught up with Cook-sey, who introduced his trainee.

"What have we got?" Cooksey said by way of greeting.

"Elderly woman stabbed upstairs," said Bentley.

Cooksey nodded. The big brown condo was one of 19 two-story look-a-likes dotting a horseshoe-shaped driveway off Continental Way. The backyards on this end of the drive sloped downward to a stretch of private lakefront called "Indian Beach." Even on a weekday morning, a few people were out in their boats.

Bentley started to see faces as he got closer to the condo. From his stint at the Perris branch of the DA's office, he recognized Detective Joe Greco of the Perris Police Department, talking with the two officers who had arrived first at the scene. Greco looked worried. Heck, Bentley thought, for a homicide detective, he looked *young*. With his slight frame and dark, wavy hair, Greco could easily pass for a college student, almost for a high school student. He tried to look older by wearing a moustache, but he could barely coax a few hairs to grow there. Bentley had been told that Greco had a wife and at least two kids, with another one on the way.

Bentley knew Greco was waiting for him to arrive. The detective couldn't have handled many, if any, homicides. But requesting another detective was futile—there were no veteran homicide detectives with Perris P.D. At 25,000 people, Perris was barely large enough to have its own police force. It had only been a few months since Perris P.D. took over the contract for police services at Canyon Lake, handling its major crimes and leaving routine patrol duties to its private security force. The district attorney's office had its lawyers make suggestions and answer questions for the investigating officer at any homicide. Bentley, who had worked at the Perris sub-station, knew Greco as a solid detective and tried to put him at ease with some gallows humor.

"Hey, I had plans this afternoon," Bentley said, walking up to Greco. "You guys are messing up my day."

Greco greeted Bentley with a handshake and a nervous smile, then told him what he'd seen inside. Within a few minutes, the ID techs, the criminalists, the deputy coroners, the officers, and the sergeant formed a loose huddle around the postage stamp–sized front yard for the briefing. Officer Lance Noggle, the first officer at the scene, ran down the facts in official jargon. Greco added a few details and Bentley asked some questions.

"O.K., let's go in and take a look," Greco said. Like a herd, the group followed Greco and Cooksey toward the condo. Hanging plants in a tasseled, macrame holder decorated the small front porch. From outside the front door, one could see the dining room and kitchen straight ahead. The stairs were·to the left.

"Wait!"

It was Cooksey. The processional stopped. From the porch, he reached around with a latex-gloved hand and flicked off the interior light switch, darkening the entryway. Taking his flashlight out from under his arm, he bent down by the front door and shined the beam at the parquet floor in the entryway, a nice oak plank, and focused the beam at an angle. When Greco bent down, he saw what Cooksey was looking at in the beam of the flashlight.

"It's a Nike," Cooksey said, recognizing the distinct trademarked swoosh on the sole. It was as if someone had sprinkled dust in a perfectly stenciled sole of an athletic shoe. The shoe print was aimed at the kitchen.

Cooksey knew that anyone who walked into that house would have had to step in that entryway. It had just been a hunch. He'd been to enough crime scenes to know that there was always a rush to get to the body. Not today.

Everyone backed out of the entryway. Cooksey walked back to the DOJ van and dug out a stack of chemically treated paper sheets and something that looked like a foot-square sponge to take shoe impressions. One by one, the officers, the sergeant supervisor and Greco—everyone who'd been inside the condo—stepped on the chemical sponge and stepped on the paper, making a shoe impression to show what he already knew would result. No swoosh.

As Cooksey was busy with the shoe impressions, the county crime lab techs set up a tripod directly over the print and aimed the camera lens downward toward the print. They adjusted the settings to take true-to-life prints that forensic shoe print experts could use to compare prints at the crime

scene with those made by a suspect's shoes. Cooksey returned to his van to get what looked like a thin sheet of firm
Jell-O suspended in plastic. When the crime techs were done
taking photos, Cooksey peeled off one layer of the plastic
wrap and unfurled the gelatin directly onto the print with
rhythmic strokes using a fingerprint roller. Then he gently
pulled the gelatin sheet from the floor and saw an eerie
shadow of dust clinging to it—deposited, perhaps, by a
killer.

"There are some people here to see you."
    The officer nodded toward an older couple casually
dressed in jeans and sneakers standing outside the yellow
tape.
    "The victim's family," he said.
    "Thanks," Greco said, making his way toward the couple.
"Go get Bentley."
    After the walk-through, everyone had been standing
around outside the condo waiting for the crime-scene techs
and Department of Justice criminalists to mark, photograph
and collect the evidence, or anything Greco and Bentley
thought might be evidence. The condo resembled a macabre
tag sale. Numbered, goldenrod-colored evidence cards were
propped up next to the blood-smeared chair on the landing,
the ripped-out phone cord, the half-empty knife holder in
the kitchen, Norma's pillboxes, her purse and the blood-
stained afghan crumpled at her feet. On the walk-through,
Greco and Bentley had reviewed with the criminalists and
lab techs what to photograph and what to collect. Greco took
photos with his own camera and wrote meticulously detailed
notes. He took the time to write neatly—there was no rush
and he wanted to be able to read his notes in the morning.
When one of the patrol officers offered Greco the use of his
own video camera, Greco borrowed it to film the crime
scene.
    Bentley walked slowly around the outside of the condo,
tossing out the usual areas for the officers to cover—he suggested they door-knock the neighborhood to ask about unusual incidents or cars, and if residents knew anyone who
had been upset or angry with Norma. An earlier check by
officers inside and outside the condo had revealed that there

were no obvious footprints in the mud outside the windows or doors, no trampled shrubs, no broken windows, no tamper marks in the doorjambs—no forced entry. Bentley had wanted to see the property for himself. If this case ever came to trial, he preferred using photos to refresh his memory, not supplant it. When the techs and criminalists had everything photographed, tagged and bagged, Greco and Bentley would go back in to examine the body in detail and to collect additional evidence, with the assistance of the coroner's investigator, who would prepare the remains for transport to the autopsy.

Greco stepped under the crime-scene tape, walked over to the couple, introduced himself and expressed his condolences. When Bentley arrived a moment later, he did the same. Jeri and Russell Armbrust said they lived nearby in Canyon Lake and had driven up to find out what had happened, and to see if they could help. Bentley suggested they speak in the couple's car, since it was chilly and had just started to sprinkle. The Armbrusts took them to their white Cadillac, parked at the curb, which would also offer some privacy.

As Greco and Bentley climbed into the back seat, both spotted Jeri Armbrust's white sneakers—Nike—and exchanged glances.

Neither Bentley nor Greco told them any details about the murder except to say that it was "pretty bad." Questions came from both the front and back seats. Who found her? Was it a burglar? The detective and the DA wanted to know when they had last seen Norma and whether she would let a stranger into the house.

Jeri was the closest to Norma and did most of the talking. She wept some, but remained calm, unlike some of the hysterical victims both Greco and Bentley had seen at crime scenes over the years.

Jeri was Norma's ex–daughter-in-law and had stepped up to take care of Norma in her later years, even though they were not blood relatives. Norma had suffered from several serious health problems and was recovering from triple-bypass surgery last fall. Up until a few weeks earlier, two registered nurses had taken turns with in-home check-ups during her recuperation. Jeri said the last time she had come over was at 6 p.m. on Sunday to drop off groceries. She'd put the groceries away and left, assuming Norma was upstairs watching TV—the volume had been up full blast, as usual, because Norma was hard of hearing. Jeri said the TV was so loud, she couldn't wait to get out of the house.

Bentley asked about Norma's typical routine. Jeri said if she wasn't somewhere with her best friend Alice, she usually stayed home and watched TV. If she was not going out, she wore a nightgown. Sometimes she would throw a blanket over her legs if it got cold, and she often fell asleep in her recliner. If she was going out or had just come back, she'd be in street clothes. Jeri said that Norma always wore slippers, even if she went out, but she never went out at night. If she was expecting a visitor, Norma would leave the front door unlocked because it was hard for her to get around. Otherwise, it was always locked.

And there was something else—Jeri said she'd left Norma's Medicare check on the kitchen counter. Had they seen it? Both Greco and Bentley said they had not seen it, but they would take note of it.

In the most diplomatic of terms, Bentley asked them to start thinking about someone in the family. Was there someone they knew who could have done something like this? This provoked quite a reaction from Jeri, a cross between shock and indignation.

"Absolutely not!" she said. "I know my family!"

Bentley said he didn't intend to offend them, but that the perpetrators in these types of cases usually come from within. There was no sign of forced entry and a frail, elderly woman was unlikely to have a high-risk lifestyle. Jeri and Russ said there had been a family fuss a few months ago over a grandson who had borrowed Norma's car and abandoned it in another city. It ruffled a few feathers because someone else had to retrieve the car. Bentley and Greco said they would check it out, but thought that it did not sound like something that would result in a murder, particularly one this gruesome.

The DA and the detective expressed their condolences again, said good-bye to the Armbrusts and ducked back under the crime-scene tape surrounding Norma's condo. Working a homicide usually means a lot of standing around waiting for the criminalists, the photographer and the coroner to do their jobs so you can do yours. That's where cops toss around their ideas about how they think the crime unfolded. It is sort of like playing the old board game "Clue." It was Colonel Mustard in the den with the knife. No, another detective says, you're forgetting this clue. It was Mrs. White in the kitchen with the candlestick. Everyone pitches their theories, partly to pass the time, partly to help solve the crime and partly as a catharsis to make sense of it all.

Bentley thought that it was obviously an inside job. Someone had to know how to get in and out of this place, past the guards and the security. Greco was an Air Force brat. He used to sneak in and out of military complexes all the time as a kid and never got caught. But he didn't say anything to Bentley. Who was he to disagree with an experienced DA?

What stuck with Greco was Jeri. Why was she still taking care of the old woman? Neither she nor Russ were even related to Norma. Jeri's marriage to Norma's son had ended many years ago, she'd said. Were they financially benefitting from taking care of her? Would they benefit if she were to die? And why did Jeri waltz in with groceries, plunk them into the fridge and leave without popping her head in the door? Pretty odd behavior for a caretaker. And their demeanor was very calm, almost icy. There seemed to be little feeling behind the tears.

Greco was excited. He might have a suspect.

The criminalists were bringing the evidence out of the condo in brown paper bags. Like a scavenger hunt, where ordinary household objects achieve inflated importance during a fevered search, so goes the criminalist's quest for evidence. In death, the tiniest scrap—a thread, a blood smear, a hair—can solve a case if it tethers a killer to the crime. The criminalists bagged the obvious items: the trash basket containing blood-spotted mail, Norma's pillboxes, the afghan and her purse, along with some hair strands found near the kitchen sink and hanks of carpet and patches from a throw rug. Evidence item number one, of course, was the shoe print. The bags were placed in the trunk of Greco's car. He would book the bags into evidence when he returned to the station later that night. As they went through the house collecting evidence, the techs dusted for prints, but didn't find any suitable for comparison.

After waiting for hours outside, Greco, Bentley and Deputy Coroner Jim Camp re-entered the condo and headed for the upstairs den. The afghan had been removed from around Norma's feet, exposing her light blue house slippers and extremely swollen ankles, a poignant contrast to the relative youth and strength of the killer, assuming he wore Nikes. Cooksey and his assistant were taking tape lifts from Norma's clothing, just like using scotch tape to pull lint and hair from clothing. Greco had never seen a tape lift and watched for a moment as the criminalist expertly swept the tape over Norma's clothing, stuck the tape to labeled evidence cards, then sealed them together in a clear plastic bag before moving to the next item of clothing. When they were done with the clothing, Cooksey took a small tool, similar to what manicurists use, and thoroughly scraped underneath Norma's fingernails, just in case she tried fighting her assailant and inadvertently collected some DNA by scratching him. He also clipped her nails extremely close. The nail scrapings and clippings were bagged and labeled.

As they worked, Greco glanced around the condo thinking how clean and tidy it was. It was well organized, pleasant. There was no doubt that an older person lived there. The towels in the bathroom were hung right where they should have been. The beds in the guest room were made. This could be my grandmother's house, he thought.

His eyes came to rest on the phone cord that had been ripped from the wall. There was no jack in the study area where Norma must have spent most of her time; an extra-long phone cord had been strung from a bedroom down the hall to reach her recliner. He saw the cord, but no phone.

Greco wondered why the killer had used two knives. Downstairs in the kitchen, the paring knife from the same set was sitting on the kitchen counter, as if pulled from the butcher's block and left there because it was too small. Did the killer stab her in the chest, then go back downstairs, leaving the blood swipe on the chair on the landing, pick up the second knife and finish her off with the neck wound? He doubted that the killer had brought both knives upstairs at the same time. Norma was probably still breathing, he thought, and the assailant returned to the kitchen for the second knife.

When the criminalists were finished, they stayed so that they could do tape lifts on Norma's clothing after she was rolled out of her chair. Deputy Coroner Camp donned latex gloves and moved closer to Norma's body to get a good look at the wounds. Greco, Bentley, the supervising sergeant and the two criminalists formed a solemn half-circle around the bloodied figure in the recliner. Greco stepped next to Camp and caught the faint but unmistakable smell of death. Camp, looking closer at the body, said that it looked as if there might be more than one chest wound. The others were hidden by Norma's black sweater. There was a solemn, collective nod.

Greco had already told Camp that he wanted him to remove both knives there instead of waiting for the autopsy, so he could get them checked for fingerprints as soon as possible. Camp wrapped his gloved hands around the far edge of the wood-handled fillet knife embedded in Norma's chest and gently tugged. It was stuck. He grasped harder, pushing his fingers into the knife to form a vise grip and tried to wiggle it slightly, then tried pulling it again. It gave. With slow, back-and-forth sawing motions, he finally worked the knife out of her chest and gave it to Cooksey's assistant to mark and place into an evidence bag. He turned his attention to the other knife. At closer look, Greco could see the tip of the knife blade jutting out on the other side of Norma's neck. It slid out easily.

Just then, Norma's head flopped forward as if the knife blade had been the only thing supporting it. Everyone froze. Camp jerked his head to look at the body. Like a surgeon handing an instrument to a nurse, Camp handed the bloody knife to the assistant, then gently placed his gloved hands on Norma's forehead. With everyone's eyes on Norma, Camp slowly pulled her head back to expose the neck wound. There was a quiet gasp as her chin seemed to lift forever skyward, unhinged from the rest of the body, exposing the deep chasm of the throat almost to the bone.

"Whoever did this almost cut her head off," Camp said quietly.

Staring in horror, Greco felt his stomach turn in shock. It looked like the only thing holding her head on was some bone and a flap of skin at the back of the neck. He couldn't believe it. Why would someone do this to an 86-year-old woman? Around him, faces were grim with disgust.

To break the mood, someone began another "Clue" discussion, this time related to the sequence of the wounds. It didn't last long. The consensus was that the attacker had first stabbed Norma in the chest, and the neck wound was the final, fatal injury. Greco offered his thoughts about the killer leaving the bloody smear on the chair on the way downstairs to retrieve the second knife.

But there was something else.

Greco had been standing close to Camp, who was awkwardly standing slightly to the left of Norma's chair in order to retrieve the knives. Greco doubted if the killer had cramped up against the railing to perform the killing. The knife had been embedded on the right side of Norma's neck at a distinct upward tilt. If the killer had been facing Norma in her chair, the knife wound would have been on the killer's left side.

Just perhaps, Greco thought, the killer was left-handed.

Two days earlier, Joanie Fulton looked at the blonde figure asleep on her couch. It looked like she was having a bad nightmare, murmuring and crying out. Dana had been drinking straight vodka since she came over that night. She'd even brought her own bottle, Smirnoff, her favorite brand. Ever since Dana lost her job, she'd been pretty much on edge, but Joanie had tried to be supportive. Joanie tried to shake her out of the nightmare and get her to go home; Joanie and her family were going to bed. Dana didn't stir. Dead drunk. Joanie covered her with a blanket, tossed the empty vodka bottle in the trash and went to bed.

Hours later, Dana stirred and winced when she looked at the clock. She swung her legs over the couch and sat up, her head reeling. She ran her hand through her chin-length blonde hair and sat for a moment until her eyes adjusted to the dark. She got up on wobbly legs and scanned the living room for Joanie's purse. Not there. She looked in the kitchen and found it on the counter. Dana dug out Joanie's wallet, slipped out a $20 bill, left quietly out the front door and drove away.

CHAPTER TWO

Who would kill this old woman? What kind of a person would savagely slice through her neck? Greco winced at his recollection of the nauseating image from the day before as he sipped stationhouse grind out of a Styrofoam cup. He stared at the neatly printed handwriting in his notebook, his mind racing. Here's this quiet, rich community and a nice, elderly lady attacked in her own home—no sign of a break-in—with her neck nearly sawed off. Her purse had $170 in cash, plus a lucky hundred-dollar bill from one of her sons that she always carried. It looked like a few drawers had been pulled out, but the apartment wasn't ransacked. The killer had ignored the nice-looking ring on the victim's finger.

None of it made sense. How was he going to pull it all together? Greco knew there was bound to be publicity and tremendous pressure to solve the case, given the clout from the wealthy, elderly residents who comprised the majority of Canyon Lake. Anything he did would be scrutinized. Particularly if he screwed up.

Last night he had returned to the station with the evidence in his trunk, booked it, and gone home exhausted. His wife was sympathetic. But he lay in bed unable to sleep, partly out of shock over seeing the violent crime scene and partly out of worry. He desperately wanted to solve this case. He'd just turned 28; this was his second homicide.

Greco had never wanted to be a cop. His dream was to be a lawyer. He'd met Darlene when both of them were working as cashiers at a drug store. She was 18, he was 21. That was December. By July, they were married and expecting their first child. Greco needed a steady job to support his new family and he thought about being a cop. No one he knew was in law enforcement, but he liked the way Hollywood movies portrayed cops getting into stuff, as he put it. They were their own bosses and did their own thing. That appealed to him. Cops seemed to get paid well, and didn't have to sit at a desk all day.

Within a year, Greco had graduated from the local police academy and was snapped up by the Riverside County Sheriff's Department. It had initiated its standard, six-month background check when the Perris Police Department also offered him a job. Although the Perris PD was much smaller, its background check took just two weeks and the agency promised he'd go straight to the streets, instead of the county jails, where all new hires for Riverside County had to work for two years. Greco chose Perris. That was in June 1988.

Greco was a hard worker, very driven and devoted. Assigned to the stolen vehicle unit, he attacked his job and recovered so many stolen cars that the state Highway Patrol honored him with nine performance awards in his first four years as a patrol officer. He got so good at spotting fingerprints and using them to track down suspects that he received another state police award five times. He won the city's Award of Valor for helping to rescue parachutists whose airplane crashed on the runway of the Perris Airport in 1992. Greco rose quickly through the small department, becoming a training officer and then a corporal—a two-striper.

At that time, another officer from a neighboring county, James McElvain, joined the department. Greco considered himself a hard worker, but so did McElvain, and the two engaged in a friendly rivalry. McElvain moved from patrol to the department's two-man detective unit, working crimes against property—burglaries, vandalism and bad checks. Several months later, McElvain asked Greco to help him with a routine pick-up. He wanted to bring in a parolee for questioning in a forgery. It would take about an hour. McElvain had been warned by the suspect's parents that he didn't want to go back to jail. When McElvain identified himself as a police officer, the parolee lunged at him, and they wrestled for McElvain's gun. Horrified, Greco hit the parolee in the back of the head as hard as he could with his

.45 Smith & Wesson. But it wasn't like TV, where the bad guy sinks to the ground. The parolee acted like nothing happened. Greco struck him again, harder, just to make him let go of McElvain, but the parolee continued struggling. The fight escalated and McElvain yelled, "He's got my gun!" Greco froze for an instant. McElvain screamed again, "He's got my gun! He's got my gun!" and Greco fired once at the parolee, killing him. The parolee's girlfriend later testified that he would have killed both officers, having told her that he would "do anything" to avoid going back to prison. An Internal Affairs investigation, a standard procedure for officer-involved shootings, cleared Greco of wrongdoing: the shooting was declared a justifiable homicide. When the family sued, the city's attorneys settled rather than going through the expense of a trial. Greco and McElvain weathered the investigation and lawsuit and became close friends.

The following year, around came a memo requesting applicants for a second detective in the unit handling crimes against persons—robbery, rape and homicide. Greco thought detective work would not only be a good change, but it would be more satisfying than working patrol. Plus, he could team up with McElvain, who shared his hard-charging zeal. He filled out the request form, hoping he would at least be considered for the job.

Greco soon realized that he needn't have worried. The stampede of applicants for the detective's job never materialized. The salary for detectives and street cops were identical and the move to detective was not considered a promotion within the Perris P.D., it was a lateral move. The only difference was the hours. Detectives worked 9 to 5. Patrol officers got alternating three-day weekends off.

Greco was the sole applicant. By default, he became a detective in May 1993. The department immediately shipped him off to a two-week homicide seminar in neighboring Orange County.

Within days, he was handed his first homicide. The victim, a prostitute and drug addict, was found spread-eagled and partially clothed behind an industrial building, by a fence at the rear property line. Animals had attacked the remains. Despite being badly decomposed, the body was spotted from the sky by recreational balloonists near the small airport in Perris. The coroner estimated that she had been dead about two weeks. She had been badly beaten, but the coroner could only guess at the instrument because of the condition of the body. The victim's boyfriend, also an addict and probably her pimp, had reported her missing eight days after she was presumed dead. He was suspect number one. Greco worked the case the best he could, but no evidence tied the boyfriend to the murder and the case remained unsolved.

And now this. Greco had barely sat down with his coffee that morning before his supervisor phoned him about Norma's murder. He'd grabbed his 35 mm camera, a notebook and a tape recorder, and pointed his teal Taurus station car toward Canyon Lake, about 20 minutes southwest of Perris. Excited and nervous, he ran through mental checklist of all the things he'd learned from homicide school about preserving the crime scene and investigating the murder. But doubt invaded his thoughts. After all, he told himself, he'd failed his first time at bat. He hadn't solved his first homicide. My god, he thought, how am I going to solve this one? Greco considered the responsibility and his stomach churned. This wasn't some dope addict or prostitute that no one would miss. An elderly victim in an affluent community like Canyon Lake would have friends and neighbors, adult children and maybe adult grandchildren, all of whom would look to him for answers—and an arrest. It was no secret that he would have to answer to them as well as his own department, but nothing would approach the pressure Greco eventually put on himself.

On his way to the scene, Greco passed the deserted rolling hills of Kabian Park, pushing the Taurus, carving up the twin black ribboned highway toward Canyon Lake. He felt tension creeping into his neck and shoulders and tried calming himself by going back to the homicide school checklist: maintain the crime scene, preserve and document evidence, photograph and collect everything for processing later, particularly fingerprints, blood, hair and fiber evidence. He repeated it over and over until common sense started to assert itself. First of all, he told himself, the responding officers at the scene will have already taped off the scene and kept everyone out. Secondly, the criminalists and ID techs are trained to take crime-scene photos and physically collect evidence. They have the tools and equipment to preserve fingerprints, blood and trace evidence.

Greco knew that part of his panic stemmed from his lack of experience with murders. You don't investigate a homicide the same way you do a car theft or a burglary or a rape. Most veteran homicide detectives have a procedure or protocol to follow—most rookies had plenty of battle-scarred older guys to follow around and ask questions. There were none on the Perris P.D. and Greco didn't know of any he could ask for help. Without the benefit of experience or a detective mentor, he had no personal guidelines, no comfortable pattern of his own. Greco couldn't resist beating himself up one more time—he was so green, he had never before called out the ID techs and county criminalists to work a crime scene. They hadn't been necessary at his first homicide.

Greco shook his head. He knew his self-doubt came from his feeling of failure, and his fear that he could have done more to solve the prostitute's murder. Wallowing in guilt and inadequacy would take him nowhere. His mother had taught him that. If you write a script for your own failure, she used to tell him, it will come true.

Greco was half-Japanese, half-Italian. His father was an intelligence officer in the air force, stationed at the Fuchu Air Force Base, when he met Greco's mother in 1957. Greco and his three sisters were typical military brats, living all over the United States and Japan, usually spending no more than a few months in each new place. Greco, often mistaken for being Hispanic, remained fluent in Japanese. As he was growing up, his mother constantly encouraged him to think positive—there was nothing he couldn't do.

As he sipped his coffee, the previous day's panic returned. Sitting at his desk on the morning after Norma's body had been found, Greco organized his notes, typed them into his laptop computer and wrote his report, poring over every detail, trying to find a direction. No break-in. No known theft. Victim lived alone. A vicious attack. Greco wished that some of the physical evidence would yield a clue. The problem was that the criminalists couldn't identify a perpetrator working only with a hair or a fiber from Norma's house. An expert has to compare strands of hair collected from a crime scene with strands of hair removed from a suspect and then determine whether the samples came from the same person. But since different people can often share similar hair characteristics, a jury is unlikely to convict a suspect based solely on hair samples. The same goes for shoeprints. Greco was estatic that Cooksey found one—Greco was so inexperienced, he hadn't even known it was possible to collect it. He'd heard of making molds of shoe impressions in mud, for example, by using plaster. He had watched, fascinated, as Cooksey had literally peeled the dusty print off the floor. The shoeprint had the potential to be a promising piece of evidence, but first he needed a suspect's shoe to compare with the one lifted from Norma's entryway.

The knives, though, might yield what Greco wanted. He was counting on getting a good fingerprint from one of them. That would be a spectacular break. A fingerprint, unlike hair or a shoeprint, can positively identify one person and only one person—if it was a good, clear, full print. That would practically guarantee a conviction. When he'd sent the knives out to the lab first thing that morning, the lab techs told him they could probably have results by the afternoon. Better yet, Greco was hoping that the killer had left behind a little DNA, perhaps under Norma's broken fingernail, perhaps from the blood on the chair on the stairway landing. DNA is as impressive and convincing as evidence can get in a courtroom, although it doesn't exactly identify a suspect the same way a fingerprint does.

DNA test results are reported to juries through statistics. For example, an expert might testify that there's a 1 in 20 million probability that another person on earth shares the same genetic characteristics as the defendant. The prosecutor usually argues that those numbers make it rather unlikely that anyone other than the defendant deposited his or her DNA at a crime scene.

He would sort through the evidence later in the week and decide which items to ship to the state DNA lab in Sacramento, hundreds of miles north. Of course he would send the knives, the fingernail clippings, the scrapings, and perhaps the carpet samples, although it was unlikely that the killer had been injured and dropped a convenient sample of blood. It typically takes a crime lab several months to perform DNA tests and interpret the results.

Greco wasn't going to wait around for a lab report when there was no guarantee of turning up the suspect's DNA. He ran through precepts from homicide school. What was the motive for attacking this elderly woman? Norma Davis had been among the most vulnerable groups of potential victims, children and the elderly—those least able to protect themselves. They were also the least likely to place themselves in harm's way. One doesn't see senior citizens or toddlers involved in drive-by shootings, lurking in dark alleys, spray-painting graffiti, selling drugs and making trouble in the streets late at night. Norma Davis was exactly where she should have been—in her own home. Greco remembered the teaching materials that mentioned domestic violence as one possible cause for extreme violence in homicides committed in the home. In fact, he remembered that one of the two homicides at Canyon Lake within the last five years had claimed the life of a woman who had been killed by her estranged husband. In the more recent case, a parolee had committed murder, then dumped the body at Canyon Lake. But Greco doubted that, at 86, Norma Davis was in a physically abusive relationship. As far as he knew, she lived alone. Greco was trained to start his search for a suspect within a close radius of the victim's home, and to consider the involvement of family numbers and caretakers. Norma's family? The only member he knew was Jeri. She was wearing Nikes, she had access to the residence, and she was the last person to see the victim alive. What did she have to gain from Norma's death?

He would start with Jeri.

Greco's head was so buried in his notes, he didn't see Wyatt McElvain standing over his desk.

"I got a call from this psychic," McElvain said.

Greco looked up. It wasn't his friend, Jim McElvain, whose life he had saved. This was the *other* McElvain. Wyatt McElvain was the sergeant who supervised the Perris P.D.'s operations at Canyon Lake and knew a lot of the residents. He had been at the crime scene the day before.

"He says there's gonna be another murder," McElvain said. "In two weeks. He says it's a woman. The murderer. He thinks it's a woman."

Greco kept a straight face. You've got to be kidding, he thought. He had more than enough work to do and the last thing he needed was to chase down some lunatic.

"You're real funny," Greco said.

McElvain offered the phone number. The guy lived in Canyon Lake. What did he have to lose? Greco paused for a second, then wrote it down.

Greco stayed glued to his desk doing paperwork; he worked on his other cases and tried calling Jeri periodically without success. He figured she was out making funeral arrangements. That morning, Greco had sent a community service officer—a non-sworn officer—to drop off the film from his personal camera at a one-hour developer. The officer returned by mid-afternoon with his prints. The official crime-scene photos were being developed by the county lab, which typically took about a week to make prints.

Greco looked carefully over his own photos, referring to them as he wrote his report. When he finished, he labeled the photos and placed them in his manila folder case file, which he put in the filing cabinet next to his desk.

During the afternoon, Greco called the lab periodically to see whether the technicians had gotten any prints from the knives. By late afternoon, they had results: No identifiable prints. Back to square one, Greco thought.

Greco decided to start interviewing other witnesses. The first stop was the hardware store, which was in a small, outdoor strip mall just outside the Canyon Lake gates. A receipt from Norma's purse showed that she'd been there just hours before the coroner estimated that she was killed on Monday, Valentine's Day. One of the employees recognized Norma's picture from her Canyon Lake membership card. She said that Norma had had two mail keys made. The time on the receipt was 11:33 a.m., but the clock on the register was an hour ahead, so Norma was actually there at 10:33 a.m.

When Greco asked if she remembered anything unusual

about Norma, the employee said, "She had a hard time walking."

Greco sighed, remembering Norma's swollen ankles and Jeri's remarks about the bypass surgery. Norma could not have escaped from her attacker if she'd tried.

Since he was in the area, he decided to take a chance and drop by Jeri's house. She lived in Canyon Lake.

He found the address on one of the development's winding streets and parked the station car in front of a house somewhat smaller than Norma's. When he knocked on the door, Russell Armbrust opened the door and invited him in. He was polite and cordial. Russell excused himself to find Jeri and offered Greco something to drink. He declined. It was a nice, airy place with a living room that, like many others in the development, overlooked part of the golf course. Greco took a seat on the couch. From where he was sitting, he could see a large painting of a clown.

Before leaving the station, Greco had drawn up a list of questions. He had reviewed suggestions from an FBI manual about preparing a homicide victimology: a compendium of the victim's personal history, family relationships, friends, employment, personal habits and behavior. FBI theory states that most homicides involve someone related to the victim. Digging out as much information as possible on the victim invariably puts you closer to the suspect. Greco considered Jeri an important contact because she would probably provide most or all of the information about Norma. He thought that his focus would have to be on the family. But since she was also potentially a suspect, Greco also wanted to spend time with her and begin establishing a rapport. Building trust would be important if evidence showed that Jeri was responsible for Norma's murder because, Greco reasoned, she'd be more willing to confide in him or confess if she trusted him. And if Jeri was not responsible, she was more likely to share information leading to a suspect. At this first meeting, Greco wanted to introduce himself and get a read on her. After delivering his standard opening and the standard condolences, he knew exactly what he was going to ask.

"Detective Greco."

Jeri looked good for a woman in her 50s. She was trim,

with neatly styled dark brown hair, and she wore casual clothes. Russ had disappeared and Jeri sat across from Greco in a recliner. He noticed she was wearing Nikes.

"I'm sorry for your loss, but it's important that we get this information so we can apprehend whoever did this," Greco said. "I need to know everything possible about Norma and her habits, any personal information that I can about her—who she regularly came into contact with, whether she had a maid."

"I'll give you whatever you need," Jeri said, addressing him formally as "Detective."

Greco started with fairly innocuous questions about Norma's medications and her pill-taking schedule, which could be critical in estimating the time of the murder. Jeri, occasionally wiping away tears, said that Norma kept two separate pillboxes, a yellow one downstairs in the kitchen for morning pills and a blue one upstairs on the lamp table next to her recliner for those she took in the evening. Both pillboxes had a separate compartment for each day of the week. Greco knew that the pills for Monday, Feb. 14, were gone from the downstairs pillbox, which was corroborated by the fact that Norma was last seen alive at the hardware store that morning. But the pills in Tuesday evening's compartment were still there. Jeri said Norma typically took her evening pills with dinner at five or six o'clock.

She got up to check on Norma's medications and came back a few minutes later with some prescription bottles which she handed to Greco.

He went through his list of questions: a nurse's log for Norma's care, a list of individuals who visited Norma at home to render medical assistance after her accident and after the open-heart surgery. He also wanted to know about the keys that Norma had purchased the morning she was killed. Jeri said that they were for the mailbox; Norma had them made so that the younger woman could retrieve her mail. And Norma did have a housekeeper, but she had been hospitalized with an aneurysm last week.

Jeri brought up the Medicare check again. She'd gone into Norma's condo after the police had left and hadn't found the check. She thought it was something he could trace in case the killer had tried to cash it. Greco said he hadn't seen it among the evidence, so they would have to subpoena bank records to find out if it had been cashed.

Periodically, Jeri excused herself to search for various pieces of paperwork. She seemed well organized and could lay her hands on Norma's paperwork fairly quickly. With every question, Jeri either answered or found whatever Greco needed without hesitation. She was exceedingly courteous and polite. At times, during the interview, Jeri cried softly, but she remained composed.

"I don't know who would do this to Norma," she said. "I can't believe this happened."

She was not merely pleasant, she was bending over backwards to cooperate. What he saw in her eyes was shock and disbelief. This wasn't his suspect.

He had one more stop—Alice Williams.

It was getting dark by the time Greco got to Alice's house. He knocked on the door, rang the bell and waited, knowing it sometimes took elderly people a while to answer their doors. Greco heard a muffled voice. He waited. Then he heard it again. She was asking what he wanted.

"It's Detective Greco from the police department," Greco shouted, pulling the badge clipped to his belt and holding it up so she could see. A bright porch light flipped on. From the corner of his eye, he saw the curtains move slightly.

He heard the lock snap and, when the door opened, a frail, white-haired woman invited him in. As soon as he stepped inside, she closed and locked the door. Greco took a quick look around. Her house was very clean and neat, just like Norma's.

Alice offered him refreshments, but Greco declined. She sat on the edge of her chair across from him. Greco could tell she had been crying. He handed her a card, gently reintroduced himself and offered his condolences with his standard opening line.

"I'm very sorry about what happened. I know this is uncomfortable for you, but it's important that I speak with you about this." Greco said. He stopped himself. Alice was trembling and her hands shook.

This woman is really frightened, Greco thought to himself. It was bad enough that murderers take others' lives but they also inflict lifelong emotional scars on the people who discover bloody, often nightmarish crime scenes involving loved ones. It wasn't fair. Alice had lived this long; she didn't deserve to see her best friend butchered. When he'd first arrived at the crime scene yesterday, he'd seen Alice cowering by her car, surrounded by Norma's neighbors. Sgt. McElvain and Officer Noggle had told him she was pretty broken up, so Greco had decided not to traumatize her with questions then. She still looked pretty shaken. Greco whisked her through the interview, keeping the questions simple.

With tears in her eyes, Alice told him she took Norma to the bank before going to the hardware store. It was Valentine's Day. Norma had gently teased the teller about the candy and the vase of flowers at her window.

"She was a beautiful lady," Alice said. "We played bridge together; we shopped together. Norma was my best friend."

Greco nodded.

He asked if she had seen anything unusual when she drove Norma home.

"Just some gardeners working in the yard," Alice said. "They were standing around talking and stuff."

As the interview drew to a close, she lingered as if she didn't want him to leave.

"I'm afraid. I live alone. I don't have any family and there's no one to watch over me. Norma was my best friend. My only friend," she said, her voice staying strong. "Do you think you could come back and visit? If you could just check up on me from time to time . . ." Greco assured her that he would.

Williams seemed relieved.

"I'm afraid the killer will come back."

CHAPTER THREE

MONDAY, FEBRUARY 28, 1994, 10:30 A.M.

If you were to walk out of Norma's front door on Continental Way, cross the street to the golf course, bisect the sixth green and jog over two houses to the west, you'd wind up at June Roberts' olive-and-white house on Big Tee Drive. June, an attractive, 66-year-old brunette, and her neighbor, Edna Barker, wheeled their golf carts over to the cluster of mailboxes near one of the community's gates to pick up that morning's mail. Like most residents of the desert community, they whizzed around the complex in their open-air electric carts to visit friends or run errands. It had been two weeks since Norma Davis' murder, but talk of the brutal killing was still a popular topic among Canyon Lake residents. It seemed as if everyone either knew the victim or knew someone who did. Even June had a remote connection—her deceased husband was best friends with Russell Armbrust, who was married to Norma's step-daughter-in-law, Jeri. June had heard from Jeri that the investigators thought it was someone from the family, and June had passed that tidbit to a friend at church.

June, after losing her husband months earlier, took care of all her own finances now and needed information about homeowner's insurance. Did Edna have a good insurance agent? Edna said she did and promised to call her with the name and phone number later in the day. The two discussed June's weekend with her daughter in San Diego, about an hour south. Sorting through their mail, June and Edna chatted a bit more, then parted ways. A canasta regular, June was headed home, then was going out for her weekly midday card game. That night, she planned to celebrate her birthday with golfing buddies.

As June drove away, a big brown Cadillac lumbered

through the Canyon Lake security gates and turned onto Big Tee Drive. Behind the wheel sat a striking blonde with slightly wavy, chin-length hair and the solid, muscular physique of an athletic outdoorswoman. A blonde 5-year-old boy was strapped into the front passenger seat. Stuffed cartoon characters Ren and Stimpy, an offbeat, irreverent animated duo, were stuck to the inside rear window with small suction cups, positioned to appear as if they were trapped inside the car. The Cadillac cruised past tall palms that rose high above the low, flat-topped homes, and stopped in front of June's house. June was raking leaves in the side yard and depositing the small piles into the trash.

"Just stay here, Jason," the driver said, pulling out a pair of latex gloves from a box half-hidden under the floor mat behind the driver's seat, and stuffing them in her pocket.

"I'll only be a minute."

Dana Sue Gray kissed Jason on the forehead and slammed the heavy driver's side door shut, then walked over to the carport to greet June. The ultra-low-maintenance front yard was cleverly landscaped with the small, green-dyed rocks favored by retirees. A small fruit-bearing orange tree and pink flowered bushes hugged the house.

June recognized Dana, Russell Armbrust's daughter. June occasionally played golf with Russell and Jeri, but had not socialized much since her husband passed away. Between the Canyon Lake Country Club, her card games and golf games, June rarely saw Dana. But when Dana had gotten pregnant last year, June, a fitness buff, had advised her about nutrition and had taken her to a health food store to pick up a few things. Unfortunately, she had heard from Russell that Dana had miscarried the baby, then heard that she had separated from her husband. Now Dana was in her yard.

June and Dana exchanged greetings and the younger woman asked if she could borrow a book on nutrition, one that June had suggested to her last year when she was pregnant.

"You know, I've been drinking a lot and I need to get back on track," Dana said. "I need your help. Maybe that book would help."

June smiled and said she knew exactly which one to get her. She disappeared inside the house and emerged moments later with the book. As she handed it over, she expressed sympathy for Dana and wished her the best.

Dana, a frozen smile on her face, glanced at the book and shook her head.

How dare you judge me? You have no reason to judge me.

"No, this isn't the right one," she said. "I think it's the other one you recommended. You know, it had to do with nutrition. Maybe I can find it on your bookshelf."

June hesitated slightly. Eager to get ready for her canasta game, June turned to go back inside, chattering away. Dana followed silently and shut the door behind her.

It will be real quick.

They walked in through the laundry room where June had plopped her purse on the dryer, down a short hallway and left into the den. June made small talk and Dana responded cheerfully, but deliberately lagged behind, quickly wriggling her hands into latex gloves while looking around for what she needed. With June's back turned, Dana quickly unplugged both the long, straight cord that connected the phone to the wall, and an extra-long, curly cord that attached to the receiver. She dropped the straight cord.

June walked around her desk and stood between it and a set of bookshelves stocked with books on religion and nutrition.

"Which one did you have in mind?" June asked, turning around to face Dana.

How dare you give me that look of disgust?

"Down there on the bottom shelf," Dana said, coming up behind June as she turned her back on Dana to scan the bookshelves.

With a minimalist's eerie efficiency and sense of purpose, Dana quickly wrapped the curly phone cord once, then twice around June's neck and jerked it backward. June's head snapped back and she clutched at her neck, clawing the cord.

"What are you doing?" June managed to croak.

Dana's eyes were cold. There was no hate, no malice, no excitement, just a look of determination.

"You can't . . . do this to me!" June gasped.

"Relax. Just relax," Dana said in a low, quiet voice, as if comforting a small child. She held the cord taut as June violently struggled. Dana assumed a wide, athletic stance, leaning backward like a water skier, using her body weight to cinch June's neck. The older woman arched back, trying to relieve the backward pull on her neck, and frantically tried, with both hands, to pull the cord away. Tanned and trim, June fought back, twisting and turning her body to shake off her assailant. As June fought for her life, her hairband was torn from her hair and her slip-on shoes were ripped from her feet. The two women careened around the small den, knocking over a heavy ottoman. In one explosive, violent move, Dana knocked June to the floor and straddled her. Weak from the fight, June couldn't stop Dana from putting her own hands around June's neck and strangling her face-to-face, sealing off her windpipe as June lost consciousness.

Dana pulled over a heavy wood chair, the match to the ottoman. One end of the curly cord was around June's neck. Dana threaded the other end of the phone cord around an arm of the chair, linking June's tethered neck directly to the chair, then tilted the chair back as leverage to keep constant pressure on the cord. Quickly scanning the area, Dana found a heavy glass wine decanter in the kitchen. She walked a few strides to the kitchen to retrieve it and came back to where June struggled vainly under the chair. She had awakened and was moaning softly and barely moving. Dana flipped June onto her back and stood behind her, close to her head.

How can you be pulling that kind of shit when you're supposed to be a friend of the family? I'm real fragile right now.

In less than a minute, June was no longer moving.

Dana left the way she came in, pausing to rifle credit cards from June's purse on top of the dryer. She tossed aside the JCPenney and the Broadway cards and chose the Mervyn's and Visa charge cards. She stuck both cards in her own purse and returned to the little boy still strapped in the Cadillac's front seat.

"Hey, Jason! Let's go shopping!"

Forty-five minutes later, Dana sipped iced tea and puffed on a cigarette at Baily's Wine Country Café in an upscale shopping center in Temecula, frowning her annoyance at the small boy running around the al fresco dining area. She ordered without looking at the menu and snapped at the waiter. She charged the scampi, crab cakes and cheesecake to June's credit card. It was too much to eat, so the waiter packed up the rest to go.

The next stop was for an eyebrow and moustache wax and a perm for herself, and a fashionable step-cut haircut for the boy. Signing the $164.76 charge "June Roberts," she cheerfully bragged to her stylist that she was going on a "shopping spree." At West Dallas, an upscale leather goods store, she spent $511 on a black, fringed leather jacket and red, yellow and black cowboy boots. She wore the red boots out of the store. Thirteen minutes later, she was Temecula's Jewelry Mart, signing June Roberts' name on a credit card charge for $161 diamond-and-sapphire drop earrings. Swinging through Mervyn's, a popular chain department store, she moved quickly, gathering up a dozen pairs of Jockey women's underwear, and three pairs of children's shoes for the young boy, $167.96; five pairs of boys' jeans and Levi's, eight shirts and a handful of boys' socks and undies, $240.80; and a set of new sheets, $40.93—all charged to June.

On the way home, Dana stopped by Sav-On to pick up Tootsie Rolls and Skittles, orange-flavored Gatorade, rawhide dog treats, dog biscuits and dog shampoo, two cartons of Marlboro Lights and two 1.75 bottles of Smirnoff vodka. Wedged into the cart was a purple boogie board, a short, Styrofoam board used for body surfing. Headed for the check-out counter, she paused by the toy aisle and tossed a $5.99 toy police helicopter into her shopping basket. Dana signed June's name on the $74.62 charge slip.

As Dana and Jason shopped, June's canasta partners waited for a while, then played without her, wondering why she hadn't called. Edna had tried in vain to reach June to give her the name and phone number of her insurance agent.

After a busy afternoon of shopping, Dana got on the freeway and took the exit leading to an unincorporated area of Lake Elsinore. She steered the big Cadillac past a run-down liquor store, with bars on the window and graffiti on the concrete block walls, and an auto parts store with cracks in the parking lot big enough for knee-high weeds to grow. In this neighborhood, there were no manicured lawns, no curbs, no sidewalks, no custom homes. Most of the homes were pre-fab or trailers. Off some of the side streets were unmarked and unlit dirt roads. On the opposite side of the street was a huge, dried lakebed with bike lanes. A few good rainstorms in the winter can raise the water level to within 50 feet of the street. Dana drove into the driveway of a brown-and-white mobile home with a brick foundation and parked in the carport. She unloaded the bulging bags from the trunk of the Cadillac but didn't have time to put everything away before her boyfriend, Jim, came home. As Dana, Jim and Jason were settling down for dinner, June's friends were knocking on June's front door, ready to take her out for her birthday. When she didn't answer the door, they used the house keys still dangling from her golf cart to get into her house.

Jim asked Dana about all of her purchases and Dana brushed him off, explaining that she got a credit card from Dennis, her estranged husband. Angry, Jim told her to cut up the card and return the merchandise. It started a fight.

After dinner, Dana fixed herself a vodka and took the drink and phone to the other room. She dialed the number for Murrieta Hot Springs, an upscale spa a couple of cities away.

"Hello. I'd like to make an appointment for a massage tomorrow morning."

"Of course. Your name?" said the receptionist.

"June Roberts."

"Hey, Rich, we've got another homicide up at Canyon Lake."

Greco was on his cell phone, standing in front of the panoramic window in June's living room. He looked out over the grassy contours of the darkened golf course. It was 7:22 p.m. He'd already walked through the scene and had just called for the county lab techs and the DOJ criminalists to come out. Bentley was his second call.

"Well," Bentley said, "there's supposed to be another DA on call. I'm kind of busy. Actually, I'm making dinner."

Over the phone, Greco could hear food sizzling and kids

in the background. His face grew hot with panic. His heart sank.

"You do good work," Bentley said. "You can do this. Why don't you just brief me in the morning?"

Greco, ignoring his anxiety for the moment, gave Bentley the rundown: an elderly woman strangled with a phone cord. Lived alone. Some rummaging in the house but no ransacking. No sign of forced entry. Great violence to the victim. Greco walked a few steps and stood at the entrance to the kitchen; he could see into the den/office area where June's bare legs, splayed at an unnatural angle, stuck out from underneath a heavy wood and leather chair.

"Are you sure you don't want to come out?" Greco said to Bentley. "It looks like there are a lot of similarities."

"Yeah, I'm sure," Bentley said. "Just go ahead and process the crime scene and brief me in the morning."

Greco felt alone and overwhelmed. All the panic from the last two weeks returned and multiplied. He was already bogged down with work on the Norma Davis homicide and here was another one for him to try to solve. He'd been typing up reports on the Davis murder when Jim McElvain told him about this one. He'd caught the call from dispatch and walked it over to Greco. Greco couldn't believe it. He thought McElvain was kidding. You're b.s.-ing me, he'd told McElvain. Greco wanted Bentley's advice from a prosecutor's standpoint. If he ever caught the killer, Greco thought, he didn't want the case to suffer because of his inexperience or because he'd overlooked something important. He needed help.

I can only do so much, Greco thought to himself. I'm a brand-new detective and I have no experience with homicides. They know that. What else can I do?

Consumed with his thoughts, Greco slowly walked back outside into the crisp desert evening and tried to focus his thoughts. Here he had two murders within two weeks, literally within blocks of one another, both elderly women and both killed with extreme violence. The murders were too close together in time and location to be a coincidence. They had to be related. Greco's mind was spinning.

Serial killer.

Oh my God, Greco said to himself. I might have a serial

killer on my hands and I can't even get the deputy DA out to the crime scene.

He dialed the local office of the FBI.

"I need assistance with a possible serial killer," Greco said. The agent told Greco that the FBI can assist a detective with profiling, but it doesn't provide agents for primary homicide investigation.

Greco pocketed his cell phone with a worried look crossing his face. He felt tired. A feeling of hopelessness shuddered through his body, but he caught it before he let it overtake him. He knew he had to stay focused and do his job. He had another hour or two before the criminalists and ID techs would get there; maybe the on-call DA would show up soon. He pulled out his phone again and called his wife to tell her it was going to be a long night.

"Good luck," she said. "And be safe."

Darlene had enough on her hands dealing with their 9-month-old twin girls and three other small children. He didn't want to burden her with his work problems. He tried to sound cheerful and hung up the phone, then figured out his next move.

Less than an hour before, Greco, Sgt. Dennis Wenker, Greco's supervisor, and Sgt. Wyatt McElvain, as the supervising officer of Canyon Lake, did a preliminary walk-through of June's house. Officer Jean LeSpade, who responded to the initial call, stayed outside to maintain a time log of people who entered and exited the crime scene. The house was largely dark, silent and still, save for a single lamp in the den.

They had entered June's house through the side door by the carport, where June's car keys dangled from the ignition of the gleaming white golf cart. Parked behind it was her silvery blue Volvo adorned with the familiar Christian logo: the word "Jesus" encased in the outline of a fish. A one-inch, rounded, rectangular piece of broken, bloody glass sat on the cement floor of the carport, a couple of feet from the side door. A few feet from that was a paper store receipt. As soon as Greco and his supervisor came in through the side door, they had seen June's open brown purse and department store credit cards strewn beside it on top of the dryer. Greco wondered if the killer was looking for something specific—why not just take the whole wallet? At that point, he couldn't assume that any credit cards were taken. He hoped the killer had left some fingerprints.

The trio went through a short, dark hallway, turned left and stood at the edge of the den, which looked like it was being used as an office. To their right was a small dining area that adjoined the kitchen. On the far wall to their left were two tall bookcases. A dusty pink velour couch with end tables on either side sat against the wall to their immediate left. On one of the end tables was a tan phone with the curly receiver cord and the long, plain cord missing. The straight cord was coiled by the end table and the curly cord had been used to garrote June. Along the opposite wall was a sliding glass door and a desk with its drawers standing open. Near the dining room area was a large potted ficus tree with a placard reading: "In memory of Duane Roberts." An eerily homey glow from the desk lamp illuminuted the disturbing scene.

Greco immediately saw that June had struggled mightily to fend off her attacker. Shattered glass littered the blood-stained carpet a few feet from the couch. In the middle of one large stain sat the stump of a wine decanter with a hinged wire top. Near the sliding glass door, a small table had been overturned. June was lying between the couch and the desk, her face horribly swollen, bloody and purplish. On top of her was a chair made of dark wood and black vinyl. Her neck had been tied to one arm of the chair with the phone, her hands still in a death grip on the cord. One piece of glass was resting on June's right hand. She was still wearing a large gold ring generously studded with diamonds on her left ring finger. Greco was perplexed by the fact that her hands and forearms bore no defensive wounds despite the lethal fight.

He could see one pant leg had ridden up to reveal a long, bloody gash down June's shin, possibly from scraping against the chair. A half-circle smear of blood ran along the side of the desk and ended at June's head on the carpeted floor, tracing her last movement where she was either pushed or fell. A plastic, tortoise-shell hairband was lying at her feet.

Greco and the two sergeants stared in silence for a few

minutes while Greco wrote detailed notes, then they quietly discussed the potential scenarios. Without any visible sign of a break-in, there was a strong likelihood that June knew her attacker. No one could explain why the killer left a diamond ring on her finger.

Looking to the right, through the kitchen, they could see the living room and an open photo album with snapshots strewn on the carpeted floor.

They backed out the way they had come and stood in the hallways to observe the other rooms. In June's bedroom one large dresser drawer had been opened and two small drawers had been removed and placed on top of the dresser. On the unmade bed was a green velour sweatsuit and a bathrobe. A few droplets still clung to the shower in the master bathroom. The trio wondered whether the victim or the suspect had used the shower. Nothing was disturbed in the spare bedroom.

With at least an hour or two before the lab techs and DOJ criminalists were due to arrive, Greco circled June's house carefully, noting the positions of blinds and curtains, whether doors and windows were open or closed, and whether lights were on or off. The venetian blinds in the den and the living room were closed. Assuming the crime occurred in the middle of the day, Greco wondered if the killer had closed the blinds. He saw two screwdrivers on a ledge outside one of the living room windows and jotted it down. He shined a flashlight on the green rocks in the front yard to see whether the murderer had left behind any evidence while fleeing. He saw none. He noted the living room's front picture window and its proximity to the golf course and made a note to himself to come back when the blinds were up to see how much of June's living room someone could see from different parts of the golf course and whether the killer could have seen June working on the photo album.

Once he'd completed the outside examination to his liking, Greco went back inside June's house and stood in the hallway far from the evidence just to get a feel for June and try to make sense of how the homicide occurred. He started in the laundry area by the side door, staring at the credit cards lying on top of the dryer next to the open purse. A small red purse, possibly for cosmetics or coins, had also been removed from the handbag. With details of the other homicide running through his mind, Greco moved through the other rooms and finished up in the den as he tried piecing together the similarities. It was interesting to him that both women were killed in a den/office area. Assuming that June had been there for a few hours before her friends found her at 6:18 p.m., both women were killed in broad daylight. Both crime scenes bore signs that the killer had rummaged around, rather than ransacked, the house.

What was the killer looking for? Why ignore the rings on both victims? Greco wasn't ruling out the possibility that something of value was taken from Norma's house. It looked like the killer was brazen enough to take time sifting through June's assortment of credit cards.

Then there was the similarity with the chairs. Perhaps the killer somehow used chairs to control the victims. The killer had passed on June's lightweight dining room chairs in favor of the sturdier wood chair. The half-moon blood smear on the desk, as well as the obvious disarray in the area, showed signs of an intense struggle. It looked as if June, in her final moments, had collapsed while she struggled to escape from the chair, leaving the smear on the side of the desk. Norma had obviously been unable to fight or flee.

Another common thread was the phone. At Norma's house, the extra-long cord strung down the hall and into the den had been ripped out but not used, and the phone itself was found under Norma's body. He had been astonished during Norma's autopsy the week before to find that Norma had also been strangled manually, meaning that the killer's hands had physically compressed Norma's throat. Greco found it strange that the killer preferred to use his own hands rather than the convenient phone cord, which had already been yanked out. In addition, Norma suffered more than the gaping neck and chest wounds. She had eleven stab wounds in all, most of them to the heart. Norma had a dual cause of death: manual strangulation and multiple stab wounds. June, it seems, had also suffered dual modes of death: ligature strangulation and bludgeoning with the wine bottle. He would have to wait for an autopsy to find out if she was also manually strangled. If she had been, there would be very little doubt that this was the same killer.

To Greco, another similarity was the brute force used on both victims. This was an earmark, Greco thought: it seemed unlikely that more than one person was responsible. How could this be the work of two people? It had to be someone working alone. And the left-handed theory? He didn't know if the coroner would be able to tell whether any of the blows were struck by a left-handed person. He made a another note to himself.

By 9:25 p.m., the county lab's photographer and ID tech pulled up to June's house. The DOJ criminalists arrived an hour later. Greco briefed them and took them on a walk-through of the crime scene. They marked evidence and laid down the taxicab-yellow numbered markers for the photographer, conferring amongst themselves and with Greco about what to collect.

With the evidence marked, the photographer took photos, and then the criminalists started collecting everything, starting in the carport with the paper store receipt and the bloodied piece of glass. For each bloodstain, bouquet of fibers and hairs, and sliver of glass tweezed from the carpet, the criminalists created what amounted to a crime-scene catalogue. A lab number given to each item of evidence would help track it on its journey from June's house to the police department, where it would be booked, to the lab, where it would be examined and tested, and sometimes to outside labs, where it might be shipped for further examination and more sophisticated procedures, like DNA tests. Years later, a prosecutor may introduce some of the evidence at a trial and show it to jurors, using the same numbers. A sharp defense attorney, faced with incriminating physical evidence against a client accused of murder, is likely to scrutinize those documents, looking for sloppy record-keeping, and pounce on any discrepancy, which could result in a judge tossing out that piece of evidence.

Hour after hour, Greco stood shoulder to shoulder with the criminalists, observing what he had only been told about in homicide school, like the tape lifts from Norma's clothing. Elissa Mayo, one of the DOJ criminalists, pointed out what she thought was a small speck of blood by the front door. Greco watched as she used a sampling kit to test the speck for the presence of blood. It registered positive and was collected to be tested later for type and other genetic markers.

When it came time to examine and move the body, the other DOJ criminalist, Marianne Stam, pointed out purplish indentations on June's neck that she thought looked like fingernail marks. They couldn't tell if they came from June trying to pull the cord away from her windpipe, or from the killer manually strangling June. They would have to wait for the autopsy.

As the criminalists slowly worked their way through the house, Greco was able to examine the scene unencumbered, finally getting a closer look at the crime scene that he had been observing for hours from the hallway. He lingered in the kitchen, poked his head into June's fridge and the cabinets, stood in her bedroom and examined her desk, trying to get a feel for June, and hopefully bringing himself closer to her killer.

Greco saw two themes in June's life—health and church. Not only did her car bear the Christian igthus, but her home was adorned with framed Bible quotations sewn in needlepoint. On top of June's desk was a Bible open to a passage from Corinthians. Some parts had been outlined with a red pencil, which was still in the crease of the book. Here's this religious woman studying the Bible, he thought to himself, and she was killed with savage violence. It was incomprehensible to him why someone would do something like this to her. The passage was bookmarked by a prayer list with penciled-in names. As Greco scanned the list, he was surprised to find familiar names: Ila Tingley, who was Norma's housekeeper, and Shirley Morrales, one of the friends who found June's body. It seemed an odd coincidence that the housekeeper of one murder victim would show up on the prayer list of the very next victim. Greco thought it was probably a fact of life in a small community like Canyon Lake that victims of tragic circumstances were so closely connected. Ila Tingley had been hospitalized when Norma was murdered. At this point, Greco had no suspects. He had no idea who would emerge as a possible suspect. He would definitely talk to Ila when she got out of the hospital.

June's passion for robust living was evident in the contents of her kitchen cabinet and refrigerator. Both were stocked with health foods. Fat-free recipes were magnet-mounted on her refrigerator. It looked like she had just opened a box containing a new food dehydrator—since her birthday was the day before, it was probably a gift, Greco surmised. The empty box was on top of the washer in the laundry area, right next to her purse. On June's desk was Adele Davis's best-seller, *Let's Eat Right to Keep Fit.*

June's desk contained the usual items—a large desktop calendar, books, a digital clock. On the far corner sat a large, clear glass pitcher with a handle. A framed picture of a mature man, probably June's deceased husband, Duane, also perched on the desk. On the living room floor, a photo album, an obituary for Duane Roberts, and an envelope of snapshots were spread out as if June had been updating the album. June's husband had been a war hero who earned the Bronze Star for bravery in World War II. There were two desk drawers open; one on the side held office supplies like a stapler and paper clips. Greco looked inside the flat center desk drawer. There lay June's checkbook, untouched.

Greco's body jolted to attention. If it wasn't money, *what was this killer looking for?* The same thought had been nagging him all night. Greco fought off fatigue and tried to focus, but nothing registered.

This killer seemed very confident and careful. Looking over at the phone on the side table by the couch, Greco saw that the longer cord had been carefully unplugged from the phone, not ripped out like the one from Norma's den. Greco rubbed his eyes, irritated from staying open all night. This killer had taken the time to remove both cords, perhaps undecided about which one to use.

TUESDAY, MARCH 1, 1994, 6:15 A.M.

Shards of daylight stung Greco's tired eyes. His head throbbed as he drove home. He was physically drained and mentally exhausted. After thinking about the crime scene all night, he couldn't think anymore. He just wanted to get home and sleep. Greco and James McElvain had waited around until sunup for one final search of June's front yard.

In the clear light of day, Greco and McElvain poked around the carport, scanned the little green rocks in the front yard and checked the shrubbery and the dirt areas around the house and under the windows. They found nothing. During the search, Greco got a call on his cellular phone from the dispatcher. June's son had suggested that they collect her handgun in her nightstand. When he and McElvain were finished outside, Greco retrieved the .38-caliber Smith & Wesson. Greco and a community service officer took the gun and the rest of the evidence back to the station, booked it, and drove home.

His mind free to wander, Greco's personal disgust at the brutality against the victims knotted the back of his throat. The image of Alice popped into his mind and Greco started to worry. She would no doubt see something about the murder in the newspaper in a day or two and would probably be petrified. Alice had been named in an earlier newspaper article for finding Norma's body and Greco wondered if the killer would come after her for some twisted reason. He promised himself that he would stop by for a visit.

As he neared his house, Greco tried to focus on thoughts of home, but the ugly images of both murders were hard to shut out. As a new homicide detective, his psyche hadn't become desensitized by prolonged exposure to multiple crime scenes. The more he tried to shut it out, the more the violent images were superimposed on his mind. Why so much force? The coroner had declared two causes of death for Norma and he would probably make the same finding after examining June's body. Why the viciousness? Easy targets, Greco thought. And for what? The killer takes the trouble to calmly remove both phone cords, uses just one and doesn't even bother to take June's checkbook?

Pulling into his driveway, Greco turned off the car engine and sat for a second, his head pounding in the morning sun. Why go overboard with overkill and leave the cash behind? And a diamond ring? And credit cards?

He wondered if the killer wasn't getting some pleasure out of this.

CHAPTER FOUR

TUESDAY, MARCH 1, 1994

The woman with the frizzy blonde hair plopped an armful of swim suits on the counter and handed clerk Kellie Jacobs a Mervyn's charge card. She seemed to be in her 30s—and in a big hurry.

It was just a few minutes after 9 a.m. Kellie thought it odd that someone would buy so many swimsuits not only early in the day but early in the season. The customer also had a black net beach cover-up and a fish-themed beach tote. While the woman fidgeted, Kellie methodically scanned the bar code on each item. The total was a few cents shy of $300. But the charge wouldn't go through. The cash register's computer wouldn't work.

"Do you have a photo ID?" Kellie asked.

"I have nothing. I don't have anything with me," the blonde woman said, frowning. "Can you hurry up? I have to be somewhere."

Kellie hesitated. The computerized cash register wouldn't let the sale go through without proper authorization.

"You know what," the blonde woman said, "just call the girls in lingerie, because I was here yesterday and they just let it go through."

Kellie became flustered. She picked up the phone to call a manager. This woman was getting upset with her and she didn't know what she was supposed to do. When the manager arrived, she asked for a home address and the woman rattled off some numbers on Big Tee Drive in Canyon Lake. But they didn't match what the computer had entered as customer June Roberts' correct address.

"I just moved there and I don't remember the address," she said with an irritated tone to her voice.

"Look, just void it out and use my Visa," she said, fishing

the card out of her purse. "I told you, I'm really in a hurry. I've got to go."

Though Kellie felt there was something suspicious about this pushy customer, her manager put the sale through using the Visa card. The woman stormed off. But she wasn't through at Mervyn's. Before she left, she bought seven pairs of boys' Levi's for a total of $154.01. The clerk in the boys' department let the sale go through.

Clerk Maria de Soto had barely opened her register at Sav-On in Lake Elsinore when a blonde woman started unloading a shopping cart full of items onto the cashier's treadmill. As Maria rung up each item, the woman talked in a loud, nervous voice with her companion, a tallish man with a slicked-back black hair and a beer belly. Kitchen trash bags. Fabric softener. A toilet duck. Carpet spray. Menstrual pads. Two 1.75 bottles of Smirnoff vodka. Four bottles of Ban de Soleil suntan lotion. Two cartons of Marlboro Lights. Maria chatted with the customer, wondering how she'd gotten a tan so early in the year, as she rang up each item.

Now that's unusual, Maria thought to herself. No one ever buys two cartons of Marlboro Lights. Or six rolls of Brawny paper towels.

The woman charged the $138.60 total on her Visa charge and the two customers walked out with the bags. It was 10:04 a.m.

Dana was in a hurry. She had an appointment for a massage at the upscale Murrieta Hot Springs resort at 11 a.m., a twenty-minute drive. Dana turned into the driveway, landscaped with indigenous cactus and succulent plants. Oversized palm trees with frothy fronds caressed the blue skies. She stopped briefly at the guard shack and continued on to the main building. She parked, checked in, bought a pool pass and was shown to one of the changing rooms where she disrobed, sheathed herself in a wrap-around towel and waited for her masseuse. Fifty minutes later, she emerged, put on one of her swimsuits and paddled around the pool for a few minutes. She got dressed, browsed in the gift shop and put a $32.33 purchase, the $50 massage and a $10 tip on June's credit card.

By noon, Dana was lunching at the Ferrari Bistro, a

racecar-themed Italian restaurant in Temecula in a new shopping center next to a string of car dealerships. She ordered so much food—calamari, tortellini with basil tomato sauce and iced tea—that she took the leftover portions with her.

At 1 p.m., Greco was at his desk, trying to stay calm. He was fending off grogginess with coffee and typing in notes from his notebook so he could write his report on June's homicide. As his fingers tapped the keyboard, he became immersed in the crime scene again.

His phone rang. It was a reporter for the local newspaper. Could he talk about the recent murder at Canyon Lake? How is the investigation progressing? Do they have a suspect?

Greco gave the reporter a quote, simply saying that the department was investigating the homicide of an elderly female, without giving any details, like the cause of death, which Greco knew the reporter could eventually get from the coroner's department. Greco hung up the phone feeling a renewed wave of panic. He was relieved that the reporter hadn't asked whether the murders were related. But he knew he would be investigating them in a political hotbox.

By tomorrow, his worst fears would be realized. The case would be in the newspapers. The residents would be up in arms. There would be pressure from the family. Everyone was expecting him to solve the case. Greco knew he had squat. He had absolutely nothing in the way of a suspect.

The Lake Elsinore Outlet Mall lures the kind of suburban shoppers who will drive more than 100 miles round trip to spend money. The 35-acre behemoth, constructed in standard-issue but fashionable whitewashed stucco, with Western-themed accents, is the unlikely desert home to 110 discount designer stores. Lake Elsinore's only other point of interest, besides the lake itself, is the Elsie Museum, containing "evidence" of a sea serpent purportedly lurking in Lake Elsinore.

Dana first stopped at Perfumania, a discount perfume boutique, for two bottles of her favorite scent, Opium. $128.11. Half an hour later, she was cruising the aisles of Famous Brands with her dark-haired male companion, stocking up on spices, blue glass bowls, golf-, cat-, and pig-themed novelty switchplates, children's scissors and extremely sharp poultry shears. Store manager Jean Smothers noticed that the blonde customer wore several rings on her left hand and seemed extremely nervous.

"Will these scissors cut bone?" the man asked Smothers. He seemed to have an East Coast accent.

"Yes, they will," Jean replied.

His companion seemed so unnerved by this exchange that she knocked down a counter display at the checkout stand. Smothers rang up the scissors, the spices and the switchplates $49.87.

Seven minutes later, Dana zoomed out of 9 West, a popular shoe store, with a pair of ladies' dress shoes. $37.68. The next stop was the Nike Factory Outlet Store, across the mall's spacious palm-lined walk-way. While the tall man held her other purchases, Dana pulled boxes of athletic shoes and exercise wear off the display racks and stacked them on the counter. The cashier, noticing that she seemed anxious and hurried, rang up the sale while Dana continued to pull items off the shelf. Paying with June's credit card, Dana walked away with white stretchy Everlast boxing tights, multi-colored exercise leggings, racer-back workout tops and bottoms, and a variety of exercise shoes for her live-in boyfriend, Jim, and herself. At 4:33 p.m., Dana and her other male friend emerged from the Nike store with $339.04 worth of merchandise charged to June. She hurried home to fix dinner for Jim and Jason.

WEDNESDAY, MARCH 2, 1994, 9:10 A.M.

"You've got some visitors."

Greco looked up from his coffee to see Sergeant Wenker standing over his desk. "It's the family of June Roberts. The son-in-law is a detective in Nevada. He works homicide. He wants to know who's handling his mother-in-law's murder investigation. They're in the lobby right now."

Greco took a gulp of coffee, put his jacket back on, walked out to the lobby and tried his best to act confident. The Perris Police building had once been a high school, and, as was the case in many of the neighborhoods in its city, several rooms were trailers. Trailers with connecting hall-ways housed the detective bureau and offices. Greco walked through the hallway to the front lobby that opened onto a small patio. Three women and two men. They looked upset and one of the women was weeping.

In a soft voice, Greco introduced himself as the investi-gator, offered his condolences and said he would do his best on the case.

A sturdy-looking man in his 40s stepped forward and asked loudly, "Who's the primary investigator on this case?"

"I am," Greco said.

Greco's words hung in the air as the man angrily stared at Greco's peaches-and-cream complexion and college stu-dent's whisper of a moustache.

Greco held out his hand.

"I'm Detective Joe Greco," he said.

"How long have you been a detective?" the man barked.

"Six months," Greco answered. "But I'm pretty tena-cious . . ."

Shaking his head, the man refused the handshake and turned away. Greco dropped his hand. His face felt hot.

A blonde woman in her 40s stepped forward and intro-duced herself as Susan Van Owen, June's daughter. She lived out of state. She and Greco spoke for a few minutes, then Greco watched them file out the door before he headed back to his desk. He didn't blame them for doubting his efforts. He didn't have much faith in himself, either.

"What's going on out here?"

"Is there some connection between these murders?"

"How come you guys can't catch this guy?"

"I'd like to report a transient in the neighborhood—I think it might be related to these murders."

By midday, Greco had fielded 15 to 20 phone calls and that didn't include calls from the press. James McElvain dropped by Greco's desk with a couple of newspaper articles and Greco read his quotes in print. Members of the com-munity no doubt read the paper; word of the newest murder would spread quickly. Some of the callers were hostile, some fearful, and some offered tips. One person who had the misfortune to resemble a transient walked through the private development and triggered more than a handful of calls. Greco heard repeat phone reports of people driving beat-up cars, and of pedestrians whom the caller didn't recognize. He fielded so many calls that he couldn't get any work done on this or any of his other cases. Of the leads he followed up on, all went nowhere. Greco chalked up some callers' hostility to a panic reaction. Canyon Lake's residents were not shy about complaining. Greco didn't know what to tell them, except to assure them that the investigation was proceeding and everything possible was being done to solve the homicides.

Greco decided to ask Sgt. Wenker for help with the calls. Wenker assigned a non-sworn officer to screen them, categorize them as complaints, comments or leads, and forward relevant information to Greco. The overflow during off-hours would be routed to an answering machine. When the news stories ran their course, Wenker said, the calls would start to die down.

As soon as he got back to his desk, the phone rang again.

"This is Charles Van Owen," he said. "You left some evidence here at the house. You need to come and pick it up."

Greco hesitated. At first he didn't recognize the voice, but quickly realized he was talking to the out-of-state homicide detective who'd refused his handshake earlier that morning. Van Owen sounded perturbed and Greco felt himself tense up. Greco knew Van Owen already thought little of his investigative skills and wondered what evidence they'd left at the house. Greco told Van Owen he'd be there as soon as he could.

When he got there, Greco found June's relatives in the middle of the disturbing task of cleaning the house. Ugly blotches of June's dried blood stained the carpet and the arc of blood still swept across the side of the desk. Greco realized that his inexperience—his having missed potentially vital evidence—probably heightened their distress. He had been right behind the criminalists the whole time and thought they had picked up everything important.

"There." Van Owen pointed. He was barely civil, but Greco didn't blame him. Who wouldn't be angry after a loved one was slaughtered in her own home? He was not about to argue with a grieving family.

There was June's bloody, brown plastic hairband, a typed list of Canyon Lake canasta players and their phone numbers, a small child's drawing with a handwritten name and address on the back and a ticket stub to a movie labelled *Do Anything*, which bore a time stamp. Any of that could be important, Greco agreed. Van Owen said some of the papers were taken from June's wastebasket, suggesting that he hadn't bothered to look through his mother-in-law's garbage. Greco let the comment go and simply agreed to collect it. He didn't have a good answer as to why the hairband and the ticket stub had not been picked up. Greco had left the homicide scene, his third, thinking he had been as thorough as possible. He slid his hands into the latex gloves from the evidence kit that he kept in his trunk, put the items in paper lab envelopes, and labeled them.

Greco worked as quickly as possible, not wanting to prolong his task as Van Owen looked over his shoulder. When Van Owen suggested that he also collect four knives in the kitchen and a pair of kitchen scissors, Greco agreed. The knives and the scissors had been laid out on the kitchen counter and could contain fingerprints.

How could we miss this? Greco thought. He wasn't sure if Van Owen knew about Norma's murder, or the fact that she had been stabbed, but judging from Van Owen's anger and stony silence, he probably did. Greco wanted to tell him that he'd used all the resources available to him and that he'd even tried to call the FBI, but decided to keep his mouth shut.

Before he left, he exchanged a few words with June's other daughter, Linda Dorsey, who lived in San Diego. The victim had spent her birthday weekend with Linda and left for home on the afternoon of Sunday, February 27, her birthday. The last time Linda heard from her mother was when she phoned to say she'd arrived home safely and to remind Linda to take the chicken stock off the stove. June was murdered the following day.

On the drive back to his office, Greco felt the strain of being watched at every turn. Not only were the public and his entire department monitoring his every move, but Van

Owen, who had many more years of experience than he did, was literally looking over his shoulder. He knew he couldn't ask Van Owen for help because it would only confirm Van Owen's suspicions that he really was incompetent. Greco tried hard not to sink into self-destructive thinking again; he would be paralyzed by fear.

The more Greco thought about it, the more angry he became that Van Owen was judging him on his looks. Yes, he looked young. But he wasn't a kid anymore. He had a wife and three children. He had done well in his career and had even been honored for his work. Just because he hadn't investigated many homicides didn't mean he couldn't solve this one. He deserved a chance.

When Greco returned to the office, he booked the evidence, then tried to call Jeri. No answer. He'd tried to reach her the day before with no luck, so he left another message. He wanted to see what Jeri had to say about why Norma's housekeeper, Ila Tingley, was on June's prayer list. Greco also found it interesting that June lived right around the corner from Jeri. He'd made a mental note of that when he went to the crime scene that night, and had later plotted their homes on a map of Canyon Lake just to eyeball the locations. Out of curiosity, he also plotted Norma's condo and Alice's house. Norma, June and Jeri all lived within a few blocks of each other.

Greco was convinced that Jeri was not a killer, but he felt she had some kind of connection to the killings. He had dropped by Jeri's house several times since Norma's murder to plumb for more information, and had completed the victimology—the summary of Norma's life, work, marriages, children and family connections. The only remarkable aspect was the fact that Jeri had taken on the responsibility of caring for Norma in her later years. Jeri had married Norma's son in 1952 and had three children, two boys and a girl. He died of a stroke in 1982 and Jeri assumed the responsibility of taking care of Norma. Jeri and Russell, her second husband, were married in 1986. Jeri's grown sons lived in a nearby county. Russell had a grown daughter who lived nearby.

Jeri said that her grandson had borrowed Norma's car over the Christmas holidays with the understanding that he had no obligation to return it immediately. In late January, the car was stolen from his house in Hollywood. Police later found it stripped. Greco took down the information. Maybe the car thieves took Norma's address from the registration slip in her car. It was worth looking into.

"So, are you ready?" Wyatt was standing over his desk. They were going to see the psychic who had predicted June's murder. Greco was skeptical about anyone claiming to predict the future, but he had two murder cases open without much in the way of a lead and he was curious about what this guy could tell him.

At least he had a really nice house. An elderly man with white hair welcomed them into his spacious, sunny living room. Because Wyatt's responsibility was Canyon Lake, he already knew the psychic so they exchanged pleasantries and Wyatt introduced Greco.

"Give me a moment," the psychic said.

He sat down with a pad of paper and, with slow, deliberate movements, began to draw in wide circles, scribbling some words.

"I see a golf cart . . . two women in a golf cart," he said. "This may or may not have significance."

Greco rolled his eyes. This man was wasting their time.

"It's a woman," the psychic said. "She has a partner, a female partner."

This guy's crazy, Greco thought. What can he possibly do, give me the killer's phone number?

The psychic looked up and asked Greco if he could get a personal item of June's. He also wanted to see June's autopsy report.

Greco had no idea whether the old man was a con artist or was actually seeing a vision. But it didn't matter. The information was so vague, it was useless. Greco told him he'd think about it and thanked him for his time.

"There's something else," the psychic said. "You're going to solve the case."

By the time he got back to the office, the LAPD had faxed the report about the stolen car. Beyond the block-out information—the time of the incident, information about the vehicle, the names and addresses of the individuals involved—there wasn't much of interest in the report.

He also checked with the community service officer about calls from the public. Officer Julie Bennett had created a note card system with the name of the caller, the reason for the call, and a return phone number. She said it seemed like fifty people in Canyon Lake all saw the same transient and called the police department. She added that the calls spanned the spectrum—some people were angry and upset and others were genuinely frightened. Those who saw the transient were convinced that the murders were committed by an outsider. Greco flipped through the cards and pulled out the few offering concrete leads that he could follow up on. He wasn't about to assume that a transient was responsible for either murder. Before he left, he tried calling Jeri again. No answer.

On the way home, Greco stopped to see Alice even though she was forty minutes out of his way. She was so frightened, he had to shout through the door to identify himself before she unlocked it.

Alice didn't look good. She seemed even more frail than she had the last time he'd seen her. Greco watched her pale, wrinkled face turn into a smile when she greeted him; it looked like she hadn't smiled in quite a while. She was extremely grateful that he'd stopped by. Greco didn't stay long. He didn't mention that he had to attend June's autopsy in the morning.

FRIDAY, MARCH 4, 1994, 12:25 P.M.

This woman could have lived another twenty years, Greco thought as he peeled off the disposable paper jumpsuit, plastic apron, and mask. She was in amazing shape for a woman of 66. She didn't have an ounce of fat on her. She would have had a long life ahead of her if she hadn't been killed by this monster.

The amount of force the killer used to brutalize June was just sick. The way the phone cord was so tightly wrapped, it looked like she had been in a lot of pain. In a way, he hoped he never got over being upset by seeing that. He was disgusted by this killer and tormented by questions. Whose hand held the bottle? Whose hands grabbed June's neck and then coiled the telephone cord around it? Having no appetite for lunch, Greco drove straight back to the Department and booked the evidence from the autopsy—June's clothing and vials of her blood. The crime lab technician who took the photos would develop the film and deliver the prints next week.

Haunted by the images from the autopsy, Greco sat down at his desk to write his report. He had to write down the start time of the autopsy and the times when certain organs were examined, to summarize and describe the findings. Marianne Stam, the DOJ criminalist, had been right. At the crime scene, she had noticed purplish marks on June's neck that resembled fingernail marks. The pathologist found that June had died of manual and ligature strangulation as well as blunt force trauma to the head. At the crime scene, Greco saw that June bore no defensive wounds. The pathologist confirmed that. Greco typed it into his report. This killer had so overpowered June that she was unable even to fight back, leaving no scratching or bruising on her hands or forearms. If the marks on June's neck did come from fingernail marks, it was impossible to tell whether they were from the killer or from June trying to pull the cord off her neck, which would explain why she bore no defensive wounds. Greco thought June knew her killer. That would explain the lack of a forced entry and why June didn't try to get her gun.

When he finished, he worked on a few leads from the phone calls, did some follow-up on the theft of Norma's car in Los Angeles and tried calling Jeri several times. Still no answer. He was starting to get concerned. Maybe she and Russell went out of town for a few days. Greco decided to stay late and work on his other cases.

Marianne Stam called late in the day with some results from the crime lab. No discernible fingerprints from the June Roberts crime scene. That wasn't unusual. Despite the frequency with which TV detectives find perfect fingerprints, getting good ones is unusual in real life. Stam was about to examine the hair and fiber evidence but had forgotten to get control samples. Could Greco go back to June's house and get a few fibers of carpet from each room?

Greco said he would, but when he hung up the phone, his heart sank. The family was going to think he was an

idiot. It was after 6 p.m. He wondered if they were still at
the house. Greco hoped that maybe Linda or her sister
would pick up the phone, but he was out of luck. He could
practically hear Van Owen smirk when he told him what he
wanted. Van Owen said he was glad Greco called, because
Van Owen was going to call him anyway. He didn't say
why. Greco said he would come out right away. This time,
Greco's insecurities were tempered by his desire to be sympathetic to the families. They were entitled to a little anger,
he reasoned, and some of it might get misdirected at him.
He wanted to be understanding, reassuring.

When he got there, Van Owen suggested that he'd missed
more evidence. Greco was horrified.

"We moved the couch and there was quite a bit of glass
there," he said, motioning to the shattered glass streaked
with blood. Greco said he would collect it.

"Aren't you going to take the chair?" Van Owen said,
nodding at the heavy chair to which June had been tied.
Greco agreed immediately, even though he thought that the
chair would yield nothing of evidentiary value. The criminalists had already tested the chair for blood—it was all
June's—and fingerprints—there were none. He was there
when the criminalists collected bloodstains from the chair.
But he wanted to appease Van Owen. Using the evidence
kit from his trunk, he picked up the glass first, then turned
his attention to the chair. There was simply no way to pick
it up without contaminating it: the chair was too large. He
carried it out the door, down the driveway, and into his
trunk, where it was certain to pick up carpet fiber and hair
from his own car.

It was so big, it stuck out of his trunk. He used rope to
tie the chair in the trunk and went back inside to collect the
carpet fibers he'd come for in the first place. Van Owen had
disappeared into the house somewhere. Greco quickly visited each room, pulled tufts of carpet fiber with tweezers,
wiping and cleaning them before collecting each separate
sample. Marianne Stam would use them as control samples,
comparing them with fibers found at the crime scene to see
if they came from a source other than June's own home.
Greco carefully labeled each envelope. Julie, who had apparently been working in another room, greeted Greco as he

was packing up his kit. They exchanged a few words and Greco left, pulling away from the curb with the chair sticking out of his trunk.

MONDAY, MARCH 7, 1994, 3 P.M.

Greco hung up the phone. He still couldn't reach Jeri and didn't know what to make of it. He'd spent most of the day doing follow-up and running down a few of the phoned-in tips; they were all dead ends. The photo lab technician said the crime-scene photos would be developed by Wednesday. Greco had avoided looking at the stack of cases that he'd largely ignored for the past two weeks while working on the homicides. He reached for the first file when the phone rang. It was Linda Dorsey. She'd returned home to San Diego over the weekend and was wondering if there was anything new on the case.

Greco told her that he was looking at every possible angle and lead, but there was still no break in the case.

"Well, what kind of progress have you made on the credit cards?"

The words stung Greco like a slap.

"What credit cards?" he asked, dumbfounded.

"Well . . . you know, Mom's credit cards," Linda asked. "We got the letter from the bank saying there was unusual activity on the cards after Mom's death. Charles said he talked to Wyatt, your supervisor."

"Well, I'm sorry I can't give you an update right now, but I'll let you know as soon as I hear something," Greco told her. "We'll take care of it from here. Thanks for the call."

Greco hung up the phone feeling humiliated. So, Van Owen went over his head and talked to Wyatt. Big surprise. But why didn't Wyatt come to him with the information? Even if a disgruntled relative goes to someone else in the department, all critical data needs to be funneled through the primary investigator. This was his investigation. Linda assumed that if her family convoyed important information to someone in the department, it would be shared. The fact that it did not reach Greco at all was embarrassing, and reflected badly on the department as well as on him. That made him angry.

Why would Wyatt leave him in the dark? And if he wasn't telling him about the credit cards, what was he doing with the information? Was he chasing down the credit cards himself? As a supervisor, Wyatt hadn't interviewed the witnesses. Supervisors ask for briefings, or they just ask how the case is going—they don't grab files or phone messages off your desk or investigate your case without your knowledge. A supervisor's function is not to take over your job.

Greco didn't want to believe that his supervisor was trying to take control of the case. He knew he had to talk to Wyatt. There were much better things to do than muck around in petty office politics. If there was some crazed serial killer out there, they needed to be pooling resources and solving these murders, not hoarding clues.

Greco started categorizing various significant points about the credit card information. First of all, the killer was one cold-hearted customer to paw through June's cards, picking and choosing, instead of just grabbing the whole purse and looking through it later. Second, it pointed to a potential motive for June's murder. The activity on the cards seemed to be high enough to trigger a letter to the cardholder from the bank's fraud unit. Last, and most important, the person using the cards, Greco hoped, had to be the killer. If the murderer had gone from store to store to store, maybe enough clerks and cashiers had seen this person and could work with a police sketch artist to create a composite drawing. It was obvious that running down the credit cards could be a shortcut to the killer.

He didn't see Wyatt McElvain until late in the afternoon.

"There was an elderly woman found dead. I think you should go out and look into it," he said.

Greco nearly jumped out of his skin.

"Where?"

"Off Wilkerson and Fourth. Found dead in her bathroom. She'd had health problems," he said. He gave Greco the address. "It's an unattended death."

Greco stopped in his tracks. He knew the address. It was

a retirement home. Why was he being asked to deal with this?

"Why doesn't James go?" Greco asked.

"He's coming with me," Wyatt said. "Besides, I think you should go."

Greco wasn't going to stand there and argue with his supervisor.

He went.

MONDAY, MARCH 7, 1994, 7 P.M.

Greco was fuming. The elderly woman had been dead in her bathroom for two weeks. It was obvious she'd had medical problems. The coroner declared it an unattended death. There was no crime scene; there would be no autopsy.

Anyone could have handled it. He'd wasted hours of his time, hours that had taken him away from doing follow-up on the murders. This was just baloney. Not that dealing with the retirement home death was unimportant it just wasn't something he needed to be spending his time on when he had two homicides. If he'd had doubts about Wyatt's intentions before, they disappeared. He was convinced that Wyatt wanted to run with his information and solve the case. He didn't want to think that the homicides were being taken out of his hands, but that was the only conclusion he could draw. Still, Greco knew that his lack of experience and insecurity jacked up his feelings of paranoia. Greco knew that solving a high-profile case could make or break someone's career. As in any office or any other workplace, politics plays a factor in police work. Neither Wyatt nor Greco was naïve about the value of self-promotion. He intended to speak to Lieutenant Henry Gaskins about the Roberts family and the credit cards. If they didn't want him on this case, then they should give it to someone else.

When he got back to the office, he ran into Julie, the community service officer who'd helped handle the influx of phone calls from the public.

"Hey, good break on the murders, eh?" she said with a smile.

Greco stared at her, wondering why on earth everyone

else knew what was going on with his cases but him.

"Yeah," Greco said. "Thanks. Do you know if Wyatt's still around?"

"I heard he was chasing down the credit cards," she said.

Wyatt and James were leaving Temecula, where they'd interviewed the owner of Baily's Wine Country Café and the theft reduction manager at Mervyn's. Both men, at the café and the department store, said they would look for the receipts bearing June's account numbers, and would tell the pertinent employees that the police wanted to speak with them.

TUESDAY, MARCH 8, 1994, 9:10 A.M.

Greco, Wyatt McElvain and Henry Gaskins were sitting around the conference table at the Perris station.

Greco started in.

"I'm trying to define what my job is here. I don't understand why he's taking the credit cards and doing follow-up without my knowledge. I should be able to do my own follow-up. He didn't come to me. He didn't tell me anything about it."

"Oh, you're overreacting," McElvain said. "I'm just here to help you."

Greco knew it was a lie.

"That's bullshit! You're not here to help me, you're here to promote yourself!" Greco said angrily, keeping his voice low. Gaskins sat back, watching, and let them have it out. He knew there had been tension between the two of them. For some reason, they didn't get along. Months ago, when they had a disagreement in the computer room, he had had to come in and tell them to cut their arguing out. Things had been simmering for a while.

"That's ridiculous!" Wyatt said. "That has nothing to do with it."

"You know what? You can have it all. If you're going to continue to do your own investigation, you can go ahead and take the whole thing. It's yours."

"Oh no, no," Wyatt said. "I'm not here to take away your

case. I'm just here to assist you. You're making a big deal out of nothing. I'm just helping you out."

"That's a lie!"

Gaskins had heard enough.

"Joe," Gaskins said. "You're the primary investigator. You're in charge of your own case. Wyatt is at your disposal. Wyatt, you're here to assist Joe. Your only responsibility is to oversee the investigation."

That didn't satisfy Greco.

"If he's at my disposal, why is he telling me what to do? Why is he keeping information about my own case from me?"

"Joe, you're the primary, it's your case," Gaskins said. "Wyatt is the case supervisor."

"All a supervisor should do is ask how things are going; and I give him a briefing or a report on my progress," he said. "At this point, I have no control over this aspect of the investigation because he kept this information from me so that he could work on it himself and try to solve the case."

Wyatt shook his head.

"I was just trying to help," he said.

The blow-up was over. Greco walked out feeling better for, if nothing else, standing up for himself. He didn't really want to give up the case—what would he tell the families? That he'd quit? He couldn't do that.

Even after all this, Greco knew he still had no control over the investigation. After the meeting, Wyatt parcelled out the Mervyn's accounts to Greco, saying they were the most important, and kept the remaining vendors. He knew that Wyatt still wanted to solve the case, but there was nothing he could do about that. He had no interest in competing with Wyatt. His race was with the killer.

Dana was knocking at her father's door.

"Hi, Jeri, hi, Dad," she said, giving each a one-armed hug. In the other arm she was cradling a pan of lasagne. "I made you my specialty."

"Oh, I see you got the flowers," Dana said, noting the arrangement in the living room. "How are you guys doing?"

Jeri nodded and managed to smile. She wasn't too talkative and neither was Russ. They were all clad in dark mourning attire.

"Well, are you ready to go?" Dana asked.

Jeri shut her eyes, squeezing out a tear, and nodded. Russell took her arm and they went outside and got in the Cadillac.

Jeri had tried to delay telling her 30-year-old daughter, Susie, the news about Nana getting murdered. Susie, a diabetic since she was an infant, was on dialysis. Her health had always been fragile and she had a particularly close relationship with her step-grandmother-in-law. When Jeri finally told her daughter the sad news, Susie's health took a sharp downturn. She died two weeks after Norma was murdered. Jeri knew that it was more stress than Susie could handle at one time. She couldn't help but blame the person who killed Norma.

"Whoever killed Mom killed Susie, too," Jeri blurted out in the car.

Dana's head whipped around. She looked startled.

"What makes you say a thing like that?"

CHAPTER FIVE

THURSDAY, MARCH 10, 1994, 1:40 P.M.

Dorinda Hawkins was on her hands and knees picking up papers when she heard the light tinkling of the bell on the front door of the Main Street Trading Post. The antique store, located in Lake Elsinore, boasted a comfortable flea-market feel. The front window displayed chairs and tables of various vintages, a lamp from the 1950s with a ruffled shade, and kitchen ceramics in a variety of decorative fowl. A window sign advertised custom framing. The rest of the store was obscured by curtains framing the merchandise.

"Hi! How are you today?" Dorinda said as she stood up, brushing the dirt from her black stretch pants.

Dana Sue Gray smiled at the 57-year-old woman as she walked through the store, passing by a 1920s metal tricycle black with age, crystal candy dishes, brass floor lamps, an open steamer trunk, lanterns, cameras, a mirrored dresser, and neon beer signs. Dana had been thinking about framing some advertising pictures of her mother, who used to be a model, and wanted to check out some older frames. On the wall near the cash register were a variety of cuckoo clocks and light blue racks holding collectable silver spoons. A windowed display case at the cashier's desk held Hummel figurines, Disney collectables, toy trains, and Oriental jade. Dana sized up Dorinda as she passed by.

Fat barfly. Crossing your arms like that makes me want to vomit. I want you to die.

"Oh, alone again?" Dana Sue Gray said as she wound her way through the store, which had a light feel because of the high ceilings, white walls, and white display cabinets. The store was somewhat narrow but very deep. Far to the back of the store was the framing area. A yellow rope,

strung between two higher white cabinets, closed off the
area to customers.

"Yes, as usual," Dorinda said. She picked up the last of
the papers and walked back to the framing area to get a tape
measure. She was helping out at the store that day as a favor
to her good friend, the 74-year-old store owner who did the
framing and matting.

Dorinda reached the back of the store and was surprised
to find her customer already back there. Dana asked about
matting and framing, so Dorinda unhooked the yellow rope
partition and stepped inside the employee area to get the
tape measure and show off the owner's work. Dana followed
her in. They stepped around another dusty vintage tricycle,
odd frames in various sizes, and a few pieces of framing
equipment on the tables. Corners of sample frames hung
along one wall and a plastic box crammed with different
colored mats sat on the counter. Dorinda walked around the
huge framing table, about five feet wide and eight feet long,
wrapped in protective brown paper and strewn with tools.

"This is a lovely example of her work," Dorinda said,
picking up a picture with three types of matting that was
leaning against the wall.

"Oh, I don't like that one," Dana said.

*What a piece of shit. I can't believe she's showing me
this cruddy frame.*

"I'm just showing you the matting and framing," Dorinda
said, quickly putting the picture back down on the floor.
Dana came up behind her and touched the back of the picture.

"Oh, that's beautiful work," Dana said, commenting on
how well the paper covered the back of the picture.

*Condescending barfly trying to palm off these pieces of
crap. Trying to act important.*

"Oh, what are those?" She pointed to two framed pictures
of hunting scenes that leaned against the wall. "Can I see
those?"

"Sure," Dorinda said, bending over to pick them up. "I
don't know if the owner wants to sell them though."

"I want to see them anyway," Dana said. "I really like
this one." It showed a group of men in vintage attire on
horseback, their steeds prancing, and dogs racing around the

horses' legs. They talked about the pictures for a moment, then Dorinda turned around to put them back on the floor, and looked for another one to show her customer.

Dorinda was still chatting when she felt something tighten around her neck. She froze for a moment, her mind going dead except for the thought that she wanted to look into the face of this person who hated her so much. As Dorinda straightened up, she saw Dana holding onto a yellow nylon rope with her left hand as her right hand pushed a slip knot toward the old woman's neck. Dorinda instinctively reached to pull the rope from her neck, and at the same time looked directly into the eyes of the stranger attacking her, expecting hatred and finding none. She saw no emotion, only a look of determination that she had a job to do and she was going to do it. She saw no hate, no malice, no excitement, no hint of a drug-crazed gleam. Just a look like she had killed before.

"Lady, why are you doing this?" Dorinda managed to choke out. She thought of pulling the rope toward her, but before she could react, Dana jerked the rope violently downward and Dorinda fell to her knees, out of sight to anyone walking by or even anyone at the front of the store. Fighting for her life, Dorinda's mind recorded many details: Her attacker had smooth skin and no make-up. The ends of the rope had been melted to prevent fraying. The six-foot-long rope was wrapped twice around her attacker's hands for a good grip. The image of her attacker's stony face became cemented in her memory.

Dana tried to force Dorinda onto her stomach. Instead, Dorinda squirmed around and fell into a sitting position with her legs bent under her. With Dana still pushing her down, Dorinda managed to get one leg out in front of her, then shifted her weight to get the other leg free so both legs were extended in front of her. Dana upped the pressure on her neck, jerking the rope, and Dorinda momentarily steadied herself with her hands behind her on the floor. With as much effort as she could muster, she kicked Dana in the stomach with both feet. The first kick caught Dana off guard, but she held onto the rope. Dorinda kicked again, and Dana nimbly jumped back. It gave Dorinda enough time to slip her fingers between the rope and her neck, but it added to the pressure on her neck, so she slid her fingers out again. As she felt the rope, she realized that her attacker had turned it around so the knot was positioned on her windpipe.

Dana's legs were spread apart and she was leaning backward as far as she could. Dorinda tried pulling on the rope to kick her attacker off balance, but Dana stood her ground. Spotting a broom nearby, Dorinda used all her strength to drag her and Dana over to where she could grab it. Dorinda rose slightly off the floor with one hand, lunging at Dana with the broom in the other, jabbing Dana in the chest. Dana dodged her second attempt as Dorinda's strength faltered and the yellow-handled broom fell uselessly out of her hands and landed on top of her. The last attempt sapped Dorinda's endurance and her consciousness lapsed. When she awoke again, Dana was on top of her with one foot on her chest for leverage.

"Lady, why are you doing this to me?" Dorinda asked again. Dana's only answer was to pull the rope tighter.

"Brian!" Dorinda cried for the shop clerk next door. "Brian!" Her voice came out in a futile whisper, a silent scream in a living nightmare.

"Be quiet!" Dana said in a calm voice.

"Oh God! I never wanted to die like this! Please don't kill me! I've got eight kids!" Dorinda pleaded with Dana. Dorinda wasn't sure that her attacker could even hear her speak or make out her words, they were so faint.

Still flat on her back, Dorinda saw that her head was near the heavy framing table. She twisted and wriggled, with Dana still on her chest, so she could grab a leg of the table, surprised that she had the strength to pull both herself and her attacker. When she got close enough, she grabbed the table leg for leverage and was able to roll Dana off her chest. Dana stumbled, but regained her stance and stepped on Dorinda's head, increasing the pressure on the rope.

"Please don't kill me," she pleaded in a whisper.

"I'm not here for money," Dana said calmly.

Dorinda flitted in and out of consciousness. When she awoke again, Dorinda croaked out, "Cash register key on wrist," motioning toward the red plastic coil around her forearm.

"I'm not after the money," Dana said again.

Dorinda was still clutching the table leg, her shoulders hunched like a turtle, and begged for her life, tears rolling down her face. She wanted to tell her attacker that she had eight children, but she could only gasp. She knew she was dying. She knew she would never see her children again. She thought of her daughter who had been raped and had survived because she went limp. Dorinda thought maybe she should go limp, too.

She felt herself start to lose consciousness again and she heard Dana say, "Relax. Just relax," in a calm whisper, as if she were comforting a child. She could feel her attacker slipping the keys off her hand. Dorinda felt like she was dying. Her brain wasn't getting any oxygen and it felt as if her head were going to burst from the pressure.

Dorinda lost consciousness.

She'll be fine. She just fainted.

Dana took $5 out of Dorinda's purse, leaving a $20 bill, used the cash register key to take $25 from the cash drawer and walked out.

FRIDAY, MARCH 11, 1994, 8:30 A.M.

James McElvain stuck the newspaper in front of Greco's nose. He had come to work early and was already buried in reports.

"Hey, Joe," he said. "Did you see this?"

"Woman Choked by Assailant," Greco read the headline aloud. The short story ran on one of the inside pages.

"Maybe it's the same person," James said.

Greco gave it a quick read. "A Lake Elsinore woman was choked unconscious by an attacker who pulled a rope around her neck during a suspected robbery at a store, police reported . . ." The attacker was described as a woman with shoulder-length blonde hair, about five-foot, two inches. The victim, Dorinda Hawkins, had been treated and released at a local hospital.

It fit. Greco knew they were getting close. For the past three days, they'd been getting the same description from store clerks about a blonde woman in her mid-thirties using June's credit cards, sometimes accompanied by a dark-haired male. It had to be related. It was a good, solid lead, but he still didn't have a name. He glanced up at James.

"Someone should go check this out," Greco said. "You want to go talk to her?"

He nodded and turned away. He didn't have the heart to tell Greco that he and Wyatt had already interviewed her the night before in the emergency room.

Greco sat back, took a gulp of coffee and took another look at the article. He'd tried hard to keep an open mind about the kind of suspect they were looking for, but he had to admit, he found it a little weird that a female had strangled the antique store clerk. How often do you hear about a female attacking someone with a rope? The assailant fit the description given by the store clerks, but Greco thought the man with the female shopper could have been the killer, or that they had committed the murders together. Now they needed to expand their focus to include the possibility of a female acting alone. Still, they were making progress. They had a paper trail of credit cards. They had information about another attack. The pieces were starting to pull together. They needed a name. It had to be the same person, but they still didn't know who it was. Greco wasn't going to allow himself to be overly optimistic. They needed a name.

Greco, James and Wyatt had gone to all of the places the attacker went with the credit cards—Mervyn's, Sav-On, the lunch spots, the spa, the Nike factory outlet store, the perfume place, the housewares store. Clerks who could remember the customer gave similar descriptions. Many claimed she'd been in a hurry, one mentioned that she'd even knocked over a display in the housewares store. She was rude to one of the waiters. She wore her cowboy boots out of the Western wear store; she had made her selections quickly when she bought the diamond-and-sapphire earrings and Opium perfume.

Opium perfume. Diamond earrings. Cowboy boots. Lunch, a haircut, pampering at a spa. Liquor and cigarettes. Greco perused the list of purchases, trying to imagine the kind of person who would beat someone to death, who would strangle someone with her own hands, and then go out an après-murder spending spree. This must be a person without a whisper of remorse. Greco found it bizarre. What did it mean that this woman killed with vicious ferocity, and then went shopping? Was it a release after the intensity of the murder?

And now, with the attack on Dorinda, she seemed to be increasing the frequency of her killing. Between Norma and June, it was two weeks. Dorinda came 10 days later. The lag time between incidents was getting shorter, Greco thought. She was like an animal that can't stop itself after its first taste of blood.

He had many questions, but no one with whom to discuss them. It saddened Greco that he and his co-workers were unable to function as a team. After Tuesday's blow-up, they split up the credit card work. Greco found it ironic that even though Lt. Gaskins had told him that he was in charge, Wyatt had assigned him to go to Mervyn's, West Dallas, Esthetiques hair salon, the jewelry store and Ferrari Bistro. Greco worked mostly by himself while Wyatt and James teamed up. He sometimes went with either Wyatt or James to interview clerks. But even though they were working with the same information on the same case, they didn't have meetings to share what they had. There was no brainstorming, no discussions about what all of this information meant and how the investigation should proceed.

Wyatt never volunteered information, but Greco played by the rules and always told Wyatt, his supervisor, what he came up with. Occasionally James let him know what was going on, but he was going to night school and usually hit the road for class at the end of the day. James had known Wyatt when they were both deputies for the sheriff's department in Orange County. James was friends with both of them and was playing it straight down the middle. Greco knew Wyatt wanted to solve the case over everything else. Greco naturally wanted to solve the case—he had gotten close to Jeri and felt bad about June's family. He didn't want to let any of them down.

Greco picked up the paper again and looked at the story about the attack. Why an antique store? He looked up the address and marked it by sticking another pin on the map behind his desk. He'd marked the murders in Canyon Lake, the shopping spree in Temecula and Lake Elsinore, and now the new attack in Lake Elsinore. He tried to set up a timeline to show the times and dates of the purchases. Greco saw that the suspect had stopped at a Sav-On in Lake Elsinore at 4:59 p.m. on Feb. 28, that she'd gone back to that same store early the next morning before going out to Mervyn's and then Murrieta Hot Springs. He'd bet the suspect lived near that Sav-On. He made the mistake of sharing that with Wyatt and James. They had poked fun at his pin map.

One of the best clues came from the hairstylists and technicians at Esthetiques, the salon in Temecula. Lisa Thompkins, the technician who did the moustache and eyebrow wax, said she remembered the woman's face so well that "If I could draw, I would draw it for you." She said she could positively identify the woman if she saw her again.

She said the woman had come back a week later, on March 7, and wanted her hair dyed red, but Lisa wouldn't do it because her hair was, as she put it, "too frizzy." When the woman insisted, Lisa bluntly told her that her hair would fall out, and the woman left.

Greco took the information down, wondering if their suspect was starting to feel pressured enough to alter her appearance. Changing hair color from blonde to red is enough to throw some witnesses off. There was no way to tell if she found another salon to color her hair or if she did it herself. They could be looking for a blonde or a redhead.

A hairdresser at the same salon who gave the boy a "step cut" also remembered the woman's face and said she could identify both her and the boy. She'd given her name as June Roberts and the boy's name as Jason Wilkins. The next day, Greco asked Julie Bennett, the community service officer, to help him scour the public schools. She found a Jason Wilkins enrolled in a local elementary school who fit the age and description. Excited about the lead, Greco staked out the apartment where the boy lived, waiting for several hours for a woman fitting the suspect's profile to show up, but when she got there, she didn't come close to matching the description. Her hair was blonde, but it was very long and she was quite a bit heavier than the clerks said she'd be. Greco talked to her anyway, but it was a dead end.

Greco thought about the name. Jason Wilkins could be a false name. But even if Wilkins was the boy's name, it probably wasn't the suspect's last name. She had told the hairstylist at Esthetiques as well as the clerk at the Western store that the boy was like her son and that she was his "other" mommy. That was another piece of the puzzle.

Before he'd started the stake-out on the apartment, he'd finally caught up with Jeri and had gone out to Canyon Lake to talk to her. She was cooperative and helpful, as always, but offered no explanation about not returning Greco's calls. Greco didn't ask, even though they'd gotten to know one another and he thought that she'd become comfortable talking with him. He hadn't spoken with her since before June Roberts died, so the first thing he wanted to do was to see if she knew June, who had lived about a block from her. To Greco's surprise, she said they'd known each other quite well.

"Her husband and my husband were best friends," Jeri told him. "When her husband died, she just seemed to keep to herself more, although she did come over for dinner. June kind of shut everybody out except for other widows. I guess she didn't want to associate with other couples."

She said that she and Russell had occasionally run into June on the golf course and at the clubhouse.

Greco sat in her living room, getting excited as he listened, trying to think. They *were* friends. That was a connection, but there had to be more in order to link it all with the woman who was using the credit cards. Greco decided to share with Jeri what they'd learned in the past few days.

"Within an hour of June's murder, there was a female using her credit cards in Temecula," Greco told Jeri. "She was youngish, maybe in her 30s, with blonde, overpermed frizzy hair and had a young boy with her, about 5 years old. He's not her son, but he could be a step-son or something.

"The suspect was sort of bragging to one of the clerks that the little boy calls her 'Mom' or 'my other mom,' but it's not really her son," he said. "Do you know of anyone who fits that description, anyone who takes care of a small boy?"

Jeri paused for a moment, thinking, but drew a blank. She said she couldn't think of anyone.

Greco remembered the tip from the salon technician and told Jeri that the suspect had asked to get her hair dyed, but the colorist refused because it would fall out. Did Jeri know anyone who had recently dyed her hair, or anyone who was thinking about it?

Again, Jeri thought for a moment and shook her head.

Greco shared a few tidbits about the credit cards—that the killer or someone associated with the killer had gone on a spending spree, buying drug store items, clothing, perfume. One of the café waiters saw her leaving in a dark car, maybe a van or a sport utility vehicle. He alternated between sharing information about the credit cards, allowing it to sink in, giving her a chance to react, and then asking a question or two before moving to another detail. He wasn't sure exactly where it would lead—he was trying to figure out the link between the cases and he had a feeling that Jeri knew something that connected these murders, but it was probably something she thought was unimportant or unrelated. He just had to keep trying to find out what it was.

The next day, after the attack on Dorinda, Greco phoned Jeri and asked if he could come out and speak with her again. She agreed and Greco drove over. When he arrived, he sat on the couch and told Jeri about the short blonde woman who used a rope to strangle the saleswoman in an antique store, leaving her for dead. Jeri said she didn't know Dorinda and didn't remember ever being in that store. Greco quietly explained there was a strong possibility that the woman who used the credit cards and attacked the antique store clerk had also killed June and Norma. Jeri nodded her head and looked down as if she was thinking.

Jeri said she'd already seen the small article in the newspaper. It was being talked about at the mail boxes, on the golf courses, at the club house, in the beauty salons and over the back fences of Canyon Lake. She didn't mention to Greco that she and Russell had started keeping loaded guns by their sides 24 hours a day.

The gardener.

A transient.

Ritual cult sacrifice.

People were frightened and nervous, and some bordered on hysteria. This was Canyon Lake. This type of thing just didn't happen here. They'd moved here to get away from murders and violent crime. Most people who lived here didn't bother to lock their doors. That was before the killings. Now, well-heeled residents didn't hesitate to pick up the phone to call police if they saw anyone who looked like they didn't belong there. Anyone they didn't recognize was a potential suspect. As the volume of phone calls increased, Julie dutifully filled out the oversized index cards on each tip. She told Greco or Wyatt about the most promising leads, but most seemed motivated by fear and nothing more. People would call in to report a suspicious vehicle or person, but the most they could provide was a description of a person or a partial description of a car. Very rarely could they supply a license plate. When someone called to report a suspicious character, Julie Bennett immediately notified the officers at Canyon Lake so they could check it out.

The murders were *the* topic of conversation at Canyon Lake. The latest theory circulating was that they were the work of a bizarre cult engaging in ritual sacrifice. Because of the level of violence, the assumption was that it had to be the sick handiwork of deranged cult-members. The weekend after June's murder, one of the golf course groundsmen found strange markings near one of the greens. Burned into the grass, possibly with chlorine bleach or pesticide, were markings resembling a partial pentagram and the word "posse." The discovery intensified the fever pitch of speculation. Flocks of elderly residents made an exodus out of Canyon Lake to live with their adult children until the killer was caught. One group of card-playing women, terrified of living alone, but determined to stick it out, created what amounted to an unofficial Canyon Lake women's dormitory and bunked together in one home, figuring that a passel of widows was a better match against a serial killer than any one by herself.

Greco chalked up the golf course markings to kids on a drunk. He knew exactly what was inside the crime scene. If it had been a ritual killing, the murderer would have somehow marked the crime scene, rather than the golf course. He also knew there was a local gang calling themselves the Club Drive Posse. That wasn't hard to figure out.

The more amusing calls were false alarms. Wyatt had been cruising around Canyon Lake in plain clothes and an unmarked car, and residents, thinking he was an outsider, called the police department to report him as a suspicious person. Twice. Even in a town where everybody knows everything about everybody, no one was above suspicion.

FRIDAY, MARCH 11, 1994, 2 P.M.

"Yeah, I remember her. She had a little kid with her. A boy," the waiter at Baily's Wine Country Café in Temecula told Wyatt and James. "The kid was running around the tables and she was getting pretty annoyed."

The waiter's description of the woman and the boy was similar to that of the others who waited on them. He said the female was about five-feet, two-inches tall, stocky, with shoulder-length dark blonde hair. The boy was blonde, about 5 years old.

"She sat right at this table out here so she could smoke," he said, pointing to the tables outside the shopping center. "She seemed to know what he wanted because she ordered without looking at the menu."

"Is there anything else you can tell us?" Wyatt asked.

"Well, just that she seemed pretty moody and anxious," he said.

As Wyatt and James questioned the waiter, a five-foot two-inch woman with blonde hair was parking her brown Cadillac at another shopping center twenty minutes away. The meandering, one-stop complex sat across the street from the main entrance to Canyon Lake. Anchored on one end by Canyon Lake City Hall and dotted with restaurants, the remaining small businesses ranged from insurance and financial services to TV repair, and included a golf cart shop, medical offices, a pet clinic and pool services. Dana Sue Gray got out of the car and walked into A Cut Above, a small beauty salon sandwiched between a travel agent and a realty office.

"Hey there!" Dana called out. "How are you feeling?"

Laureen Johanson, a manicurist, was waiting for Dana at a work table behind rows of pink, red, tawny and purple nail polish.

"Much better, thanks," Laureen said. She had finished up with her last customer and had been waiting for Dana, whom she hadn't seen in a month because she'd had a cold and had to cancel all of her appointments. Dana looked very different, she thought, like she'd put on ten pounds in the space of a few weeks, which was not like Dana at all. She was so active. She liked taking her dog for bike rides on the beach and worked out so often that she usually wore her gym clothes to the salon. Dana was proud of her muscles and sometimes rolled up her sleeve to show off a flexed bicep. "See how strong I am?" she'd say. Suddenly, it hit Laureen that maybe Dana had finally become pregnant like she'd yearned for all these years. Laureen decided not to say anything. Dana had lost one baby last year and had become depressed; she'd told Laureen then that she needed medication to help her sleep. The other thing Laureen noticed was that bad, frizzy perm, something she knew Dana would never tolerate. She was so meticulous about the way she wore her hair, and getting her hair color just right, that Laureen couldn't imagine Dana walking around looking like that.

"Well I'm glad to see you," Dana said. "I had to go the whole month with shit-for-nails."

"Sorry about that," Laureen said. "But look at you! What did you do to your hair?"

Dana ran her fingers through her blonde curls and mumbled something about having to use up a gift certificate to get a perm at another salon. Dana said she wanted to get her hair cut again.

Dana quickly changed the subject and lapsed into her usual joke-telling mode with Laureen, who rarely understood her sense of humor. Laureen sensed that Dana still didn't seem herself. Dana usually came into the shop after work, when no one else was there, because she liked the solitude of an empty salon. Dana often told Laureen that she liked the one-on-one attention—a bit of pampering at the end of a long day. But this time, it was the middle of the day and the shop was busy with chattering customers. Laureen saw Dana look around uncomfortably at the other customers in the shop and figured she needed some personal attention.

Laureen sat Dana down and got started with the manicure and pedicure. As usual, Dana wanted a rich purple nail color. Purple was her favorite color. If she didn't get purple nails, she chose bright colors or blues. As a nurse, Dana liked her nails fairly short.

Sitting at a small work table across from Dana, Laureen held Dana's hand and cleaned off the old polish. Then she noticed something else about Dana. She was wearing a loose-fitting black-and-white dress with brand new black cowboy boots. In all the years she'd known Dana, she'd never once seen her in a dress. As she sat there cleaning off Dana's old polish, she realized it was probably a way to camouflage her weight gain, so she decided not to say anything about it.

Laureen decided to change the subject to something relatively safe—like the murders. Everyone was talking about them. Frankly, it was making Laureen uncomfortable. Canyon Lake was such a small community, the murders seemed magnified in importance because everyone thought it was a local resident. It was the kind of eerie feeling that made you look twice at everyone you saw and think, "Could that be the murderer?"

"I've been kind of out of it since I had this cold," Laureen said. "But have you heard about the murders here? What do you think?"

"Oh, I heard that they're connected to the two in San Diego," Dana said.

Laureen nodded, her head down looking at Dana's nails. She didn't read the papers much, so she hadn't heard that.

"Really?" she said, wanting to hear more.

Dana said nothing. Laureen looked up and Dana looked away.

"Did I tell you Jason and I went shopping?" Dana said. "I bought Jim three pairs of shoes and Jason needed pants so I bought him a bunch of jeans and shoes. He goes through them so fast.

"And I took him to lunch," Dana said. "He drove me crazy the way he was running around the tables."

"He's such a cute kid," Laureen said. "They've got so much energy at that age. I bet he runs your legs off."

"Yeah," Dana said. "He calls me 'Mom' now. His mother lets him call me 'Mom.' And then sometimes he calls me his 'other Mom.' That's cool too."

Laureen sometimes wondered whether Dana was getting

too close to Jason. She'd warned her about that before, but this time she let it go.

Dana talked on about fixing up the house she shared with Jim, trying to turn it from the kind of place where a single man lived with his son into a family home. She cleaned and organized. She cooked. She re-arranged. She shopped. She bought curtains. It was shaping up.

As they finished up, the hairstylist came over to guide Dana to the hair-cutting area of the salon.

"Dana," said Sharon Callendar. "I heard that your grand-mother was one of the, you know, that she was one of the ones who was killed."

Laureen looked up sharply. She'd been sitting with Dana for an hour and thought it was peculiar that Dana hadn't mentioned that. Weren't they just talking about the murders?

"Well, she was actually my step-grandmother-in-law . . ." Dana said.

"I am so sorry," Sharon said.

So, Laureen thought, that's why Dana was acting funny. She got up from her seat and walked a few steps toward Dana to give her a hug. But as she hugged her, Dana re-coiled. During their friendship of eight years, Laureen had never hugged Dana, but she instantly felt strange about Dana's cool response. Laureen felt uncomfortable and wished she hadn't tried to hug her.

"Thank you for your concern," Dana said stiffly, "but, um, we weren't that close."

CHAPTER SIX

WEDNESDAY, MARCH 16, 1994, 9 A.M.

"Name?"

"Dana Gray."

"What's your number?"

"34-7036."

"O.K., have a seat and a counselor will be with you in a moment."

Dana sat down in a black plastic consular chair. A handful of other people were already waiting. Since losing her nursing job in November, Dana had gone out on a few interviews arranged by the Employment Development Department, the glorified name given to the state unemployment office. When Dana had called to check in the day before, her counselor had found two job leads. She'd only been half-heartedly looking for work. In the last week, she'd filled out applications at a Sav-On drug store, and the Von's and Albertson's grocery stores in Lake Elsinore and Temecula. But if she wanted unemployment benefits, she had to dance to the tune of the EDD's drummer and go on their job interviews.

A harried counselor called out her name and she was led into a cubicle. He had two computer print-outs from employers that the EDD had matched with likely candidates. He handed the print-outs to Dana, who scanned them. She frowned. The first job opening was for a part-time janitor at a business in Brea, a city in neighboring Orange County that was about 30 minutes away. The counselor had circled the name of the contact and the phone number.

A janitor? This is what they think I'm good for? From a nurse to a janitor?

The second one was a part-time waitressing job at Murrieta Hot Springs for $4.25 an hour.

"Thank you," Dana said icily as she walked out the door.

9:30 A.M.

"Joe?"

Jeri's voice was tentative.

"I've been doing a lot of thinking about all the things you've told me, you know, about the suspect," she said quietly.

She paused. Joe could hear her taking a breath.

"It sounds a lot like my step-daughter."

Joe could feel his hand tighten around the phone.

"What's her name?"

"Dana Sue Gray."

Joe was excited, but cautious. He wanted to get the information from her and then think about it first before jumping to conclusions. He asked Jeri if Dana spelled her name "Gray" or "Grey." She gave him the basics—her date of birth, address, phone number. As she gave the address, Joe noted that her home was about a mile from the Sav-On drug store where the suspect had used June's credit cards on February 28 and again the next morning, March 1. He also made a mental note that the antique store where Dorinda was attacked was not far from Dana's house. He asked for a description. Jeri said that Dana was five feet, two inches and had blonde hair. So far, that fit the description of the suspect. Of course, as Russell's daughter, she knew Norma Davis, who was Jeri's step-mother-in-law, as well as June Roberts, but there was no connection to Dorinda. Greco vaguely recalled hearing about Dana when he was going through Norma's victimology with Jeri, but figured she had certainly passed over Dana as someone worth mentioning to a homicide detective. Dana and her husband, Jeri told him, once lived in Canyon Lake, but had moved out last summer. They'd had money problems and had separated. But she still had her resident permit and could go in and out of Canyon Lake without raising any suspicion. In addition, Dana had a key to Nana's condo.

Joe realized that Jeri was speaking in a monotone as if she was numb or in shock. Joe thought it took a great deal of courage for any parent—or step-parent—to make this kind of a call. Despite the obvious stress she was under, Jeri sounded somewhat hesitant, but remained poised.

"Tell me about her," he said gently.

"Well, she just recently changed her hair color," Jeri said. "She told me that she'd just cut the split ends off a bad perm."

"What color did she dye her hair?" Joe asked.

"Red. She just dyed it red. We just saw her this weekend," Jeri said. "That's one of the things that made me think. Remember what you said about the hairdresser who wouldn't color the woman's hair red because it would fall out?"

Joe remembered. He wanted to know about the boy. Did she have a step-son?

"She lives with her boyfriend and his son. It's not her step-son, but she just told me that he's now calling her 'Mom,' " Jeri said.

Joe wanted a description of the boy and Jeri told him—5 years old, blonde. So far, everything matched. He was getting anxious. This was it. This was paydirt. For all the times he'd gone up to talk to Jeri, this was the information that he sensed Jeri knew. From his desk, he could see Wyatt talking with Lt. Gaskins in the detective bureau across the room. Joe couldn't wait to tell them.

"What's his name?" Joe asked. He'd never told Jeri the boy's name.

"Jason."

Joe asked for his last name, but Jeri didn't know. She said she would find out and call back. A few minutes later, she did.

"OK, his last name is Wilkins," Jeri said. "Dana's boyfriend's name is James Wilkins. His son's name is Jason Wilkins."

It was her.

"That's a lock," Joe said.

Joe felt elation and panic all at once. Oh my God, he thought, I have a suspect. I've got to get moving. I've got to get this person into custody. First he wanted Jeri to come to the station. He didn't want to talk about this on the phone.

"No, I can't," Jeri said, her voice staying strong. She was still at work. She mentioned leaving early. How was she going to tell Russell?

"What's going to happen to her?" Jeri asked. "What are you going to do?"

Greco explained that he had to obtain a search warrant, which involved writing down a detailed explanation of the evidence that would convince a judge to allow them to enter a suspect's home to search it. The judge had to read it, ask questions, and then sign it before anyone could search Dana's house. After that, he would take Dana to the station and question her. If there was enough evidence, he would arrest her, then send the case with a summary of the evidence to the D.A.'s office so they could make a decision whether to file charges. If there was enough evidence, a prosecutor would file charges against her for murder and from that point the case would be in the hands of the courts.

Jeri told Greco that Dana would be home after 1 p.m. today. She'd told Jeri and Russ that weekend that she had a new job.

"O.K.," Greco said, trying to keep his mind from leaping ahead. "I'll call you and let you know as soon as there's a decision either way about filing charges."

Greco wanted to ask Jeri a favor. He asked if she would delay telling Russell about Dana's impending arrest until after she was in custody. He didn't want Dana's father somehow getting ahold of her and tipping her off. Jeri agreed. Then she asked Greco for a favor. Could Greco keep her name out of the newspapers? Greco promised that he would.

Jeri could barely breathe when she hung up the phone. What she didn't tell Greco was that she was afraid of Dana. And she had no idea how she was going to break the news to Russell. Dana was Russell's only daughter. On Sunday, when Dana showed up with newly dyed red hair, something clicked. All of the details Greco had been telling her over the past few weeks suddenly fell into place in the most horrifying way. She tried to put it out of her head. It could not be, she had said to herself. This can't be right. After a sleepless night, Jeri went to a neighbor's house to examine a

composite sketch of the woman who had attacked the antique store clerk to see if she could recognize even a hint
of Dana's facial features in it. She tried to tell herself that
the sketch did not resemble Dana, but it stuck in her mind.
Then one last detail nagged her—Greco had said that a stove
clerk had seen the suspect driving some sort of black van
or sport utility vehicle. On Tuesday, she asked her son what
kind of vehicle Dana's boyfriend drove and he told her that
Jim drove a dark-colored pick-up truck. Oh my God, Jeri
said to herself. She became very agitated and anxious and
finally realized there were too many similarities for this to
be a coincidence. She confided in her son. He had insisted
on calling the police, but she refused. If anyone has to do
this, she told him, it's me. *I will do it.*

Now Jeri was confused about what to do next. She was
frightened that she would be Dana's next victim. She was
afraid to go home. She couldn't decide whether to hide out
at her son's house or go home. The hard part would be
telling Russell. She decided to go home and wait for him
so she could break the news. But she would be prepared.
She wasn't going to let Dana do to her what she'd done to
Nana. Jeri left work early and drove home. The minute she
walked in the front door, she set the cordless phone on a
table next to her chair in the living room, put the dog on a
leash and sat in her chair with a gun in her lap waiting for
Russell to come home.

10 A.M.

Dana drove through the well-trimmed gates of Murrieta Hot
Springs, down the long drive lined with huge palm trees,
and parked by a small sign designating the personnel office.
She was wearing a dark flowered print shirt and dark pants.
She was neat, clean and professional-looking.

"Hi, I saw an ad in the paper for a waitress."

"You want an application?"

Dana sized up the woman behind the counter. The last
time she had been here, Dana was wearing a brand-new
bathing suit, carrying a brand-new beach bag, and getting a
massage. She doubted that anyone in the administration office of the resort would recognize her.

"Yes, thank you," Dana said. She reminded herself that she was only doing this because she was trying to get unemployment benefits. It was humiliating.

The woman behind the counter pulled an application from a set of pigeonhole shelves behind her and turned around to hand over the form. She noticed the intense blue eyes of the woman asking for the application. Dana moved over to the side, fished for a pen in her purse, and started filling it out, placing her name, address and phone number in the boxes. She filled in her educational history and put down Jim and Jeri as references. In the work history section, she listed a job at a pharmacy between 1979 and 1981 and a staff nursing job she'd held from 1981 through 1987. For the last job, she put down that she was the owner of "Jungle Printing," a silk-screen business she had run from her home from 1988 until 1993. She didn't mention the last job she'd held at a local hospital during the same period of time. She signed and dated the application and left.

10:15 A.M.

Greco was ecstatic and panicked all at once. He hung up the phone and walked over to where Wyatt and Lt. Gaskins had been talking. Lt. Gaskins had returned to his office. Wyatt was still there.

"I know who she is," Greco said.

"Oh?" Wyatt said. "How do you know?"

Greco looked at him. His face was expressionless. It was no surprise that Wyatt was not as excited as Greco, but Greco was feeling too good to notice. He wanted to catch her. He wanted to move.

"Ahh, I had an informant who told me this is the suspect that did it," he said quickly. "They ID'd the kid and the names matched." He wanted to move. "Let's go tell Lieutenant Gaskins," Greco said.

Gaskins was on the phone in his office. They sat down and waited. When he hung up, Greco filled him in, told him about the phone call from Jeri and told him the name of the suspect.

"I want to go out to the house and see what we've got

so I can write out a warrant and make the arrest," Greco said.

"Ahhh," Gaskins said. "All right. Good. Go take care of business."

Before they left, Greco wanted to call Deputy District Attorney Rich Bentley and fill him in.

"Rich," Greco said. "I have a suspect. Her name is Dana Sue Gray." Greco told him what he had: Jeri had named her step-daughter, who'd just dyed her hair, matched the description of the woman using June's credit cards, knew June and Norma, and was taking care of a young boy seen with the suspect using the credit cards.

Bentley listened, then said, "I don't think you have enough."

The words deflated Greco's excitement. It made him backtrack for a minute. Didn't he have enough evidence to arrest Dana? Wasn't there enough for a search warrant? As the seconds ticked by, he tried to think. He couldn't speak.

"Maybe we should keep investigating it first before we get a warrant," Bentley said.

Greco was in no position to question Bentley's judgment. At the same time, he was convinced he had the killer. It was Dana. He was certain.

"Well," Greco said slowly, "if I go ahead and write the search warrant, would you still want to come out?"

"Yeah," Bentley said. "Why don't you go ahead and write it up and see if you can get it signed, then give me a call?"

Greco told Bentley he would and hung up the phone slowly. He felt the same pangs of self-doubt that he'd been working hard to suppress. He thought he'd solved this thing and for a few moments now that certainty teetered in the balance. No one thought he could solve this case, not Charles Van Owen, the homicide detective who was June's son-in-law, not Rich, not Wyatt and, for a while, even he didn't think so. Greco took a second to straighten himself out. A few moments ago, he'd wanted to roll out of there as fast as possible to arrest this murder suspect and here he was again, wondering if he was doing the right thing. His knew in his gut that he was right. It *had* to be Dana. He shook off the negative feelings and focused his attention on what he had to do.

Greco grabbed a Polaroid camera and his keys and he and Wyatt hit the door for Dana's home on Mission Trail. It was important to preview a location before serving a search warrant. First of all, the law requires the officer filling out a search warrant affidavit to provide a precise description of the location they were asking permission to search, whether it's a home, an office building or a warehouse. And, since he was planning to arrest her at her home, he didn't want to walk into any situation blind. No cop likes surprises. He wanted to know if anyone else lived there, like Dana's boyfriend, and if she had any dogs that could prevent their entry. He would look at the position of the doors and windows to see if someone inside the house could see down the street, or if there were places through which a person could escape or aim a weapon. There's no telling what a person would do to evade arrest once they saw a horde of police officers in raid gear knocking on their front door. Jeri had told him that Dana and her boyfriend lived with his child, Jason Wilkins, and that the child would probably be present when they served the warrant. It would be preferable to get a look at everyone in person first.

It took about twenty minutes to get to Lake Elsinore. On the way, Wyatt suggested that they call ARCNET, Allied Riverside Cities Narcotics Enforcement Team, a task force comprised of area police departments, including Perris', that specialized in undercover narcotics work and particularly in surveillance.

"Why don't we get them to sit on the house while you write the warrant?" Wyatt said.

Greco nodded his head.

"That's a good idea, thanks," he said.

Monitoring Dana's movements while Greco got the paperwork signed would allow the service of the search warrant to go smoothly. Once Greco and Wyatt got what they needed for the search warrant from observing Dana's house, ARCNET could pick up on the surveillance and keep tabs on her. By the time the warrant was written and a judge reviewed and signed it, ARCNET would by then, hopefully, have a line on Dana's whereabouts and could assist in executing the warrant.

Wyatt used his cell phone to call the ARCNET office in Hemet, about an hour away. Fortunately, the seven-member task force was able to take the assignment. By this time it was close to 11 a.m. Wyatt and Greco planned to watch Dana's house for about an hour. ARCNET said they could be there by early afternoon.

Wyatt, driving Greco's aquamarine Taurus, turned down the street where Dana lived, flanked by trailer homes on one side and by the vast, dried lake bed on the other. When they got to the house, Greco snapped pictures as Wyatt slowly cruised by. No brown Cadillac, no dark pick-up. They saw no cars in the carport, the driveway, or in front of the house. Looked like no one was home. A chocolate-brown labrador retriever and a light-colored dog with brown and black spots milled around inside a fenced backyard. McElvain parked down the street and they watched the house for a while. No one came in or out. Greco took down the license plates of a Chevy and a Nissan parked down the street in front of neighbors' homes. After a few minutes, Wyatt went farther down the street, turned around and parked directly in front of the house. Greco took more photos. They stayed for a while, then moved the car again down the street to watch the house some more, to see if anyone came home, before eventually going back to the station. No one came or left during the time they were there.

Greco found it ironic that, after all their strife, Wyatt was with him to catch this woman. But he was too excited to care. He wanted to catch this woman so bad. The only thing he had on his mind was to get Dana Sue Gray into custody and talk to her. Why, he wanted to ask her, are you killing helpless old ladies?

10:49 A.M.

"Good to see you, Mrs. Beebe."

The receptionist greeted the 87-year-old woman as she entered the eye doctor's office, holding her cane in one hand and opening the door with the other.

"How are you today?" she answered.

The receptionist jotted down the time on the office log: 10:49 a.m. She showed Dora Beebe into a waiting room and, within a few minutes, the ophthalmologist came in and examined her eyes. The appointment didn't last long. On her way out, the receptionist made another appointment for Dora to return in six weeks. It was 11:10 a.m.

It took Dora about five minutes to drive from her eye doctor's office to her home in Sun City, an entire neighborhood of low, flat homes. Dora's house had bright orange shutters and a garden full of rose bushes and irises. It was fifteen years to the day since her husband, Ernest, had died. She was active in the community, a prominent member of her church and involved in in clubs. She stayed current with the news and liked keeping statistics on football and baseball games. She rarely missed a golf tournament on TV. She was expecting a call from her daughter, who lived in Brentwood, a tony suburb of Los Angeles. Despite the sadness of the day, she would see her longtime companion, Lou, later in the day and take him to a doctor's appointment.

She pulled her white Toyota station wagon halfway into the driveway, got out to open the garage door, then eased the Toyota into the garage. Since she was planning to leave again in a few hours, she left the garage door open. She also left her cane in the car. She had only been carrying it for a few months, and hated using it. Besides, she had another one in the kitchen.

A few minutes after she'd gone into the house, a brown Cadillac slowly pulled up in front of the house with the bright orange shutters. A stocky woman with reddish-brown hair hopped out of the driver's seat, walked to the house and knocked on the front door. Dora was normally cautious, but she opened her door to the woman standing on her front porch.

"I'm so lost!" the woman said. "Can you tell me how to get out of here?"

"Well, I'm not sure," Dora said. "But I have a map book inside that you can look at. Why don't you come in?"

"Thanks!" the woman replied, her intense blue eyes shining brightly.

12 NOON

"Excuse me, can you tell me where the Dayrunners are?"

An attractive but somewhat stocky woman with reddish-brown hair, wearing a dark shirt and dark pants, had been wandering around Sun City Stationery for about 15 minutes.

"Yes, they're over here," said clerk Dennis Valencia.

A few minutes later, she asked about the briefcases and Valencia helped her make a selection.

She put the Dayrunner and more than a half-dozen other stationery items in the black leather briefcase, wrote a check for $110.05, signing the name "Dora Beebe." She waved off the offer of bagging the briefcase and headed for the health food store across the way.

12:45 P.M.

Greco had written exactly one search warrant. This was his second. He knew that if the police seized something that tied Dana to one of the murders, maybe a blouse with Norma's blood on it, that evidence could be tossed out by a trial judge if he found that the warrant was legally faulty. On the other hand, he knew that it didn't have to be perfect. As long as it was served in good faith, the police officers had a little leeway. The main thing was that he wanted to avoid making a fatal error. There was no one on the department who was an expert on search warrants, but he knew James had done countless searches on drug cases, so he asked him for help with some of the wording.

The search warrant generally fell into four major components. The first was the search warrant itself, which was a full, legal description of the location they wanted to search and an explanation of exactly what they were looking for. Joe typed in: "32524 MISSION TRAIL, IN THE CITY OF LAKE ELSINORE, COUNTY OF RIVERSIDE: further described as a single wide mobile home, white and brown in color. The number '32524' is in black on the front of the mobile home. The home is on the east side of the street . . ." James told him that he had to spell out specifically what he was looking for. "Credit cards in the name of June Roberts, purchases made from the use of the credit cards, trace evidence, handwriting samples, keys, telephone bills, papers and documents . . ." Greco was required to provide a description of his career in law enforcement, referred to as the "hero sheet." He already had his input saved on the computer from the last warrant. Now he inserted his hero sheet, about a page and a half, into the computerized document. From cop to cop, they all read about the same: "Your affiant is Joseph K. Greco. I am currently employed by the Perris Police Department as a police officer and have been so employed for more than 5 years. I currently hold the rank of corporal . . ."

12:47 P.M.

A poster outside the door of Crain's Health Foods advertised a natural weight loss product. The red-haired woman in the dark shirt and dark pants wandered around the store for a while, then approached the store owner.

"You've got a sign outside that says something about losing so many pounds," the customer said. The customer picked up a bottle of Thermagenics, described as a weight loss aid for $29.95, as well as a dozen other bottles of vitamins.

She wrote a check for $133.20, signing the name "Dora Beebe." When the proprietor asked for her phone number, she gave a phony one.

2 P.M.

The seven-member ARCNET team, each in separate, unmarked cars, had spread out around Dana's house. One officer sidled up to a liquor store parking lot several blocks down the street. Another was at a car wash a half-mile away in the other direction. One car was parked far down the street, but within sight of Dana's house. The others were spread out, but close to major intersections. The officers had tiny binoculars, microphones, earpieces and radios. If anyone spotted the brown Cadillac, they would radio the team and let them know her location and direction and the officer closest to the direction in which she was headed would pick her up. At 2:15 p.m., the two officers closest to her house changed positions so the second officer could watch her house, but from a distance. Jeff Smith, a Perris police officer, had been assigned to ARCNET for a year. The other officers were from other local departments in Riverside County. The cities of Banning, Beaumont, San Jacinto, Hemet as well as the state Department of Justice contributed officers. They rotated positions a couple of times an hour.

At 3:10 p.m., Smith spotted the brown Cadillac.

"The subject pulled into the entrance to the driveway," he said over the radio. "Subject matches the description, dark blue pants, blue shirt. She's alone . . . checking the mailbox . . . getting back into the car. She's pulling into the carport."

Another agent took over watching the house and reported that she was pulling out of the driveway again at 3:40 p.m. That officer stayed behind to keep tabs on the house and the other six mobilized to follow the brown Cadillac. To avoid making it look like a parade of cars following Dana, the officers hung back and allowed other cars to get between them and the suspect's. Only one person needed to be in eye contact; one person could relay the information to the others. Dana drove out to Sun City, about 15 minutes away, and pulled into the drive-up window of Provident Bank at the corner of Sun City and Cherry Hills Boulevards. One officer followed Dana and another stopped short of the bank and turned around. The others continued up the street past the bank and fanned out in different directions. The officers couldn't get close enough to observe exactly what kind of business she was conducting, except that some papers seemed to be exchanged. Five minutes later, she pulled away, drove up the street to an adjoining shopping center, to a Von's grocery store parking lot. She pulled into a parking spot, got out, looked around and got back in her car and drove away.

That was not normal behavior. The officers assumed they'd been seen. They didn't discuss the situation on the radio because they never knew who was tuned in to their frequency, but each of them thought she was wary. Even if they'd been spotted, they weren't about to halt the surveillance.

3:15 P.M.

It wasn't like Dora to be tardy.

Louis Dormand had been "going with" Dora for eight years. She was a religious woman, a prompt woman and a very private woman. If there was something going on with her, she just might have kept it to herself. But it wasn't like her to be this late.

Louis had a doctor's appointment at 1:30 p.m. and she'd promised to drive him. But she never showed and he finally drove himself. Now she wasn't answering her phone. He was starting to get worried. He was contemplating going over to her house to see if she was OK, but he could imagine her scolding him for going over there to check on her.

He decided to do it anyway, got his car keys and headed over to her house.

4 P.M.

The last part of the search warrant, the toughest part for Greco, was to summarize the murder investigation so far, describing the evidence linking Dana to the crimes. Greco wrote in the bare facts of the murders of Norma Davis and of June Roberts, the link to the credit cards, the description from the store clerks of the suspect and the boy, and the desire of the suspect to dye her hair red. Finally, he wrote that an informant told him the name of a woman and a boy who matched the descriptions and that the female suspect knew both victims, had access to Canyon Lake, and had recently dyed her hair red. The name of the boy known by the informant also matched the name of the child on the hair salon's appointment calendar. He ran some of the language by James, who made a few changes.

The last thing he had to do was attach photocopies of the credit card receipts and the Polaroid photos he'd taken of the merchandise.

4:25 P.M.

Bright red fire trucks clogged the street in front of the house
with the cheerful orange shutters. The firefighters had been
waiting several minutes when the black-and-white patrol car
pulled up. They briefed Riverside County Sheriff's Deputy
Diane Stuart before she went in, letting her know exactly
who had entered the house, what they had touched, and what
they had seen. As soon as she crossed the threshold, Deputy
Stuart could see the legs of a prone woman to her left and
dark red stains on the light gold carpet. She walked carefully
through the living room and saw that the victim was lying
in a fetal position. Her upper body lay just inside the bathroom and her lower body lay in the hallway. There was so
much blood on the bathroom door, against the wall, and
pooled around the body, that it was impossible to estimate
the age of the victim, except by her gray hair. A four-inch
tear had ripped the scalp at the back of her head. A shiny
iron splattered with blood sat in the bathroom sink, its cord
dangling from the counter. Covering the faucet was a
scrunched-up washcloth, bright red with blood. Under the
woman's left leg was a blood-smeared telephone.

Deputy Stuart backed out, radioed dispatch for a homicide detective, and cordoned off the house. Then she went
over to speak with the distraught elderly gentleman sitting
in the blue Dodge Diplomat parked in the driveway.

4:30 P.M.

With a half-dozen officers trailing behind her, Dana drove
back down to Lake Elsinore, to another Von's grocery store.
A female officer followed Dana into the store and saw her
purchase a few small items and cash a check for $50 over
the price of the purchases. She came out five minutes later
and went into the Sav-On drug store next door. She emerged
a few minutes after that with two bags and got back in her
car.

She left that parking lot and went to Stater Brothers, another grocery store in Lake Elsinore. Fifteen minutes later,

she wheeled a shopping cart with several grocery bags to her car, drove home and unloaded her purchases.

Smith knew something was going on, he just didn't know what. Why go to the grocery store all the way out in Sun City, to another one in Lake Elsinore, and then to still another? Smith thought she was trying to pass a stolen credit card or use someone's check-cashing card. During a surveillance, they often had to follow drug dealers and rapists to the post office, a grocery store or a movie theater. He'd even had to sit through movies just to keep tabs on a suspect. His team ran into that all the time. It wasn't their job to decide now whether Dana was committing more crimes or simply running errands. Their job was to document her activity without letting on that they were following her every move.

4:35 P.M.

With the search warrant complete, Greco and James McElvain walked across the street to the local court house, Three Lakes Municipal Court, which had two judges. First they went to the office of the court clerk, where the warrant was assigned a court file number. They waited about 15 minutes in the courtroom while the judge finished his calendar, then called the two officers into his chambers. The judge carefully read the warrant and Greco's affidavit while he tried not to fidget. Then he swore Greco in to attest that his affidavit and the warrant were true to the best of his knowledge. The judge signed it at 4:58 p.m. Greco and McElvain returned to the clerk's office where the clerk time-stamped the warrant and made copies, giving Greco the original. The clerk kept a copy and gave Greco a copy to give to the suspect.

When they got back to the station, Greco called Bentley to let him know the warrant had been signed; he told Wyatt the same thing. Wyatt got on the phone to tell the ARCNET team. Everyone agreed to meet at a grocery store parking lot down the street from Dana's house while one of the team members kept an eye on the house.

5:34 P.M.

"The time is 17:34 hours. The date is 3-16-94. I'm at 28080 Pebble Beach, Sun City. This is file number . . ." Riverside County Sheriff's Department homicide detective Chris Antoniadas looked at his paperwork and read the numbers into his hand-held tape recorder: "SW94075044. The weather is as follows: Clear with a slight breeze, 70 degrees. I'm in the Sun City area in a residential neighborhood. I'm standing in front of a residence which is a cream-colored single-story residence The garage door is open and a white vehicle is parked in the garage, license plate 2SGY513. Parked behind that vehicle in the driveway is a Dodge Diplomat, blue in color with a license plate of 1FVH876, which belongs to the victim's friend, Louis Dormand.

"Upon my arrival, the screen door was standing open, as was the front door. There is one newspaper in the driveway. The front doors have shutters on them; they are open. The windows appear to be closed.

"I'm now looking at the rear of the residence . . ."

5:45 P.M.

During the quick briefing, each team took turns exchanging information. The ARCNET members recounted Dana's activities, from the business she'd done at a bank in Sun City to her shopping excursions at various drug and grocery stores in Sun City and Lake Elsinore. It looked at first as if she could tell she was being followed, but maybe she hadn't known after all. Greco said that he wanted Wyatt, who was going to handle the search on Dana's house, to grab all the Nike shoes he found, regardless of size. He was hoping to match one of Dana's shoes to the dusty shoeprint in the entranceway of Norma's house. He also asked him to take anything that looked like it had belonged to Norma.

The plan was to do a calm, low-profile entry. Half of the ARCNET team would approach one side of the house, and the other would come up on the other side. Greco would go up to the front door, knock, ask Dana to step outside, then hand her the warrant. She would be handcuffed immediately. Dana, Jim and Jason would be transported separately to the Perris Police Department. Greco would take Dana back to the station himself. If she agreed to be interviewed, Greco, James and Bentley would talk to her.

The ARCNET officers pulled on helmets, bulletproof vests and their navy blue nylon raid jackets that spelled out POLICE in white letters on the back. They strapped on extra ammo and handcuffs. One of them would carry a hand-held battering ram, just in case. Greco wore his Perris Police Department vest and no helmet. He already carried his gun, badge and handcuffs. Bentley would stay back until Dana was in custody and the premises were secured.

They rode four to a car and parked several houses down the street on either side of Dana's house. It was already getting dark. They quietly got out of the cars and approached the mobile home from each side, single-file, with guns drawn.

By the time Greco knocked on the door, the ARCNET team members had positioned themselves in formation behind him. After a few moments, the door was flung open and Dana was standing in front of him, looking frumpy in a dark housedress, barefoot, her mouth agape. Greco saw her face turn ashen as her ice-blue eyes saw the collection of police officers in her front yard.

"I think you know what this is about," Greco said.

CHAPTER SEVEN

Grocery bags still unpacked covered the gold linoleum floor in Dana's kitchen. The brown bags rimmed the kitchen floor and covered part of the living room. Greco and Bentley wanted to do a quick walk-through of the house while Dana waited in the back seat of Greco's car. Jim, tall and lanky with a sandy blonde pony tail and jeans, had been escorted from the house and was sitting handcuffed in a police car, looking around, bewildered as he watched his home become a hive of activity for people in uniforms. Jason, a tow-headed boy with an elfin grin, was being kept occupied by an officer in an unmarked car. Each of them would be transported separately to the police station.

There were so many grocery bags, Greco and Bentley had to step around them to get to the rest of the house. Greco peered into a few of the bags as he went by. He saw cake mixes, dinosaur cake decorations, bottles of spice, Baxter gourmet soups, diet drink mix, Shake 'n Bake, Bake 'n Fry, Kibbles 'n Bits dog food, Knorr sauce mix, batteries, olives, capers, hair coloring, a saute pan. And vodka and cigarettes. The pantry shelves were crammed so full that a loaf of wheat bread, mayonnaise, rice cakes, pasta noodles, canned corn, tea and plastic bags had spilled in a jumble on the floor. As Greco walked through the house, he recognized the other housewares purchased from June's credit cards—the golf and pig switchplates, poultry scissors, dog shampoo, the blue glass plates.

In the hallway he saw the left side was lined with boxes that were clearly Dana's. More boxes filled with Jim's belongings lined the right side. It looked to Greco like they had a line dividing the house or maybe that she just hadn't finished moving her things in. He thought it was odd.

Aside from the clutter, it was a nice home. A big, comfortable black leather couch dominated the living room. By the modern block-style coffee table sat exercise equipment. Off to one corner was a desk surrounded by breathtaking pictures of Dana in her sky-diving days, dangling thousands of feet in the air from a rainbow-hued parachute. Greco was a little appalled but not surprised to see a grinning plastic skull on top of a stereo speaker. Bizarre. Fashionable whitewashed oak cabinets set off the kitchen. The dinette had a round kitchen table with a white lace tablecloth and four white chairs resembling those at an old-fashioned soda fountain. Dana had put the brand-new blue sheets on the bed in the master bedroom. Stuffed animals sat on top of the wood cabinet that made the headboard. There was more exercise equipment and a fold-up floor mat. The bottles of Opium, still in their boxes, were on her dresser. Her closet was crammed with new workout clothes, some with hangtags still attached, the black, fringed leather jacket, boxes of expensive Nike shoes, and two new pairs of cowboy boots. The multi-colored fish tote bag held the black fishnet beach cover-up, the new bathing suits, and the Murrieta Hot Springs massage receipt. The purple boogie board was propped against a wall in Jason's room. His closet held stacks of new Levi's, new shirts and new shoes.

The house reminded Bentley of Christmas morning, before everything was put away. A glint of steel in Dana's closet caught Bentley's eye. It was a Trek mountain bike, a nice one. He took a closer look at the aluminum frame. As a mountain bike aficionado, he knew that it cost upwards of $1,000. Bentley wondered where she'd gotten it.

As they headed back to the car where Dana was sitting, Bentley volunteered to drive while Greco sat in the back seat to keep an eye on Dana. Greco's car was equipped with child-safety locks, so no one but the driver could unlock the doors from inside the car. Their intention was to interview her. Bentley suggested handcuffing her to the front instead of the back so she would be a little more comfortable. Greco agreed.

While Greco and Bentley were gone, another officer had been watching her. The color had returned to her face and she had recovered her composure to the point of being rather nonchalant, given the platoon of officers invading her home, and that she was sitting handcuffed in the back of a police car. One of the back-up officers who'd arrived later had retrieved a pair of white Birkenstock sandals from her bedroom and had put them on her feet. He noticed that she had perfectly manicured purple toenails.

"What's this all about?" she asked as Greco and Bentley approached.

Her question caught Greco a little off-guard. He didn't want to start talking to her right then. He had to follow procedure. He had learned a whole routine for interrogation that had worked for him in the past. He had used it to get quite a few confessions and he wanted to start from the beginning and do it right.

"Let's talk about it when we get to the station," he said.

He got into the car with Dana. She sat directly behind Bentley. Greco sat right next to her and turned slightly to face her so he could keep an eye on her. In the bright glow of the car's dome light, Greco saw that Dana was wearing a very loose-fitting, tie-dyed purple, orange and yellow dress. It was a handmade batik-print dress from Indonesia, a fashionable, somewhat expensive item often sold at art fairs, but Greco regarded it as an ugly muu-muu. He scanned her face, arms and hands for bruises, cuts and scratches but saw nothing. He also caught a whiff of soap. She must have just gotten out of the shower.

Bentley got in the car and started the engine. He thought it was a good sign that she was asking questions because it probably meant that she'd be more open to being interviewed. From his point of view, he thought it was important to establish a rapport and to make the suspect feel comfortable. He wanted to keep her talking. He and Greco hadn't taken the time to discuss how they would handle the interview.

Bentley said something about making certain her rights were protected, so they didn't want to discuss anything of any substance before they performed a formal interview. But he was curious about one thing.

"Was that your mountain bike?" Bentley said. "I liked your bike."

"Thanks," Dana said.

"You do much mountain biking?" Bentley asked.

"Yeah, I do," Dana said. "I just got that for Christmas."

"Yeah?" he said.

"It *is* a nice bike," she said. "It's a Trek. I put it on layaway and Jim paid it off and got it for me for my Christmas present."

Bentley nodded his head and, glancing at her in the rearview mirror, caught a glint of something.

"Where do you like to ride?"

"Well, sometimes I go down to Newport and take my dog," Dana said. "He loves going. He loves the beach.

"How long is this going to take?" she asked. "You know, Jason has a bedtime and it's really going to mess him up if he isn't in bed on time."

"He'll be taken care of," Bentley said. "Don't worry about Jason. We all have kids, so we know how important bedtimes are . . .

"So, do you go down to Newport Beach a lot?"

"Yeah, I do silk-screening and I sell crafts down there," Dana said. "I go down there quite a bit—about every other week. I was just down there, as a matter of fact."

Bentley glanced in the rear-view mirror again. This time he caught the glint. It was her earrings. She was wearing diamond drop earrings. He wondered if they were the same ones she'd bought with June's credit card.

7:05 P.M.

The ringing phone startled Jeri.

"Hello?"

"Hi, Jeri. It's Joe. I just wanted to let you know that we have her, we have Dana in custody. She's here at the police department. We're going to be talking to her."

"Thank you," Jeri said, hanging up the phone.

This was the moment she had been dreading. Jeri had thought about it all afternoon and wanted to break it to Russell as gently as possible.

The police had arrested the person they thought was responsible for killing Norma and June, she began carefully. "It's the person that Jason calls 'Mom.' "

"You mean Jason's mom did all this?" Russell barked.

"No," Jeri said, shaking her head. "It's Dana."

Russell refused to believe it.

Jeri knew that Russell would probably never understand this tragic turn of events, but she took a deep breath and tried her best to explain it to him.

7:25 P.M.

Greco was nervous. But at the same time, he felt strangely confident. He was hoping she'd confess.

Dana was sitting in the interview room by herself; James and Bentley were outside the door waiting for him and half-keeping an eye on her. Instead of bringing Dana in through the enclosed garage, which was the usual procedure for transporting prisoners, Greco and Bentley had brought her in through the back door of the police station and walked her down the hallway to the interview room. Other than asking, "What is this all about?" she was very cool. Greco just kept putting her off until he finally sat her down in the room where she settled into a big, comfy armchair. He politely asked her if she needed to use the ladies' room or if she wanted a glass of water or some coffee. It was weird. Here was a brutal murderer and he was playing the host and being nice to her. But being nice would make her comfortable, maybe comfortable enough for her to talk to them. He didn't want to lose this case. The stakes were too high. This was it. This interview could make or break the case.

Dana had asked for water and Greco told her he'd get her some. But first he walked over to the detectives' wing to a file cabinet behind his desk. On the view camera there, he could see Dana fidgeting in her chair and blowing her nose into a tissue. Dana didn't know it, but she was being videotaped. The interview room in which she was sitting had a tiny, hidden camera and a state-of-the-art microphone that would pick up her voice even if she whispered. The controls and the videocassette were hidden in the file cabinet. He wanted to check on the equipment and insert a blank cassette. Greco saw that the camera was working, though it wasn't recording, and he could hear Dana's sighs and nose-blowing, so the microphone was also functioning.

Greco walked back to the supply room to grab a couple

of blank videocassettes. As he walked by the report-writing room, he recognized a Riverside County homicide detective who was on the phone, and asked him what was going on. The detective cradled the phone, and told him that an elderly woman had been killed in Sun City that afternoon. Greco nodded, got a handful of cassettes, loaded one into the machine by his desk, got a Styrofoam cup of water and joined McElvain and Bentley outside the room. He wanted to make sure they were all on the same page in terms of their approach during the interview.

Greco felt uncomfortable with the prosecuting attorney in the room while they were interviewing a suspect who hadn't even been formally booked. He thought that would reduce the chance of her telling him everything, and he also thought it would be harder for her to talk with three people asking questions instead of just two. Or maybe just him. He feared that she would think they were ganging up on her. But he didn't feel like he had the authority to tell Bentley he couldn't come in. Greco still felt a bit of insecurity and didn't feel comfortable confronting Bentley while his suspect was in there waiting for them. This was the woman who left knives buried to the hilt in Norma Davis's body, who strangled a woman in broad daylight and strangled and bludgeoned June Roberts, only to go on a dizzying, two-day shopping spree. They walked into the room.

Dana was curled up in the comfy armchair, her knees drawn under her chin, her arms draped around her leg. There was a table to her left. She straightened up when they walked into the room. Greco, McElvain and Bentley introduced themselves by their first names and they sat down facing her, their backs to the camera. Greco started right away with questions. He intended to go by the book and ask a series of questions from the interrogation seminar that he and James had attended. He wanted to get her talking and get a personal history—the correct spelling of her name, her address, employment history, education, family history, where she was born and raised, her marital history. This took a few minutes and Dana answered dutifully: She was born about 50 miles away in Pasadena, earned Bs and Cs in school, became a nurse, was fired and now took care of Jason, who was Jim's son from a previous relationship. She said she was awaiting paperwork from the court that would make final her divorce from Tom Gray, whom she married in 1987. Dana said she was "job searching. I've done a few screen-printing jobs but I've been interviewing and phone calling and going to the unemployment office."

"How do you feel today?" Greco asked.

"Today? Right now?"

"Right now."

"Depressed. I want to know what's going on. I'm really worried about Jason," Dana said as she started to cry.

It was her first show of tears. Greco watched her carefully as she reached for the tissue box and at the same time he attempted to comfort her.

"OK. That's why we're here. That's why we're here. I'll explain everything, OK?" Greco said.

With no prodding, Dana volunteered that she was on her period, said she had been depressed as a result of her separation and divorce, was visiting a psychiatrist and a counselor and was taking anti-depressant medication. She gave Greco an alphabet soup of medications she had been taking and spelled out the names of the drugs—Paxil, an anti-depressant; Darvocet, for back pain and cramps; and birth control pills. She admitted having had a vodka and water that evening.

A discussion of Dana's medication got Bentley thinking about her defense options. If Dana was taking an anti-depressant like Paxil, available only by prescription, that meant she had to be undergoing some kind of treatment by a psychiatrist. If you put the medication together with the counseling, the intense brutality of the murders, and the post-killing compulsion for spending, Bentley expected her attorney to mount a mental defense or even have her plead insanity.

At the same time, Greco was trying to make sure that if Dana decided to discuss the killings, her remarks would be admissible. He didn't want to get some great statement from her and then find that he hadn't asked the right questions to determine if she had been under the influence of alcohol, medication or anything that would give a trial judge a reason to find that she was unable to make a clearheaded decision when talking to police. Greco thought the videotape of her calmly answering questions would also show that she was in a rational state of mind. Satisfied that she was not under the influence of alcohol or drugs, Greco decided to discuss her Miranda rights.

"We do this with everybody, OK? You have the right to remain silent. Anything you say may be used against you in court. You have the right to talk to an attorney before and during any questioning. If you cannot afford an attorney, one will be appointed for you before questioning if you wish. Do you understand each of these rights I've explained to you?" Greco held his breath for a second.

"Yes," Dana said.

"OK, having these rights in mind, do you wish to talk to me?"

"Well, I don't mind talking to you, but I'd like to call my dad."

Greco breathed a sigh of relief.

"OK. You will get your phone calls," he said.

"What am I being charged with?" Dana asked.

"I—I need to find out a little bit more about where you're coming from 'cause I really don't understand the clear picture either. OK? I need to put this together in my mind," Greco said.

Dana had verbally agreed to the Miranda rights, but he wanted her to sign the form to prevent a defense attorney months down the road from challenging the interview in court.

He asked for her signature and she signed.

"OK, Dana," Greco said. "Can you tell me in your own words why you think we're talking today?"

"Well, it obviously has something, um, to do with the search warrant," Dana said. "With, with June."

"OK."

"With June Roberts."

"OK," he said.

"That's what I saw on the search warrant," Dana said. "It was a little description. That's why they were searching my house."

"OK, how do you feel about talking to me about that?"

"I'm comfortable," Dana said. "I just, I don't understand, you know, why you guys are talking to me in connection with her." Dana started to cry again. "I mean, she's been a longtime friend. She went to our wedding. I met her husband before he died. And you know, we talked a lot about health stuff because she was really knowledgeable. She used to help me with recipes and stuff like that."

Greco let her cry for a few moments, watching her. This is just the beginning, he thought. Dana's display of raw emotion suggested that she finally realized she'd been caught. None of those tears were for June. She was crying for herself.

"If you had anything to do with this, OK, I want you to tell me now," Greco said.

"Do with what?"

"What do you understand about what we were looking for?"

"I understand they were looking for stuff of June's in my house," Dana said. "But I don't know what."

"Basically, we were looking for items that were purchased, OK, so if you had anything to do with that, I need, I need to know now," Greco said.

"Purchased what?" Dana said. "I mean, 'items that were purchased'?"

"Yes," Greco said.

"I don't understand."

"With June's credit card. OK? So you don't know who did this?"

"Who did?"

"Did this with June's credit cards," Greco said.

"No, I don't."

"OK. Do you have any idea who did it?"

"I have no idea," Dana said. "I'm kinda still in shock over that, you know. It was a big deal for our family."

"Is there anyone you can eliminate from this investigation as a suspect?"

"Well, I don't know who would be a possible suspect," Dana said, quickly recovering from her tears and beginning to gesture, a wadded tissue in one hand. "I mean, you know, Jason and Jim didn't know June, and so they would be eliminated. My parents would be eliminated."

Greco and James immediately knew that Dana had a guilty conscience. Greco had just asked one of those trick interrogation questions. When an innocent person is asked who can be eliminated as a suspect, they shout out, "Me!" A guilty person, unless they're extremely sophisticated, will hem and haw.

"Um, June was kinda, after her husband died, she went a little strange, you know. She just got more, like, secluded to herself and stuff, and you know, when we all golfed together, she was more gregarious when Duane was alive, and she just seemed a little snippier later. But we still talked and stuff, you know.

"But it wasn't as . . . like it was when he was alive. It's like when you lose someone. They just get a little cooler. I can't say who to eliminate 'cause I don't know. I don't know her circle of friends, 'cause her circle of friends are my father's circle of friends."

Greco was appalled. She was sitting here trying to minimize June as a person, like it was some perverted way of justifying why she killed her. To Greco, she was making an admission just short of a confession.

"Tell me why you didn't do it," Greco said.

"I didn't do what?"

"With the credit cards."

" 'Cause I wouldn't do that."

"Do you think you're capable of doing something like this?"

"No," Dana answered.

"No? OK. Did you ever seriously think about doing something like this?"

"Well, I, I seriously thought about, well not, not with a credit card, because we didn't have any before we went through bankruptcy right before my divorce, foreclosure, miscarriage, bankruptcy, all in one year. But I thought, that I was angry with my husband, you know, and I wanted to make him pay for things that financially, that I haven't paid for. But I couldn't do it. I got stuck with it. But we didn't have any credit cards . . ."

Bentley thought that if he was a defense attorney, he'd go for the insanity defense. Not that Bentley thought she was insane. Once a defense attorney heard that she'd weathered all of these hardships leading up to the crimes, that was the most logical defense. It might work with a juror or two, but all a defense attorney needs is one vote to hang up a jury.

"OK," Greco said.

"I paid [the bills]. Well, actually, my parents paid . . . and I paid them back for our divorce and our bankruptcy and I left him with, um, some utility bills that still aren't paid.

"I'd like to wring his neck, you know, and grab him by his long hair and make him pay that stuff, you know?"

As she spoke, Dana placed her fingertips and thumbs in a circle as if she were strangling someone. It made Greco feel sick inside, but he tried not to show it.

"Is there any reason why somebody would say that they saw you using the credit card?"

Dana's face went blank.

"Well . . ."

"Is there any reason why someone would say that?" Greco asked.

"Well, I think I've been told that I look like a lot of other people," Dana said.

Greco tried hard not to roll his eyes or show any reaction. He had expected her to be evasive. She was also throwing out a lot of baloney, but the more she talked, the more she was likely to say something incriminating.

"I have a lot of people come up and say, hey, you look just like so-and-so, or, or, do you have a sister, or do you have a brother, so-and-so," she said, gesturing again. "I think I have a pretty common face."

"OK," Greco said.

Dana wasn't done.

"I've been in the valley a long time, too, you know, maybe they've seen me around and you know, with a familiar face. I've been out here for a long, long time."

It was obvious that Dana thought she could talk herself out of it and be home in time to put Jason to bed. Greco decided to change tracks. He learned during the interrogation seminar that you can measure a suspect's veracity by asking whether he or she would be open to taking a polygraph test. If the suspect is eager to take a polygraph, then barring a con artist's overconfidence, he or she is probably telling the truth. If they throw out a lot of excuses, they're probably lying.

Greco asked what she knew about "the incident" at Canyon Lake with June.

"I heard about it, but I don't really know any of the details," she said. "Um, my dad said that they were keeping a lot of stuff quiet because they didn't want to wreck the case . . . He said that she was murdered and um, he said that she was, um, strangled just like, um, Nana was, and I said, I didn't know Nana was strangled. I thought she was just stabbed. I didn't even know."

"OK. Did you, uh, tell anybody jokingly that you did it?" Greco asked.

"Why would I say that? I didn't do it," Dana said. "No, no, I wouldn't joke about anything like that. That's sick. This is my family."

"OK. Are you willing to take a polygraph? You know what a polygraph is?"

"I want to say yes, but I don't really believe in 'em, you know, and I don't think that they're 100 percent," Dana said.

"So is that a yes, no or maybe so?"

"I don't really believe in them," Dana said.

"Then you would not want to take a polygraph to verify your truthfulness? If you took the polygraph, what do you think the results would be?" Greco asked.

"I have no idea," Dana said. "I just don't know, but I know there's been a lot of cases where, however they read them, they're like wrong and sometimes they're right and sometimes they're in the middle. I just don't think it's a very accurate measurement. I just don't."

She was lying. Her answer to his question was exactly what he'd expected. Now he was going to lay a little trap.

"Um, is, is there any reason why you would be on a videotape using June's card?" Greco asked. "At Mervyn's, let's say."

"No," she said. Dana's face was blank, expressionless.

There was no videotape of Dana at Mervyn's. But the law allows investigators to mislead a suspect into thinking that evidence like fingerprints or an eyewitness links them to a crime scene.

"There's no reason that you would be on a videotape using June's card at Mervyn's? No?" Greco said as Dana shook her head, watching him.

"OK, let's all break," he said, getting out of his chair.

As Dana sat immobile in her chair, eyes straight ahead, McElvain and Bentley also got out of their seats. On his way out, Greco said it would be a minute or two while they went to the men's room. McElvain asked Dana if she wanted more water and she said yes. The three men left the room, but instead of going to the men's room, Greco, McElvain and Bentley hovered around the video monitor by Greco's desk to watch Dana.

It was a ploy. Greco wanted to give her a reason to think they had information and then look at her reaction when she thought she was alone. Sometimes suspects will shake their heads, wring their hands, or talk to themselves. Greco recalled one suspect who shouted, "Oh, crap!" as soon as he left the room. When something like this happens, it gives him an edge when he returns to continue the interview because he knows the suspect is under stress, and he can use that to persuade him to discuss the crimes. It's also interesting to show it to jurors.

But Dana was a cool customer. She wiped her nose, shifted into different positions in the chair and wiped tears from her eyes. Other than heavy sighing and sniffling, she said nothing.

She was very, very smart and cagey. Confronting her about being followed that day to Provident Bank was the last thing they were going to do. Instead, they would keep her talking by feeding her tidbit after tidbit, some of it not true. Once she either denied her involvement or got locked into a story, then they would give her another tidbit and see if she changed her story. The more she became tethered by her different stories, the harder it would be for her to deny her participation in the crimes. But first they wanted to apply a little pressure.

After watching her for a few minutes, James went into the room with the fingerprint kit and a handwriting exemplar package. His specialty was paper crimes and he had administered the handwriting samples to suspects on many occasions. He rolled each of Dana's fingers, reassuring her that her prints and a sample of her handwriting could be used to clear her as a suspect. He took the handwriting forms out of a folder and spread them out on the table. The first one was a generic form in which the suspect writes numbers and letters of the alphabet in various combinations, using both upper- and lower-case letters. The second sheet was specifically geared toward Dana and had the name "June Roberts," "Hemet Savings and Loan" and the words "dollars" and "cents," a dollar sign, and the words "bank," "savings," "federal" and "loan." Dana even complied with signing June Roberts name as if it were a signature.

"OK, in this box and in this box, sign the name 'June Roberts,'" James said. "Like you were signing a check."

"OK," Dana said.

"Now, instead of printing, put it in signing, like, uh . . . you'll cursive-write," James said. "You know what I mean by cursive?"

"Yeah," Dana said, "but that's how I cursive-write. See, this is what I do. You know, that's what I was trying to do."

"Do you know how to, how they make J's, like this?" James said, demonstrating a handwritten "J" with a loop at the top.

"Yeah, but I never do," Dana said.

"OK, well go ahead and try and write your J's that way also," he said.

"OK. But I never do that," Dana said. "And, um, I usually just, N-E, see, I don't connect all the time on the letters."

"OK. Do the same thing with the cursive 'J,' right here. 'Roberts,'" James said.

"I'm just not used to writing like that," Dana said.

"OK."

"I'm a printer."

While McElvain worked with Dana and Greco watched them on the monitor, Bentley picked up a phone in the detective bureau and called one of the best forensic psychologists he knew, leaving an urgent message asking him to call as soon as possible. If Dana was going to plead insanity or a mental defense, he wanted to be ready with an experienced psychiatrist to administer a full battery of tests and a full examination as soon as possible.

It took a few more minutes, but Dana finished up with the handwriting exemplars. She then announced that she had to go to the bathroom. Before she went, she asked what was next.

James told her that Greco was going to come back in and they'd talk some more.

Greco had been watching on the monitor. He had expected her to try disguising her handwriting—shaping her J's differently, balking at cursive instead of print writing. By now, Dana had to know they had information on her about June's credit cards. Greco knew it might take a while to convince her to tell the truth. He had already been getting resistance from her—answering his questions with questions. Right now, it seemed as if she was testing them, as well. She wanted to know how much they knew.

8:31 P.M.

Greco, McElvain and Bentley walked in with solemn faces and took their seats without saying a word. Dana looked up at them and sat forward in her chair.

"Dana, what I have here clearly indicates that you're involved in this," Greco said, raising his voice a little. "So I'm asking you to start telling me the truth about what's going on here. You understand me? What's going on? What happened?"

"What do you have that clearly indicates that I'm involved?" Dana asked steadily.

"You tell me what's going on!" Greco said, raising his voice.

"Please don't raise your voice at me," she said in a low, calm voice.

"OK. Well let me, let me explain to you that we understand a lot of things that have occurred, OK? And I'm sure you've probably figured this out in your mind. And right now, you are playing games with me. I want you to tell the truth—about what's going on here. Why were the purchases made? How were the purchases made? How did you get the card?"

At this point, Dana paused and looked at all three men sitting in front of her.

"I don't think . . ." she began. "I'm actually being questioned like this without my lawyer here. I feel like you're trying to badger me. I don't, I mean, I've been very cooperative. I feel very badgered."

Greco's heart sank. He'd pushed her too hard. Once she invoked her rights and asked for a lawyer, they couldn't use anything she said after that in court. He looked over at Bentley, who picked up the ball and continued questioning her. Obviously, he felt it wasn't a complete invocation. They were good to go.

"Why don't you show her the receipts?" Bentley said.

Greco rummaged though his folder and pulled out copies of the receipts that were stapled together, and held them at an angle so Dana, leaning forward in her chair, could look at them as he slowly turned the pages.

"We got sales receipts that were signed 'June Roberts' from every store, OK?" Greco said.

"Uh hum," Dana said, looking at the receipts.

"The only problem is . . . June Roberts was dead. Did you know?" Greco asked.

"Yes, I know," Dana said, starting to cry again. "She was family. She was at our wedding."

"OK. The people from where these purchases were made said that you made those purchases," he said.

"Me?"

"Yes. With the credit card," Greco said.

Dana's tears disappeared.

"Did they describe *me*?" Dana asked in a nasty, nasal tone of voice.

"They described you," Greco said softly. "We found several items that were purchased from the stores in your residence. So let's do lots of explaining. I'm not, I'm not accusing you of killing June. You understand what I'm saying? I want to know about that card stuff, because if, well, maybe there's somebody out there that needs to be stopped. You understand where I'm coming from?"

"Yeah."

"OK. And you may be able to help us. In finding this person," Greco said.

"Well, I mean, I've done some purchases, you know, with the money that's left over from my retirement savings," Dana said. "You know, stuff. Just, uh, the clothes for Jason and stuff."

Dana insisted that she didn't use June's card; she used cash.

With each of them holding a list of stores and purchases and the dates she visited each store, Bentley and McElvain started drilling her on the stores she visited and the things she bought. Like a teenager caught using her parents' credit card, Dana admitted buying only a fraction of what she really bought, then insisted that she'd paid cash. At the Nike Factory Outlet, Dana said she only paid cash for shoes on sale which she claimed she bought for Jim. She admitted having gone to Ferrari Bistro and Baily's Wine Country Café, but said she hadn't been to either of them recently. She said she bought underwear and socks for Jason at Mervyn's "within the last month." She denied getting a massage at Murrieta Hot Springs, but admitted she'd been there earlier that day to fill out a job application. She denied getting Jason's boogie board at Sav-On and claimed she paid cash for it at Kmart. She denied knowing about Famous Brands, the housewares store, and "didn't remember" going there. She admitted buying her favorite perfume "in bulk" at Perfumania. "The only perfume I wear is Opium," she said.

Interestingly enough, Dana admitted buying earrings at Jewelry Mart, but said she'd purchased them as a birthday gift for herself months ago.

"Do you know where those diamond-and-sapphire earrings are?" James asked, looking straight at Dana.

"Um-hum," Dana said.

"Where are they?" James asked.

"They are in my ears," she said. "You want me to take them off?"

"Yeah, I'd like to take a look at them, if you don't mind," James said.

"These are the ones I got," she said, taking out the right earring and handing it to James.

"You bought these a year ago?" James asked, looking at the earring, then handing it to Greco.

"Yeah," she said. Greco had been to the jewelry store and seen exactly what she had purchased. These were the same. He hadn't noticed her wearing the earrings until then. The fact that she actually had them on was compelling. It was neat how things were falling into place.

As he handed the earring back to Dana, Greco opened his mouth to ask a question. Before he could, Bentley started asking about the boots she bought at West Dallas. Inside, Greco was seething. He had finally established a solid line of questioning and Bentley was changing the subject. He wanted to continue asking her about the earrings because that was something solid they could catch her on. Once they started talking about the boots, it would be too awkward to change the subject back again to the earrings. He wished he was talking to Dana alone.

Dana said she never bought boots for either herself or for Jason at West Dallas, but that his mother, Rhonda, had bought boots for Jason.

"Does she look like you?" Bentley asked.

"Well, you know, she does kind of, uh, gosh, she changes her hair color a lot, she just recently cut it," Dana said. "She has shoulder-length, kind of sandy blonde hair. And a little bit of a shag. But just recently, ummm, she shaved the top like a flat-top."

"She the same height, the same size?" Bentley asked.

"Yeah, we're close," Dana said. "She might be about an inch taller than me. And she is a little . . ."

"What's her name?" Greco asked.

"Rhonda."

"Where does she live?" Bentley asked.

"She lives up by the hospital," she said, "in a mobile. And, uh, well it's Wildomar. They have a dirt road and uh . . ."

There was a pause. Dana was obviously trying to get them to focus on Rhonda, but Greco didn't want to go there.

"Now this salon, though," he said. "Esthetiques. Somebody who looked like you was, was in there . . . on the twenty-eighth," Greco said.

"Of?" Dana asked.

"Of February, two weeks ago," James said as Dana emphatically shook her head.

"Can you tell me why Jason, um, says that he knows the name of the person at the salon? And he gives the name of that lady. Can you tell me why Jason gives me that, that name? About getting his hair cut there. Is that a mistake or . . ."

James wanted to give Dana as much of an opportunity to make excuses as possible. Once she locked herself into an explanation, they could use it further down the road. If they ever do confess, criminals rarely admit their crimes in one quick interview. First they deny, then they blame someone else and make up stories about why incriminating evidence really doesn't point directly at them. They try to minimize. Sometimes they'll admit one small part, then maybe another piece. If nothing else, the rationalization and excuses tell how a given criminal thinks.

"He gets his hair cut at, uh, he confuses a lot of salons. I always take him to California Styles," Dana said. "He makes up a lot of stuff."

"But, but what I'm saying is he knows the name of, this is not something that's made up. Because we have a real person here," Greco said.

"Well," Dana said.

"That was at a real place that cut his hair and he really remembers the name of a lady," Greco said, "How can he remember the name of the lady?"

"I don't know," Dana said. "He makes, fabricates stuff, sometimes, you can't tell."

Bentley cut in. "We're trying to get an explanation, that's what we're trying to do. OK, these people, a lady fits your description comes in with a credit card from your friend. You see the problem that we're looking at?"

"Your friend couldn't have done it, 'cause she wasn't here, right?" Bentley said, referring to June's murder.

"Well, I don't know exactly what day that happened," Dana said.

"OK," Bentley said. "But the point is, it fits your description. So, if you were in there . . ."

"Well, like I said, I've gone in there for waxes . . ." Dana said. "At Esthetiques 'cause it's the only place that you can go, or that I found locally that I can get a bikini wax. Lots of people can do your eyebrows, and I went there, uh, the beginning of February maybe, and, you know, a lot of times I go on the day with Jason and he would, runs around and makes friends with everybody in the salon."

"So he was in there?" Bentley asked.

"At, I, at the last time I got waxed, he was," Dana said.

By the same circuitous route, Bentley got Dana to admit that she'd taken Jason with her to Mervyn's "many times," but said the last time she was there was in January. She specifically denied being at Mervyn's on February 28. Greco, James and Bentley knew what it meant when, three weeks later, she could instantly recall a specific date when she had not been at a department store. But now was not the time to confront her on that. Bentley wanted to continue pinning her down on specifics that they could use to catch her later in the interview. They knew she'd been in the hair salon and that was as far as he could push her there.

Next, he wanted to discuss her whereabouts that afternoon because he knew exactly where she had been that day. That was the typical strategy—get her lying on the known factors and then confront her piece by piece to get her to change her story.

He asked what she was doing that day from noon on.

Dana said she had gone to the unemployment office, then drove out to Temecula to fill out an application for a waitress job, then stopped at Sav-On and Albertson's in Temecula to see about work.

"I was home about, uh, 1 p.m. and then I stayed home, and had lunch and drank, fed the dogs, uh, called back a few people and then, uh, the only other time I went out is when I went to Thrifty's to get my, I forgot to get my birth control pills. I ran out and did that, uh, 4:30 p.m."

"And, and then you were at home until we came by?" Bentley asked.

"Yes. I was getting ready to make dinner when you guys showed up. We watched *Roseanne* and then we made dinner," Dana said.

"OK. So, I just wanna back up," Bentley said. "Noon. From noon on, I want to get it clear, OK? Noon on, what places were you?"

"I was at home," Dana said. "Like around 12:30 p.m."

"OK, OK. Even at 1 p.m., you were still at home?"

"Yeah, and I didn't leave," Dana said.

"You remember that? You remember that for sure?" Bentley asked.

"Yeah. I was tired from running around and I wanted to sit back and watch some TV," she said.

"From one until two, you were still at home for sure?" Bentley asked.

"Right."

"Two to three?"

"Yes."

"Three?"

"Yes. I didn't leave again until 4:30 p.m."

"4:30. Where'd you go?"

"Thrifty's to get my birth control pills."

"And then you went back home and then we showed up?"

"Uh-huh," Dana said.

"You're absolutely sure from what you told me from noon until 4 p.m."

"Uh-huh," she said.

"Let me ask you this—do you know, were you driving today, the only car you drive is a Cadillac, right?" Bentley said. He wanted to eliminate her later saying that she had loaned her car to someone else that afternoon.

"Uh-huh," she said.

"Did anyone else drive the Cadillac?"

"Not that I know of."

"Now tell me this, you talk about using cash and it's kind of hard for me to understand this—you sound like you made a lot of purchases. How do you go about carrying cash? What do you do?" Bentley asked.

"I put it in my purse," Dana said.

"Well, no, that's not what I mean," Bentley said.

"Well, I don't know what you mean."

"OK, what I mean is, you go . . . you have a big bank account with ten grand in it, you grab five hundred bucks . . ."

"I cashed it when I got, when I got off my job and, uh, Thanksgiving, that weekend, I had a large amount from my savings, then I had an annuity that I cashed. I had a tax shelter annuity for $7,000 from my, uh, Grandpa, and I cashed it. In cash," Dana said. "I paid off a lot of bills with it, I bought my new screen cleaning equipment with it, and now I'm dwindling down to the last little bit."

"OK, where do you bank?" Bentley asked.

"Hemet Federal Bank. It's in Canyon Lake. 'Cause, see,

I used to live there and I'd stay with my folks and I go and cook for my dad."

"OK, so then you'd go up to Hemet Federal to get money when you need it, then?"

"Yeah. Or I can use, I have my, my card . . . that's to my bank."

"What other banks do you use?"

"Uh, I've used Household," Dana said.

"Ever used Provident?"

"No."

"Ever go to Sun City?"

"Sun City, yeah," Dana said.

"Do you know where Provident Bank is in Sun City?"

"No."

"You never been there?"

"Uh-uh. I know where the Von's and the Stater's and the health food store, and, uh . . ."

"But you've never been to the, the Provident in Sun City?" Bentley asked.

"Uh-uh," Dana said.

"Never."

"Never ever. I don't even know what it is. I mean, there's lots of banks around there."

Bentley decided now was the time to break the news.

"Today, OK, from 12 noon on, what was it, 1:30 p.m. on? Sometime today, OK, 1:30 p.m., I think, on. And they saw you go to the Provident Bank. OK, now in my mind, you kind of, with a straight face, told me a lie. If, if—We had somebody saw you, and I can't believe an officer that's following you is lying to us," Bentley said.

Dana stared at them.

"You were surveilled this afternoon," James said.

"OK, so why did you go to the Provident Bank and why didn't you tell us about it?"

Dana dropped her head and began sobbing. There was a long pause.

" 'Cause I was scared."

"Of what?" Bentley asked.

"Well, I'd found a purse."

"Where, where did you find a purse?"

Dana sighed deeply.

"Over by the Albertson's," she said, sighing again.

"Albertson's where?" Bentley asked.

"In, uh, Elsinore," she said.

"What was in the purse?"

"A bankbook."

"From whom?"

"Uh, a lady. I think her name was Betty, Bebe or something."

Beebe, Beebe. Betty Beebe? Who the hell is she talking about? Greco thought to himself.

"Where did you find it?"

"I found it, uh, this afternoon right before I went home."

"Where?"

"At the Albertson's."

"Where at Albertson's?" Greco asked.

"Uh, there's a parking lot and a cleaner's and stuff, and it was just kind of, uh, thrown by the side. There's a dirt driveway by Boston Market."

Betty Beebe. Greco had heard enough. He was starting to put two and two together. He got up, excused himself and walked out of the room.

"OK, what time did you find the purse?" Bentley asked.

"I found the purse at about, um, right before I got home, so, twelvish," Dana said.

"And how did you find the purse? I mean, how did that happen? You see it and then you pick it up?" Bentley asked.

"Yeah. I was, I was pulling out, I was pulling out of the Albertson's and I saw it . . . so I picked it up."

Outside the interview room, his heart in his throat, Greco half-ran down the hallway to the report-writing room. The Riverside County Sheriff's homicide detective was still sitting there.

"Hey," Greco said.

"What's up?" the detective asked.

"What's the name of your victim?"

"Our victim? Her name was, um, Dora, let me look," the detective said, looking at the paperwork. "Here it is. Dora Beebe."

It was like cymbals crashing in Greco's head. His heart was pounding so hard, he could hardly speak.

"OK," he said evenly. "We have your suspect in custody."

CHAPTER EIGHT

WEDNESDAY, MARCH 16, 1994, 9:15 P.M.

He was wondering when the killer was going to hit their side of town. Detective Chris Antoniadas, stocky but nimble enough to step lightly through the crime scene, had been expecting someone to get whacked in his part of town. If this killer was targeting the elderly, Sun City was an obvious choice. It was one of several cities built around the country just for retirees. Just as Canyon Lake was built around a man-made lake, the homes in Sun City were literally built around a golf course. But unlike Canyon Lake, there were no walls, no guards to check visitors and no on-site police sub-station. Most of the homes had no-maintenance lawns of decorative rock and all of the homes were one-story to allow ease of mobility among residents using canes, walkers and wheelchairs. The community service center offered shuffleboard, lawn bowling and card groups as well as an array of service clubs. It was a well-stocked pond for a killer targeting the elderly.

Antoniadas had been a cop for fifteen years, the last nine as a homicide investigator for the Riverside County Sheriff's Department. His curly dark hair flecked with gray, he was 100 percent Greek and proud of it, speaking nothing but Greek until he was 5 years old, when his parents sent him off to school. He'd lost his accent a long time ago, but he loved good, authentic Greek food and still celebrated Easter the old-fashioned way—by slaughtering a lamb and cooking it in the backyard on a spit. The neighbors had called the cops on him once because they thought he was cooking someone's dog.

He had been a street kid, had run with a tough crowd and got into a lot of trouble before joining the Marines. They straightened him out in a hurry. When he got out, a friend encouraged him to join him in law enforcement, so he applied and got a job. At about the same time, one of his friends asked to borrow $5,000 to start a copy business and Antoniadas agreed. Then he begged Antoniadas to be his business partner, but Antoniadas argued with him. How the hell are you gonna make any money turning out three-cent copies? His friend found other partners and they started Kinko's. Antoniadas still goes to visit his buddy at his million-dollar penthouse office overlooking the ocean. He teases Antoniadas: "How the hell am I gonna make money turning out three-cent copies?" But Antoniadas doesn't regret his choice of staying with police work.

From 1988 on, he worked out of the Lake Elsinore station, which had jurisdiction over roughly 1,000 square miles, including unincorporated county areas and cities like Sun City that didn't have their own police departments. The region was sparsely populated, but it led the county in violent homicides. There were murders, and then there were ugly murders. Biker gangs cutting people's fingers off before killing them. A mental case stabbing his mother so many times, he ended up hacking her head off. For some reason, dirt bags came to Lake Elsinore to kill people. He thought it was partly that and partly the meth.

The things he'd seen had changed him. The last thing that had shocked him was seeing his partner shot to death. He was assigned to investigate the case. When he went to the autopsy and saw his partner laid out on the metal gurney with the holes cut into it and a tray underneath to catch the spillover, he joked, "I always wondered what he looked like from the inside out." Black humor relieves stress. What was he supposed to do, sit there and blubber?

He was the kind who worked a case until he ran himself into the ground. Most of the time, he just worked, all day, all night, for days on end, barely coming home to sleep. His wife didn't like it, but that was her problem. The effect it had on his health was an annoyance. At 42, he was too young for his heart to be giving him problems. He was out on a surveillance for his undercover unit one time with his partner, waiting for a guy to come out of a bar. They knew the suspect carried a sawed-off shotgun in his car. When the guy came out, Antoniadas stepped on the gas and at the same time, a local reporter and his photographer, also in a car, had found out where Antoniadas was and inadvertently blocked his way. Alerted to the trap, the suspect got his gun and started shooting. Antoniadas' partner got shot, Antoniadas had to shoot and wound the suspect. As it turns out, they all got a ride to the hospital. Antoniadas hadn't been shot, but the strain on his heart caused him to go into tachycardia—his heart was beating 200 times a minute and got stuck there. The doctor told him to slow down. Antoniadas didn't know how.

Antoniadas had investigated more than 100 homicides and this scene was one of the worst. Looking around Dora's house, Antoniadas saw the obvious signs of age: the walker, the cane and the calendar marked up with doctors' appointments. On the first walk-through, he assumed the victim was old because every single person who lived in that area was aged—and she was the companion of Louis Dormand, the elderly gentleman friend who discovered her body. It wasn't until after they found her ID that they checked her date of birth. Dora was 87.

There had been very few murders in Sun City; Antoniadas found that the suspects in the cases he investigated around there were sons, grandsons, nephews or other relatives killing their parents or grandparents for an inheritance. Sometimes the victim was a resident who surprised a burglar. Antoniadas took one look at Dora's mutilated corpse and knew this one was different.

In the first place, most murderers, particularly those who kill for profit, during a burglary, or to settle a gang score, just kill and get out. They don't sit there and endlessly bludgeon the victim. On the walk-through of Dora's house, he saw the results of a prolonged beating that went far beyond what was needed to kill a victim of this age. One blow would have done it. This was a definite overkill with the severe beating and obvious signs of ligature strangulation. He was past feeling horror at seeing the victim's face battered beyond recognition, her hands still raised to ward off her attacker. It wasn't his job to feel. His job was to catch who did this and to calm down the people who were frightened of becoming the next victim. As he walked through, he considered the possibilities, trying to determine the sequence of the attack as well as the killer's motives. Though law enforcement doesn't have to prove a defendant's motive in court, it's usually helpful in identifying a suspect. Antoniadas saw a lot of rage in the way that Dora had been brutalized. Given the extent of the beating, one possibility was that the killer was venting anger on the old woman personally. Since there was no sign of a forced entry, it was possible that Dora knew her attacker. But the killer could also have conned his way in. If he did, he didn't attack her at the front door, because there was no indication of a struggle in the entryway or the living room. It also didn't look like Dora had surprised a burglar who had gained access to her home, because nothing was ransacked. Antoniadas didn't think this killer was there for monetary gain. Very little effort had been spent searching for valuables and far too much time had been devoted to brutalizing the victim. He could have dispatched her with one blow. This guy could be mentally disturbed like the guy who stabbed his mother. Or he could just be extremely violent. Maybe he had a fetish against old people. He knew it wasn't Louis Dormand. The old guy didn't have the strength to do this. Whoever it was, was definitely out of control.

When Antoniadas first arrived at the murder scene, he had dictated his observations into a tape recorder, documenting everything, starting with the weather and temperature, the open garage door, whether the day's newspaper had been picked up or not and which doors and windows were open, closed, locked or unlocked. Dormand said the front door was closed, but not locked. There were no broken windows, no scratch or tool marks that would indicate a forced entry.

After a hundred homicide investigations, he had no idea whether the time of death would emerge as the primary issue of the case. He had no idea how long that woman had been dead. He had no idea whether they would ever find a suspect or what was going to be important years from now at trial. The outside temperature, the temperature inside the house, open doors and windows and the setting of the thermostat could be important if the coroner had to estimate the range of time in which the murder occurred. It was impossible to pinpoint the exact time of death. But if the homicide investigator records the ambient indoor and outdoor temperature at the crime scene, as well as details like thermostat settings, a deputy medical examiner can plug those figures into a formula that calculates the amount of time it would take a body to cool, providing a span of several hours during which the murder most likely occurred. It isn't an exact science. But Antoniadas had seen clever defense attorneys at murder trials insinuate that detectives were sloppy if they missed a piece of evidence at a crime scene, and he'd seen them make points before a jury over evidence that wasn't important.

He once found himself on the witness stand at trial of one of his homicide defendants who was accused of bludgeoning his wife with a hard object. In his opening statement to jurors, the defense attorney had woven a tale of a sloppy police investigation and shoddy detective work. At the crime scene, years earlier, Antoniadas had dutifully documented, photographed and collected all of the objects that could have been used to strike the fatal blow, like fireplace tools, a hammer and a heavy candlestick. But under cross-examination, the defense attorney produced a crime-scene photo showing a large baseball bat that Antoniadas had never collected and hadn't mentioned in his police report. Antoniadas calmly acknowledged that he, indeed, never mentioned the big bat. Turning to jurors and waving the photograph in front of them, the lawyer finally asked why he never picked up the bat. Antoniadas testified that it was a plastic toy bat. The bat contained numerous holes in it to play Wiffle Ball and was designed to prevent injury if a child was accidentally struck with it. The bat could not possibly have been used to murder the victim. After the jury stopped laughing, the defense attorney slinked back to the counsel table. His client was convicted. Antoniadas would have told the lawyer about the bat before he got on the witness stand, but he never asked, and Antoniadas didn't volunteer it because he didn't know the lawyer was going to make some insignificant detail the centerpiece of his case. Antoniadas had no patience for that. He was not about to be shot down in front of a jury. That was why it would take 15 to 18 hours to process this crime scene.

He had another problem. The old folks were coming out of their homes to gawk and ask questions. Not only were they frightened, they were angry. They were former accountants, lawyers and business owners who, by the time they retired, had had multiple employees answering to them. They'd reached a point in their lives where they wanted to live out their years in comfort and safety. It was not acceptable that a murderer was stalking their neighborhood. There was nowhere they could go to escape, unless they left the homes they had worked for all their lives. These were the people who voted in every election, read the newspaper and had the time to phone the gas company when there was a problem with their bill. Now they wanted to know what the hell was going on. He'd talked to a handful of them when he arrived, but he was in no position to tell them anything of substance. The best he could do was to say yes, there'd been a homicide, they were working on it, and then try to reassure them that the police would do everything to catch the killer, and as soon as they knew anything, they'd let the neighbors know, but at this point, there was no reason to be concerned about safety. It was b.s., of course. Hell, they had a Freddie Krueger character on the loose. They had every reason to be afraid. But he couldn't tell them that.

As the evening wore on, the number of onlookers seemed to increase as more and more people found out about the murder and showed up at Dora's house. There must have been about 40 of them altogether, arriving a handful at a time. Antoniadas remained in the house most of the night, but the deputies keeping watch outside let him know.

By this time of night, the ID tech had placed numbered yellow placards by each piece of evidence. Antoniadas and the tech had started from the outside and searched around the side and backyards for anything of evidentiary value, like a shoe or some foot imprints on the lawn or the driveway, snapped or broken twigs, or marks in the dirt under the windows showing that someone had been outside looking in. Anything at all that simply looked disturbed or out of place. They found nothing.

Antoniadas found the home clean and orderly. From the front door, the living room was directly ahead and the kitchen was to the left. The living room was a mix of colorful but tasteful furniture. There was a floral sofa with soft blue stripes, a light blue velour recliner and a matching ottoman, an Oriental rug, a 1970s lamp and a few antiques. Framed portrait-style family photos of a man, a woman, a child and a teenager hung on the wall. The kitchen held a few clues—there was a half-eaten sandwich on the kitchen table and a half-glass of orange juice next to the sink. On the counter that separated the kitchen from the living room lay a daily calendar with the page exposed to March 16, a few clipped coupons, a church newsletter, a grocery list and a pair of bifocal glasses. A GTE phone book was open and lying face-down on the kitchen floor in front of the sink. A cane hung from the doorknob of the kitchen pantry. On one kitchen wall were more family snapshots—a baby in a red corduroy jumper, a school photo of a young boy, and a picture of Louis Dormand. There was an empty phone jack on the wall, but no phone.

From the kitchen, a hallway led to the bathroom and the master bedroom. Dora was lying on her right side, curled against the bathroom door jamb. Her legs protruded from the bathroom and into the hall, where they rested beneath a dozen family photos. Her left hand was raised against her face, and her fingers—stiff from rigor mortis—were outstretched, frozen in an unsuccessful attempt to ward off the attacker. Her hands, fingers and forearms bore multiple bruises and cuts; blood was caked under her fingernails. She was wearing gray stretch slacks and a light pink shirt. Blood had soaked through the soft gold carpet in the hallway, had splittered low on the walls, had pooled on a purple towel in the bathroom, and had matted the area around Dora's head. So savage was the attack that hanks of gray hair lay on the carpet. Dora's pearl clip-on earrings and her glasses, worn around her neck with a beaded neckchain, had been ripped off during the struggle and had landed on the carpet near her feet. Yellow placards, like dozens of small easels, littered the floor, numbering the beige princess phone and the cord, tied in a slip knot, that lay under her bent left leg, the jewelry, her glasses, the hair and numerous bloodstains.

A gruesome trail of blood splatters and smears and overturned furniture in the master bedroom told Antoniadas where the attack had begun. He thought Dora was assaulted in the bedroom, where a little blue lamp had been knocked off a white-and-gold–trimmed dresser and a metal chair had been overturned. A pencil-holder on the desk was also up-ended. The attacker probably surprised Dora from behind, strangling her. After that, the struggle moved into the hall-way where blood splatters reached hip level along the walls. Dora must have been doubled over when she was struck in the back of the head with the iron. Years ago, when Anton-iadas was a young cop on patrol, he had to use his baton to strike a suspect on the shoulder, but when the man turned to run away, Antoniadas struck him squarely on the head, causing blood to spray everywhere. He knew head injuries caused spatters.

Later, when he started investigating homicides, he got many first-hand looks at the forceful spray and the profuse gushing that comes from a hard blow to the head. Just like clusters of stars suggest to an astronomer the origin and velocity of celestial bodies, the constellation of bloodstains dotting Dora's white walls chronicled the order and direc-tion of the attack. Coming up with precise data about space from millions of miles away is about as difficult as looking at a crime scene and deducing an exact order of events that accounts for every injury, every piece of evidence, each blood drop, smear and spatter. Murder scenes have puzzling pieces that don't seem to fit because the action that occurs during a frenzied attack rarely makes much sense. Never-theless, detectives pride themselves on the hypotheses they form about how murders occurred. While their deductions may never make it to court, they can help them track the killer.

The first set of splatter marks was on the wall just outside Dora's bedroom, slanting slightly downward from left to right. The second set was to the right, covered the door to the linen closet, and slanted at a similar angle. There was much more blood and it covered a larger surface area than the first set of dots. At its lowest point, the dots were much closer to the floor, indicating that after the first blow, when Dora was crouched over, the second blow was delivered while she lay even closer to the floor. The third set of splat-ter marks on a second door in the hallway showed that the struggle continued to the right. It was about the same level as the second set. The largest bloody carpet stain, at about the center of the hallway, showed where Dora probably collapsed to the floor, bleeding from multiple blows.

From there, the assault moved toward the bathroom. Judging from her body position, it looked as if she had tried to crawl into the bathroom, but she could have been dragged there with the phone cord around her neck. A fourth set of blood splatters had sprayed on the hallway wall just outside the bathroom, indicating that she was on the ground by this time. Those marks were congruent with another large carpet stain. Dora had either continued crawling away, or she'd been rolled over. Next to the open bathroom door, directly across from where she lay, the imprint of her blood-matted hair smeared against the door at floor-level. Next to it was a towel so soaked with blood that one could barely see its original purple color. Dora had come to a rest directly against the bathroom doorway. Bloody smears on the wall inside the bathroom, close to the floor, showed that something had rubbed against the wall. By that point in the attack, Antoniadas thought Dora had to have been either unconscious or dead. The smears could have been made by the killer, whose clothing who would have had a fair amount of blood on it. Dora was left with both eyes blackened and her scalp literally split open. Antoniadas thought that the killer dragged Dora, with the phone cord around her neck, into the bathroom to beat her. It probably didn't take long. Less than a minute. The killer was probably in and out of the house in 10 minutes.

The small bathroom was outfitted with matching light pink chenille for the toilet, rug, and bath mat. Small, pink guest soaps were arranged by the tub. Blood spots lightly dotted the wall, toilet, counter and rug, probably flung when the killer was cleaning up. The yellow numbered tags marking the blood dots were hanging from the wall and the toilet tank; they were propped up on the counter for the photographer. Next to an array of lotions and hand soaps which Dora had put in flowered containers next to the sink, lay the Black & Decker iron, black on top, and shiny, bright chrome on the bottom. It had been neatly deposited in the sink and a bloody flowered towel was hanging from the faucet. Resting next to the iron was a clear bar of golden-hued soap. The hand towel was twisted, wrung out, and plopped over the cold water faucet handle. When an ID tech removed the iron to allow the photographer to take a picture, Antoniadas saw that the left side was dented.

The master bedroom held clues about what happened after the murder. Wallpaper, white with an airy pattern of blue flowers, matched the bedding. Dora's nightstand was largely bare save for a small flashlight, a phone, a clock radio, a tissue box, and three containers of cold remedies. A bulletin board on the wall next to her bed held a big map of Indiana adorned with family photos. Dora's large black purse was unzipped and sitting on her bed, its wallet missing. A desk drawer containing financial statements from Provident Bank had been pulled open. It was the only open drawer. A large black jewelry box on top of a dresser was undisturbed. There were just three small blood dots on the dresser, next to Dora's walker and an old-fashioned hair salon–style bonnet hair dryer. Another tiny blood dot was on a white jacket hanging from the door. More blood dotted the carpet in front of the closet door. Antoniadas thought these drops were, in police parlance, cast-off, meaning that those spots were inadvertently flung from the killer's hands or clothing during the search for valuables after the murder.

As Antoniadas walked through the crime scene with the ID techs, putting together the scene in his mind, he continued stumbling upon details. An ironing board was set up in a second bedroom. The door to that bedroom was shut when the police got there and was one of the areas sprayed with blood in the hallway. Did the killer see the iron in the bedroom and then neatly shut the door before attacking Dora? The iron also could have been stored in the hall closet, which meant that the killer had shut the linen closet door before attacking Dora. But that left the question of why the killer, needing a viable murder weapon in a hurry, would choose to rummage through a linen closet.

The other odd detail was the phone cord. Not only was it still attached to the phone, it had been removed from the victim's neck. If the phone cord had been ripped from the wall, why hadn't the killer unplugged the receiver instead of strangling the victim while it dangled from her neck? Antoniadas thought the cord could have slipped off the victim while the killer used it to drag Dora to the bathroom.

There was no sense in driving himself crazy. He'd seen too many crime scenes, too many blood smears he couldn't explain. Murder defied logic.

"The sheriff's here to see you."

The deputy surprised him. Antoniadas turned around.

"The sheriff?"

"Yes. *The* sheriff," the deputy said, referring to Sheriff Cois Byrd, the elected sheriff of Riverside County. He rarely came out to crime scenes unless one of his deputies was shot. Antoniadas knew the sheriff was here because he was expecting a lot of publicity. The press would be all over the place in the morning and, with the additional publicity, the community would be in an uproar. Byrd wanted to know what was going on. None of this worried Antoniadas. He was just the detective. Byrd was the politician.

"I'll be right out," Antoniadas said.

It was 9:41 p.m. Antoniadas stepped outside the house and ducked under the yellow crime-scene tape to greet the sheriff, who was wearing a business suit. He was alone. No entourage—no press people, no secretary, no assistants.

Antoniadas briefed him so that he would be informed enough about the case to talk to the media. This was the third killing of an elderly person in a month. Counting last Thursday's assault on Dorinda Hawkins, it was the fourth attack.

Byrd asked if Antoniadas needed anything and told him what he already knew—they wanted to see this case solved and he had the resources of the department at his disposal for the asking.

A moment passed. Antoniadas asked the sheriff if he wanted to make a walk-through of the crime scene.

Byrd was an elected official, more comfortable making small talk at a political dinner than he was processing a crime scene, but at heart, he was still a cop. Byrd asked, "Is that a good idea?"

"No," Antoniadas said, breathing a sigh of relief. He didn't like lookey-loos anyway.

Antoniadas went back to work and Byrd stuck around for about an hour. After he left, the sheriff had hamburgers and coffee delivered to the crime scene.

* * *

When Greco got back to the interview room, Bentley was still questioning Dana about the bankbook. Greco used a yellow, lined legal pad to write a note to James.

Dora Beebe was killed in Sun City today, he wrote. James was careful to register no visible response. He scribbled a quick note back to Greco.

"And you see, uh, a checkbook, and you go, 'What the hell, I might as well cash it,' right? How much did you cash it for?"

"I went to the bank for $2,000," Dana said.

"Where is the $2,000?"

"At home. I can get it back. I haven't spent any of it."

"Well, well, that's nice. So, you go in there and you write a check, you, you just show them her I.D. then?"

"No, I didn't," Dana said. "I didn't have her I.D. I just had the bankbook . . . I asked her for a savings withdrawal form and I signed it and that was it. They did not ask me for any I.D."

"And what was the lady's name?"

"Beebe. Beebe."

"Beebe what?"

"Dora Beebe, or something like that."

"How do you, how do you spell Beebe?" Bentley asked, also registering no response.

"B-E-B-E," Dana said.

"OK. What time was that?"

"Let's see. I don't know. I don't know, I can't say. About an hour or so after I . . . I had her purse when I thought about it, you know, 'What should I do?' and . . ."

"Did she . . ." Bentley began.

"I saw the bankbook and I was tempted," Dana said.

"But you knew it was wrong," Bentley said.

"Yes, I knew it was wrong, but I was tempted by that bankbook," Dana said.

"OK."

"But I did not take or spend anything of her credit cards or nothing."

"Now where, now where are all the credit cards and everything?" Greco asked.

"Well, I took the ones I thought," Dana gave a little laugh and a sigh, "I would try and use, and I put 'em in my house. But I didn't use any of them. I just put 'em away."

"OK. Where are they in your house?"

"They're in my sock drawer," Dana said.

"OK," Bentley said. "This person, you didn't happen to know her?"

"Uh-uh," Dana said. "Never seen her before."

Greco shot a sideways glance at McElvain. Dana had just slipped. If she'd just found a bankbook lying around a supermarket parking lot, then she never would have seen the person from whom it was stolen. It was a very incriminating statement. They were sure that Bentley caught it, too, but no one wanted to challenge her yet. They just wanted to keep her talking.

McElvain switched subjects. They knew she'd killed someone today. Today. A few hours before, she was killing Dora Beebe. She had to be feeling some stress. He wanted to push her a little and at least get her to admit using June's credit cards. One of the tactics he and Greco had discussed involved creating a scenario in which Dana would be comfortable admitting that she had used the cards, like saying she was financially strapped or saying that everyone makes mistakes. Suggesting a few excuses can make a suspect comfortable admitting some small steps. Then they could build on those steps and, hopefully, keep pushing the suspect into admitting her entire role in a crime.

"Earlier, you know," he said slowly, "you were stating things that are contrary to the evidence that we have."

"Yes," Dana said. "I think so."

"And it's not a 'maybe' mistake. It's not, well, maybe someone looks like me," he said. "It's definitely you. It's, uh, a lot of us get into positions where we make mistakes, we do things, because of financial difficulties. And that's . . ."

"I admit I've been very, very stressed," Dana said.

"OK. And, and I can understand that," McElvain said. "We've all been in those positions where we get . . ."

"When I saw that bankbook," Dana said, interrupting, "I just thought, 'Yea!' 'Yippee!'"

That's sick, Greco thought. She knows full well that she just killed this lady and she's acting like she hit the lottery. That was worse than just lacking remorse. It was as if she were celebrating the murder.

"I, I understand, I understand," McElvain said. "Hear me out here. We've all seen financial situations. I don't know what I would do if I got my back up against the wall. And I'm sure Joe here doesn't know what he would do. We both have families, we have kids, we understand those financial difficulties. But, but if you flat-out deny doing this, it's, it's hard for me to understand.

"We've all made mistakes and that is understandable," he told her. "But for you to flat-out and deny you're lying to my face . . . it's hard for us to understand and try to work with you."

They waited. Dana looked down and sniffed into a tissue. Greco thought he'd keep up the momentum.

"I mean, I understand the position, too, for being depressed and, and, that you, you know, you just recently went through a divorce," Greco said.

"It's much more than that," Dana said.

"OK. Maybe you can explain to us, what happened with these, these other incidents?" Greco asked.

"I don't know. What incidents are you talking about?" Dana said, staring back at them. She was crying, but at the same time, her face hardened. She wasn't giving an inch. Bentley decided to confront her.

"Well, let's, let's go back and start with, uh, this is what's happening, OK? We have a police officer who 100 percent saw you at Provident Bank," Bentley said.

"OK," Dana said.

"OK," Bentley said.

"I mean, they may have saw me, but I did admit that I took the book," Dana said.

"OK," Bentley said. "OK. Now these other things sound real similar."

"But those are the credit cards," Dana said.

"Well, they're very similar," Bentley said. "The people are obviously not police officers, but they're positive, OK?"

"I've been, I've been in those places," Dana said.

"But they're positive that you're the one," Bentley said. "And I'll tell you what else we're going to do. He's gonna take that handwriting, he's gonna compare it . . ."

"Go ahead, I know that's why you have to do that," Dana said.

"Let me put it this way," McElvain said. "Purchases that were made at various locations are items that you have at your house. The exact items. We went and checked the, the codes, on the receipts, pulled the items from the shelf . . . the name brand, the style, the color. You have the exact same items in your house.

"It's, it's now beyond coincidental. Way beyond coincidental. And for you to continue to deny, it's like we don't have a relationship here. . . .

"I mean, you had these financial difficulties, you've been under a lot of stress, is it just that this came over you and it was an opportunity? That's understandable. But for you to deny and lie, that's not understandable," he said.

Dana, crying again, paused.

"There are a lot of things in there that are not me," she said.

"Well," McElvain said. "I know right now it's hard for you to just come out and say that you have done something . . ."

"I did wrong things in my life before," Dana said.

"And remember back to those things. Doesn't it feel like a, a weight's been lifted off your shoulders?" McElvain asked.

"Yes, about the bankbook, yes," Dana said, pausing again.

"Well, OK. I want to get back to this," Bentley said. "Is there some way you could have her credit card, that she let you use it, that something happened to her and you just took the cards? Is there something that could have happened that you're not telling us? That you visited her that day or . . ."

"I've visited her off and on because I told you, you know, she teaches me about vitamins and cooking . . ." Dana interrupted.

"OK, did you visit her in February, the beginning of February?"

"Somewhere in February. I don't remember the date. It was . . ."

"Your prints will be in her house, obviously," Bentley said.

"Yes, my prints would be there . . ." Dana said cautiously.

"Now, prints don't last a long time," Bentley said.

"Um-hum," Dana said. "I saw her, um, shortly before the, that ac—ac—."

"It wasn't an accident," Bentley said.

"Yeah, I was just gonna say the right words."

"Did you ever argue with her?"

"Never."

"Did you ever try to borrow money from her?"

"Never."

While Bentley was taking this line of questioning, James McElvain quietly excused himself and left the room. He wanted to call Wyatt and tell him to look in Dana's sock drawer for property belonging to Dora Beebe.

"OK. Prints don't last a long time, so how close to the time that she was murdered were those prints there?" Bentley asked.

"I visited her within a day or two."

"So you think you were there the day or two before?"

"It could have been. Yeah. Well, it coulda, 'cause I know the next week I heard about it, but it was days after so I wasn't sure when the day it happened," Dana said.

"When you saw her, how was she doing?"

"Fine. Just, she's just, she's just gotten a little kind of reclus-ish, you know."

"She grumpy?" Bentley asked. Greco hated seeing Dana portray June in a poor light. But it revealed what she was thinking.

"No, not grumpy, just kind of not as the way she used to be when her husband was alive. You know, just trying to keep busy."

"Know why you were there that day?"

"To talk to her about vitamins because I have been trying to stop drinking and I wanted to know what kind of vitamins, like B vitamins, or what kind of things that I should take to help me," Dana said.

"Then that would explain why your prints were there?"

"Were they there?"

"I think so," Bentley said.

"Well, then, that would explain it."

Another pause. Greco picked up from there.

"There's no way by accident that you came across June's credit card. Not if you . . . not like you did the purse," Greco said.

"You know that I'm very scared," Dana said.

"I understand that. I do understand that and I don't wanna, I don't wanna pressure you or force you, OK? But . . . it's like a weight that's lifted off your chest. And I understand that you felt at least somewhat better about telling us about the purse, right?"

"Yeah . . . I was at my bank and I saw a man throw a little coin purse thing in the trash where the, by the Ready Teller. And I looked in it, but I didn't think those were, it was her," Dana said.

"OK." She was lying again. Her story now was that she had found discarded credit cards belonging to one woman, and a bankbook, belonging to another, both within an hour of their owners' separate murders. *Just keep talking, Dana,* Greco said to himself. *Just keep talking.*

"I had no idea. And, uh, I took a Mervyn's card and a VISA and that was it. I threw the rest in the trash."

"So you did make those purchases?"

"I made some of the purchases, but not everything you have listed."

"OK, what did this guy look like?"

"Medium build. Uh, kind of sandy, blonde hair with a kind of, the kind, like a construction worker, kind of grubby, kind of low-life–looking guy," Dana said. "Faded T-shirt and jeans and stuff."

Dana had finally admitted using June's credit cards. They got as far as Mervyn's and the Nike Factory Outlet before they got hung up on Murrieta Hot Springs. First she denied using the card for a massage. Then she admitted that she went and used the pool with her own pool card but insisted that she'd paid cash for it. The next story was that Jason's half-sister, a 10-year-old, had taken June's card out of Dana's purse before Dana disposed of it.

"You know, sometimes this little girl comes in the house, we let her . . .'cause she's Jason's uh, half-sister, and she, I forbade her to come anymore, because she steals stuff from Jason," Dana said.

"Who is she?" Bentley asked.

"The little 9-, um, 10-year-old, uh, I'm sorry, I'm so freaked out. Taby. And she's stolen stuff and she was around then. So I used the pool one day, but I didn't get a massage."

"Can you explain why we have a carbon copy of a VISA purchase?" James asked.

"Who knows? With this little girl, I don't know," Dana said.

"How old is she?" Greco asked.

"She's 10 and she's slick," Dana said.

James McElvain had returned from talking to Wyatt. He'd been on the phone when a deputy walked over to the sock drawer. Sure enough, there were ID cards and an auto club card of Dora's in Dana's drawer.

"Now that's you, you, you're going off the wrong way again," James said. "It's, it's not the little girl. It's you. . . . What you keep doing here, you keep pointing here and pointing there and you're still not being totally honest with us . . . So far, you're giving us bits and pieces of that. We want the total truth."

"Well, I'm scared," Dana said, starting to cry again. She finally admitted using the credit card there for a massage.

"Why were you hiding that?" Bentley said. "That's like, stupid!"

"Well, I'm scared," Dana said again. *Way to go, Bentley,* Greco thought. *How can you build trust like that?* He couldn't believe the prosecuting attorney, who was supposed to help establish a rapport with the serial killer, had just called her stupid. He wanted to be alone with Dana, but it was too late now. He winced as Bentley continued.

"OK, Dana," Bentley said, "but you knew we had proof."

"I was just scared and I've never done this before and I'm just scared," she said, starting to cry again. When she calmed down, they went through the list of stores—West Dallas, Baily's Wine Country Café, the Esthetiques, Sav-On drug store, Perfumania, Famous Brands, the housewares store, Ferrari Bistro. They got hung up on the diamond earrings. Dana admitted going to the Jewelry Mart, but insisted she bought the earrings with a check. They let it go.

"OK, here's what I want to ask you then," Bentley said. " 'Cause here's what's really weird to me, OK? We know when June was killed."

"Um-hum," Dana said.

"And that darn credit card was used within an hour at Mervyn's. OK? Now I submit this . . ."

"Well, I can't say . . ." Dana interrupted.

But Bentley interrupted again. "Let me finish, let me finish. And I'm gonna tell you who I am. I'm a Deputy District Attorney, homicide. OK? And they asked me to come out here and I've probably been out to 150 murder scenes. And I've never seen a woman kill somebody like that. Men I've seen happen. OK? And then I'm sitting there looking at the timing that you finally, you finally came forward so close in timing. That timing is so close, OK, so close in time, plus you know the person, makes me think if you didn't do it, you were there and knew who did it."

"No, I did not."

"OK, that's what it makes me think."

"Uh-uh," Dana said.

"OK, now, then explain to me why I'm wrong," Bentley said.

"Because I went to the bank, saw the guy throw those in there, took the cards and went shopping," Dana said.

"Dana," Greco said. "Dana, the only other, the only other, I guess really odd or unusual coincidence is that this person, this Beebe person that you used to cash her check. Do you realize that she was murdered today?"

"No," Dana said. "No."

"She was murdered pretty much the same way June was murdered," James said.

"No, I don't know anything about that," Dana said.

"How do you explain this coincidence?" McElvain said. "Two homicides. And you find a credit card from June and then the next thing you know, a couple of weeks later, another homicide and again, you find this person's purse."

"I don't have an explanation."

"Are you, are you extremely lucky?" James asked.

"I think it was purely coincidental. 'Cause there's no way . . ."

"OK, OK, let me ask you this," Bentley interrupted. "You knew June 100 percent, right?"

"Yeah."

"This person that you cashed the check on, you're 100 percent sure you did not know her?"

"I'm 100 percent sure," Dana said.

"Did you happen to see her driver's license in there, in her purse?"

"It was mixed in with the other stuff," Dana said.

"And what did she look like?"

Dana laughed. "Like an old lady," she said with a soft laugh. "I didn't look at it very closely."

That made Greco's skin crawl. She just killed this woman today. Now she's laughing about her looks. He wondered if she had something against old people.

"Do you realize that your opportunity is very suspicious? Your opportunity lies around two elderly females that were murdered," McElvain said.

"If that's what you say, yes," Dana said. "I mean that's from what you said, yes."

"It's such a coincidence," Greco said.

"I know, but I'm telling you, I didn't do anything but make some purchases."

"But you, you would have to know something. You would have to know something!" Greco said, raising his voice.

"I don't know! Well, like what?"

"A person. Somebody you suspect."

"Ah, the only . . ." Dana said, sighing. "I don't know. There's bad elements at Rhonda's house, but that's really the only . . ."

"That's the, see, that's the only problem with this whole case scenario, is that everything centers back to you," Greco said. "See what I'm saying? Uh, as far as purchases and everything else that happened, my, my intention in this, in this investigation was to get to the bottom of this, to get to the truth."

"Well, I've given you, I've, I finally broke down and I gave you the truth now."

"Well . . . is there any reason why your prints would be in Beebe's house?" Greco asked.

"No."

"Would you, would you think that, uh . . ."

"I don't think they're gonna find anything," Dana said flatly.

"Would you, would you think Jim would do something like this?" Greco asked.

"Absolutely not," Dana said.

"If you're responsible for this, I don't wanna see the pendulum swinging the other way pointing towards Jim," Bentley said.

"He doesn't have any idea," Dana said.

Greco thought that was probably the most truthful statement she'd made to them all night.

"Jim's gonna be sitting in this same chair you're sitting in, answering probably the same questions," Greco said.

"Tonight?" Dana said, looking alarmed.

"Yes," Greco said.

"I told him when I got the, um, when I got the card from the trash, that my husband had gotten a card in the mail. And, um, that's when I told him," Dana said.

"Now this is your husband's card?" Greco asked.

"I never got a card for my husband, I just needed to explain, I really wanted to, you know, get some things for Jim. He's been taking care of me an awful lot and that's it, really, that's all."

"And this is, this is the most important part. Is that if you're involved in this and for some reason, and there's gotta be a reason, if there was some reason that, that made you do any of these things, that reason would be very important," Greco said.

"My reason for . . . ?" Dana asked.

"Well," Greco said. "I'm not talking about the card purchases."

"Oh."

"I'm referring to, specifically now, I'm referring to the deaths."

"I don't, I can't do that."

"You never get so desperate that . . ."

"No," Dana said. "I wouldn't . . ."

"Not even for money?" Bentley asked.

"No, no. I've been working my ass off trying to get jobs and stuff, even menial shit, you know, and I've been frustrated with that and that's why, you know, I saw that bankbook and I went, 'Yippee!' But, uh, no, I couldn't kill," Dana said, putting her hand to her nose and taking it away again. "But the person, if I was going to kill anybody, I would have killed my husband. I would never, he's the only one that I was so mad at that I could, I could think about something that drastic. But no, I wouldn't kill." The hand came to the nose again and stayed. "I'm used to taking care of people, not killing them."

Greco wanted to use her rather odd admission about wanting to kill her husband as a springboard. Could she think of any reason why they now considered her a suspect?

"No. My unemployment got denied and that's why I was so desperate with the shopping. . . . I'm still on appeal for that, but," she said with a sigh, referring to being dismissed from her nursing job, "I'm not a killer. I am not a killer." The hand came up to the nose again.

"Do you know who is?" Greco asked.

"No, I don't. I do not know," Dana said, changing the subject. "I'm trying to get a job, and you know, and you stand in the unemployment line and you bullshit and stuff." She said she was tired of nursing and wanted to work— screen printing or even waiting tables—while Jason was at school.

"All through nursing school, I waitressed," she said, bursting into tears. "I'm so sorry. I'm so sorry. I've got such a problem. I'm so embarrassed. It's gonna hurt him so bad."

"Listen, it's gonna hurt who?"

"It's gonna hurt Jim because he's tried so hard and he's done so good for me. It's gonna make him feel, well, I'm sure there's gonna be some mistrust and stuff, but I just feel so bad. I just wanted to get some stuff for Jason and us.

"You know, if you look at the purchases, it's mostly for them, you know," Dana said, now fully sobbing. "I didn't get a lot of things for me. I didn't go clothes shopping and stuff. I got some boots and perfume. Everything else was for them."

Greco was attempting to comfort her, but he was revulsed. Sure, he thought. It was all for them. Does she really think we'll believe that? Let her think we do . . .

When she settled down, Greco asked about June. Dana denied having had a fight with June, that she had not told Dana anything was bothering her.

"No, she, she's very flighty, and said she'd be in and out for a few days and this and that. You know, she, uh, didn't catch where she was or anything. But she said she'd just gotten home after being out a couple of days, but I don't know where she was.

"I don't know if she was with family or, I don't know. That miffs me. It really miffs me."

Here she was blaming June, Greco thought, but it sounded like she was about to say something significant.

"Why?"

" 'Cause, 'cause . . . I can't imagine it; that somebody . . . it's just so weird. I mean, I'm sorry about what happened to that other lady, but you know, I don't, it's not like what happened to June and Nana, you know. I just can't imagine."

She's miffed? She's comparing the murder of Dora to the murders of June and Norma?

"That's, that's why I'm trying to understand what's going on," Greco said softly.

"I got desperate to buy things. Shopping puts me to rest," Dana said with a chuckle. "I'm lost without it."

CHAPTER NINE

WEDNESDAY, MARCH 16, 1994, 10:04 P.M.

Jim Wilkins had been cooling his heels for three hours in a cell. He didn't know why the hell cops were crawling all over his house or what they were looking for. He didn't know why he had been handcuffed and dragged to a police station as he was sitting down for dinner. That made him cranky and hostile. Tall and lanky with a dirty blonde ponytail and sideburns, Jim was the quintessential blue-collar guy, a mold maker who punched a time clock at a machine shop every weekday from 7:30 to 4:30. No lunch hour. He skipped it so he could pick up his kid at daycare by 5 p.m.

With expletive-laced sarcasm, Jim insisted that he had no idea why the detectives wanted to talk to him. Mostly, he was pissed because he couldn't smoke in the cell and had gotten yanked out of his house before he'd had a chance to grab his cigarettes.

Greco thought of that as he walked out of the lock-up area, where he'd just placed Dana in a cell. She didn't act the same way Jim did. Jim was confused and angry and maybe a little scared; he was protesting about being in a cell. Dana didn't say a word. She didn't yell, she didn't ask why, she didn't whine about being in a jail cell for the first time in her life or holler repeatedly that she was innocent and couldn't handle being locked up. The difference between Jim's and Dana's reactions made sense to Greco. A majority of criminals just accept their fate. Of course, not all suspects caught red-handed willingly go to jail, but for the most part, if they do something illegal and get caught, they know they'll have to go through the justice system and pay the price. Greco saw that Dana had accepted her fate and her future. It reflected her guilt—*Hey, you got me, now see what happens in court.*

After Greco put Dana into her cell, James McElvain took Jim out of his. Because of the configuration of the lock-up, neither knew the other was there. McElvain walked Jim to the interview room, where he and Greco started asking detailed questions about his background, much the same way they'd interviewed Dana. His deep voice reflected a combination of irritation and incredulity that the police had arrested him, with guns drawn, so they could ask him, among other things, about his report card. He complied, telling them that he had been a horrible student "if the teacher was an asshole," but did well if he liked the teacher. He brushed off questions about whether he was ever in the military: "With my attitude?" He told them, "I don't do sports," and, "I don't fight." Asked about prior contact with police, he told them that he had been arrested for smoking pot when he was 14 but was told never to tell anyone because the record was sealed. "Personally, I don't give a shit," he said.

Jim said he met Dana after he started playing in a band in September of 1992. She was still with Tom, her husband. Jim and Dana first got together as a couple in May of 1993, and she flip-flopped back and forth between Tom and Jim for the next few months until she took a trip to Sweden that fall. Dana returned to her husband briefly, then finally left him for Jim. They'd lived together ever since at his house on Mission Trail. "Tell you the truth, I'm a bit confused, because I don't know why the hell I'm here," he said, exasperated. "I don't smoke pot, I don't do drugs, I don't own a gun," he said, pausing. "Might have a fillet knife in my fishing box."

Greco jumped.

"What's the fillet knife have to do with anything? I don't understand."

Jim laughed.

"You asked me if I've got in trouble before, right? And so I'm tryin' to tell ya, I don't do drugs," he said, ticking off each point on his finger, "and I don't fight. I don't own a gun, I don't own knives. I mean, what could I be in trouble for?"

"OK, can you tell me in your own words why we're talking today? Do you have any idea?" Greco asked.

"I don't have a clue."

Greco told him about purchases made using a homicide victim's credit card and asked if he was aware of the two murders in Canyon Lake.

"Yeah," Jim said. "One of them was Dana's grandmother . . . in-law or something."

"Yeah," Greco said. "The second one was a lady by the name of June Roberts . . . Well, it's those purchases on June Roberts' VISA and Mervyn's card that we're so interested about. The day that she was murdered, and the day after, somebody made purchases on June Roberts' VISA and Mervyn's card."

"You're kidding," Jim said.

"No I'm not kidding. I wouldn't kid about something like that," Greco said.

"Well, if I had to take a stab at it, I guess you might be talkin' about Dana," Jim volunteered. "But I don't understand why she'd go out and get someone else's credit cards. Shit, she had mine."

"OK, well . . . that's the answer that I was trying to get from you. How do you feel about talking to me about that?" Greco asked. Greco suspected that Jim really didn't know what was going on, but he had to make sure. Jim had just turned on Dana in a heartbeat. A relationship of convenience rather than romance perhaps, Greco thought. Still, Greco couldn't get a read on Jim's involvement. Had he been there, or did he participate in the murders?

"I don't have a problem with it 'cause I don't, I don't have a clue," Jim said.

"If you had anything to do with this, I want you to tell me now," Greco said.

"I don't have anything to do with anything," Jim said. "I've got a job, I make money, I go, I play, I have fun when I can."

"OK. Do you have any idea who did it?"

"No, I don't think so."

"Well, you just told me that Dana might, right?"

"Beats me. She didn't like credit cards up until a couple of weeks ago."

Jim said that Dana had access to his credit card and had used it to buy things for herself, clothes for Jason, and household necessities. As he spoke, he continued to distance himself from Dana. Greco wondered whether Jim was involved, and was trying to keep attention focused on Dana, or really was clueless.

"Is there anybody you can eliminate from this investigation?" Greco asked.

"Eliminate? Me. I ain't charged nothin' except on my own. Actually, I haven't bought anything for months."

That was the same question they'd just asked Dana. Jim just gave them the textbook response of someone who was innnocent.

"What about Dana?"

"Yeah, she bought me some shoes the other day," he said.

"No, I mean, can you eliminate her from this investigation, or can't you really say?"

"I, I don't know," Jim said slowly. "I'm at work all day long, what she does while she's out lookin' for jobs or whatever she's doin', I don't know."

Greco decided to take a leap and get personal.

"Do you guys have a really close relationship or what?"

"I think we do," Jim said, pausing. It seemed like he was really thinking about it. "Sometimes I wonder."

"OK," Greco said.

"I mean, wouldn't you?"

Greco was eyeing Jim and Jim was eyeing him back.

"Now, can you tell me why you didn't do it?"

"I had no reason to," he said. "I just got my tax return the other day. I have two thousand dollars in the bank. Why would I need to get money somewhere else?"

"Do you think you're capable of doing something like this?"

"Me? No. Bad conscience."

"Did you tell anybody, even jokingly, that you did it?" McElvain asked.

Jim turned in his chair to face McElvain, shooting him a look.

"You gotta be kidding."

Greco tried the polygraph question, but he couldn't even get the sentence out before Jim agreed to it. When asked what he thought the result would be, Jim said he didn't know.

"That depends on how much it irritates me. I hate being

accused of things that I didn't do," he said, pausing. "And being here is an accusation, isn't it?

"You should have talked to me at home about all of this shit instead of draggin' me down here," Jim added.

"Well, what about Dana? Do you think that she's the type of person that could do something like this?"

"It's hard to say, hard to say," Jim said. "Sometimes she gets pissed off and on a roll."

Jim complained that he needed a drink of water, so they took a break. Outside the room, they watched Jim on the video camera. He sat quietly, one ankle crossed over his knee. Greco, McElvain and Bentley discussed where they were headed. He had been openly hostile at first, but seemed to be answering their questions. Not the kind of guy to get excited about anything, not even when his live-in girlfriend's accused of charging up a dead woman's credit cards. Dana had already told them that he knew nothing of the purchases and they assumed he also knew nothing about Dana's involvement in the murders. There was still a very remote possibility that he was involved with the credit card fraud. The interesting thing was how quickly he had distanced himself from Dana. Maybe they could use that. Greco, McElvain and Bentley went back into the interview room.

"How you doin'? I'm Rich Bentley."

"I'm dry mouth and pissed off," Jim replied.

Bentley plunged in and asked him where Dana got her money and where she banked. Jim said he'd been paying all of her bills as well as giving her cash.

"OK," Bentley said. "She's admitted a lot of stuff to us. And she's lied about a lot of stuff, OK? She's admitted a lot of, of using credit cards. And a lot of that stuff is in your house. A lot. You must have wondered where all this shit came from. So what do you know about all this stuff that's showed up in your house?"

"She just told me today she got some money from her aunt . . . a couple hundred dollars," Jim said.

"Did she show it to ya?"

"No, she didn't show me anything—except her new briefcase," Jim said.

Bentley asked Jim whether he'd been at work that day

The Perris Police Department sketch of the female attacker who strangled Dorinda Hawkins. RIVERSIDE COUNTY SHERIFF'S DEPARTMENT

Criminalist Ricci
Cooksey spotted a faint
shoeprint in the foyer
of Norma Davis'
Canyon Lake condo.

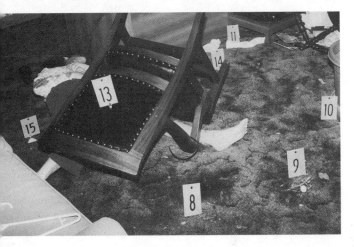

At the scene of June Roberts' murder, detectives spotted obvious signs of a violent struggle: an overturned chair, broken glass, and massive blood-stains on the carpet. RIVERSIDE COUNTY SHERIFF'S DEPARTMENT

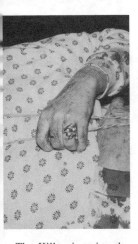

The Killer, ignoring the diamond ring on June's finger, didn't appear to be motivated by theft . . .
RIVERSIDE COUNTY
SHERIFF'S DEPARTMENT

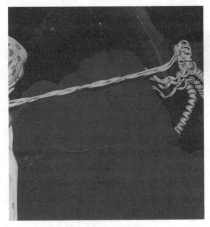

. . . but took enough time to anchor June to a chair with the phone cord.
RIVERSIDE COUNTY
SHERIFF'S DEPARTMENT

The attack on Dorinda Hawkins took place in the very back of this deep-set antique store, located in a charming section of Lake Elsinore's small downtown. RIVERSIDE COUNTY SHERIFF'S DEPARTMENT

Dana Sue Gray chose a very confined area to strangle Dorinda Hawkins, who tried to defend herself with the broom.
RIVERSIDE COUNTY SHERIFF'S DEPARTMENT

This Black & Decker iron was dented in the attack on Dora Beebe. RIVERSIDE COUNTY SHERIFF'S DEPARTMENT

Blood was splattered on the door jamb and on the wall of the bathroom during the murder, and smeared when the killer attempted to clean up afterward. RIVERSIDE COUNTY SHERIFF'S DEPARTMENT

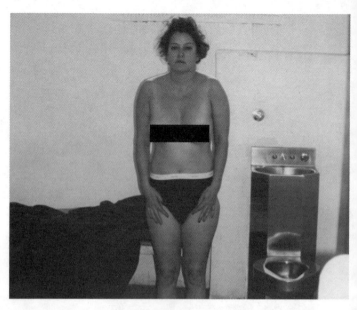

Dana, in her cell, after Joseph Greco arrested her. Her face bloated from hours of crying during her interrogation, Dana posed nearly nude. Authorities were hoping to find evidence of bruising or scratching incurred during the murder of Dora Beebe hours earlier.
RIVERSIDE COUNTY SHERIFF'S DEPARTMENT

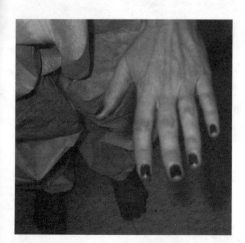

Dana had killed Beebe without marring her perfectly manicured purple fingernails.
RIVERSIDE COUNTY SHERIFF'S DEPARTMENT

Riverside County Sheriff's Department criminalists carted bag after bag of merchandise out of Dana Sue Gray's house the night she was arrested.
RIVERSIDE COUNTY SHERIFF'S DEPARTMENT

Detective Joseph Greco.

Detective Chris Antoniadas.

Deputy District Attorney
Richard Bentley.

and whether anyone could verify that he was there the entire
day. Jim seemed almost relaxed and told him to call his em-
ployer and look at his time card. McElvain took the number
and left the room to call while Bentley continued asking questions. Jim couldn't remember whether he was at work on February 14th or the 28th but remembered taking one day off
within the last two months because he didn't feel well.

Bentley wanted to know what Jim thought about Dana.
If she was hardened enough to commit murder, she must
have an interesting home life.

"OK, tell me about her," Bentley said. "Does she get
mean, violent, bitchy, anything like that?"

"Yeah, she was a little bitchy last night," Jim said.

"OK. What happened last night?" Bentley asked.

"Well, actually, she got lit and passed out," Jim said.

"What do you mean by 'lit'? Drunk?"

"Yeah," Jim said. "We were sittin' around talkin' about
windsurfers and all of a sudden, she's noddin' off, tellin'
me, yeah, ya gotta have a good relationship with your boy.

"I'm goin, what the *fuck* are you talkin' about?" Jim said,
gesticulating. "It was beyond me."

"She's a physical person?" McElvain asked.

"Yeah, she likes to run into me and throw me down and
shit."

Bentley's eyes opened wide. Jim had just given him some
ammunition, he realized. Immediately, he thought of three
ways he could use that statement before a jury. If she'd been
moody and angry the night before a murder, that testimony
could be used as evidence at trial. If this wound up being a
capital case, which Bentley believed it would, and the defense brought in someone to say that she was a nice, kind
person, he could put Jim on the witness stand to contradict
that testimony. The third way would be if Dana mounted an
insanity defense. If her lawyer put on some expert to say
she was insane, Bentley could put Jim on the stand to show
that when she was at home, and not being interviewed by a
sympathetic psychiatrist hired by the defense, she was
moody and angry, with a combative personality. At any rate,
Bentley thought, it looked like they'd arrested the right person.

"Now, you puttin' us on or is this true?"

"I mean for fun," Jim said. "You know, like you might wrestle with an older, older kid, you know."

"Like two teenagers or something . . ." Bentley said.

"Yeah. Don't stand too near the couch, don't stand too near the bed, you might get attacked," Jim said with a laugh.

"Between her and her husband, were they violent? Did she ever bop him, he bop her, that you know of?"

"Not according to her," Jim said. "He used to let her hit him in the shoulder when she got pissed off."

"Yeah? Is that what she did to you?"

"No, I don't go for that shit."

"Did she ever try and strangle ya?"

Jim sat back in his chair. He seemed more amused than alarmed.

"Hmm-mm," Jim said, shaking his head no.

"Pull a kitchen knife on ya?"

"No. She's never done anything like that. She's been extremely pissed off at me."

"Do you think there's anything unusual about her?"

"Occasionally I wonder, but I tend to give people the benefit of the doubt," Jim said flatly, triggering laughter from everyone. The interview had quickly turned from a tense question-and-answer interrogation into a bull session—the kind a bunch of guys would have over beer in someone's living room, griping about their wives or girlfriends. Now this is good police work, Bentley thought.

"In the last month, has she ever came home with any injuries? To her arms or anything like that? Scratches?" Bentley asked.

"No, not that I know of. I haven't seen any," Jim said.

"OK, when she came home today, what was she doing?"

"I don't know. I wasn't paying any attention at all."

"Shoes. What shoes was she wearing?"

"I don't know."

"You're a big help," Bentley said, triggering another round of laughter.

"I told you you'd love me for this, but . . ." Jim joked, shifting in his chair. More laughter.

Bentley asked whether Dana had washed up that day or whether she'd done her laundry. Then he leaned forward in his chair and tried to form his words carefully.

"If, if I told you that I thought she killed somebody, what would you say?"

Jim considered the question for a moment.

"I'd be shocked. But then again, I've been through a lot of other, of other weird shit. I supposed maybe it wouldn't," he said dryly.

Bentley, McElvain and Greco looked at him. He wasn't finished.

"I don't think she would kill anyone. Ever. What would she gain from it?" Jim said.

So, Greco thought, he gets up in the morning with this woman, goes to bed with her at night, lives with her, lets her take care of his kid while he works . . . they share lives together, and he doesn't ruffle an eyebrow when police ask whether she might be a killer?

Jim wasn't easily shocked; the answer he'd given was probably the only answer one could expect from him. If he wasn't so even-tempered, he would never be able to have a relationship with Dana. When she had her mood swings or when she physically attacked him, he probably showed no reaction, which probably set her off even more.

Bentley filled Jim in. But instead of just telling him what they suspected her of doing, Bentley told him that Dana at first had lied to them and denied using the credit cards, then told them that she'd found the credit cards in the trash by the bank. Those cards, Bentley told Jim, were used within an hour of June Roberts' murder.

"Obviously, does that sound like a lie to you?" Bentley said. "That sounds like bullshit, right? I found a credit card of someone who was just murdered. But here's a clue. We're tryin' to say, who was this guy, you know? Now here's the clincher, though, let me give you the description of the person she gave us. The person that had that purse was about six foot, looked like a construction guy with sandy blonde hair and kind of thin.

"Now, I never saw you before today, but guess what? The first thing that came to my mind when she gave that description . . ."

"Oh, geez," Jim said.

"OK, now, I don't believe her," Bentley said. "I don't believe her. And she didn't say you. But you see what I'm sayin', she didn't say my height, you know, my color hair, she said your height, your color hair. So, so, here's what I think. I think somehow she gets a card one hour after somebody was murdered. Either she knows who did it that fits that description and she helped them, or she did it. OK?"

"That's fucking wonderful," Jim deadpanned.

"OK, so my next question to you is, can you help us figure it out? 'Cause you just told me you didn't think she would do it, but then she gave a, I mean, does that fit your description?"

"Oh yeah, it fits my description, I guess, but . . . do I look like a construction worker?" Jim asks, grinning slightly.

"Well, I, to me you do," Bentley said, surprised at the response.

"Shit," Jim said, pausing. "Guess I'll have to get a new job."

The men erupted with laughter again.

No matter what they threw at Jim, he remained unbelievably even-keeled, Greco thought. He was a working drone, getting up and going to work every day. He was probably more than happy to have someone looking after his kid while he was at work. They weren't looking at romance here as much as convenience.

After less than 20 minutes, Bentley felt they'd established more than enough of a rapport with Jim to turn the corner on the interview. He decided to take him into their confidence and ask him for advice on getting her to confess. First, he asked Jim if they could examine his timecards from work to verify his whereabouts on the days of the murders. Jim agreed to cooperate. Then, Bentley sketched out how he would resume the interrogation of Dana.

"We're gonna bring her back in here, OK? . . . She first lied about the credit cards and while you're sittin' there, she finally says that [she used them]. So here's what I'm afraid of. We get her back in here and we start pointing more fingers at her 'cause we got all kinds of evidence against her. What's she gonna do? What do you think she's gonna do?"

"Well, when Dana's angry with me, she breaks down hysterically crying," Jim said.

"She's either gonna point the finger at you or somebody

else. So my question is, what can you give us? I hope you got an alibi. It makes it easier for me. The second thing is, what else can you give us to get her straightened out when she starts doin' that? She's copped to most of it. She's copped to the credit cards . . . How do you get the credit cards and not know about the murder? She hasn't copped to the murder. But I think when we get her back in, she's gonna say, finally say she did it, or she's gonna say, she's gonna blame somebody. That's why I asked you who her girlfriends are."

Jim skirted the larger question, but said that Dana hadn't seen her friends much lately, except for a visit with David and Joanie Fulton a month ago. "She was going to spend the night and she ended up coming home, like, real early in the morning. She was upset and crying hysterically over having lost her job and all kinds of shit."

OK, so he wasn't the go-to guy for sympathy, Greco thought. They weren't there as relationship therapists.

Bentley asked Jim if Dana had ever mentioned visiting either Norma Davis or June Roberts, and he said she hadn't. He asked if Dana ever mentioned getting nutritional advice from June, and Jim, again, was disdainful. "What's she need a nutritionist for? She's got a cabinet full of every kind of vitamin you could imagine."

Bentley and Jim reviewed some of the purchases Dana had made, like the boots and the shoes for him and his son, then asked where Dana got her money.

"I don't have a clue, as far as I know, she didn't have any money," Jim said. "I've been paying all of her bills."

"What if I told you we found $2,000 in a sock in your house?" Bentley asked.

"Oh, fuckin' great," Jim said. "I'm goin' into debt paying her bills and she's got money. Nice. No, I paid everything, uh, except today she gave me twenty bucks. 'Cause she said her aunt sent her some money and she tried to give me more and I'm goin' hey, fuck this."

"What would happen if you confronted her about what happened?" Bentley asked. "What do you think she'd do?"

"I don't have a clue. Probably either break down and cry or accuse me. Some shit."

The interview took on the aroma of a locker-room bull session.

"That's the least she's gonna do," Bentley said sympathetically.

"I think she'll probably just bald-face lie," Greco said.

"She might," Bentley said.

"I, I just don't see a real close relationship there," Greco finally said. "I mean, did you guys talk about anything or did she just come home and say, hi, how's it goin' . . . ?"

"No, actually, we talked a lot about a lot of things . . . windsurfing, surfing," Jim said.

"I mean, did she seem sane to you?" Bentley asked.

"Well, she had her moments after she lost her job because she was freaking out," Jim said. "All of a sudden, she didn't have an income." That was right after Thanksgiving. Then they took a four-day trip to Mammoth Mountain, the largest ski resort in Northern California.

"Did she lie to you a lot?" Bentley asked.

"That's hard to say."

"To your face, she lied? Did you ever catch her lyin' to ya?"

"I've caught her twistin' things once or twice, but that's it. But it didn't amount to anything, you know."

"She ever come in in clothes with blood on her in any way?"

"No, I've never seen her come in bloody."

McElvain asked whether any clothes had disappeared from Dana's wardrobe recently.

"No, she's like the jeans, the T-shirt, or the shorts and T-shirt kind of person, so you know, shit, there's probably twenty-five white T-shirts in that damn closet. Half of them probably say 'Impeach Clinton Early,' " Jim said.

Greco asked Jim about their relationship and where it would head.

"I think I'm a little irritated at her," Jim said.

"A little?" Bentley said, chuckling. "Well, I mean, we're asking for your help, because I'm telling you right now . . . we're gonna have her here for a while and if we catch her in some more lies, I mean, we've caught her in a bunch. And that she admitted it. And that she started playing games and making excuses, I mean, outrageous excuses.

"So, my question is, how can you help us before she does something to you? Or tries to do something to you?"

Jim again avoided Bentley's attempt to rope him into helping them.

"Well, I don't know how hard it is to condemn the innocent, but maybe she could do that."

"I guarantee you, she tried," Bentley said, trying to trigger some response from Jim.

"I don't know what I could tell ya, other than the fact that she has access to my truck," he said.

"Well, we're gonna confront her again, so we'd kind of like to have you hanging around. I know, there's a nicer place you can sit," Bentley said.

"Like without handcuffs and where I can have a cigarette?" Jim asked.

"Yeah, yeah, sure," Bentley said. "Let me ask you this. There's a bunch of cigarettes inside your cabinet in your house. Who bought those?"

"Dana. Today."

"So, that's how we'd like to do it," Bentley said, explaining the tedious process of asking a reluctant suspect a question, waiting for a lie, and confronting them with a "gotcha!" response to make the suspect aware that the police know they're lying and encouraging a truthful response.

"Yeah, sometimes she doesn't offer information," Jim agreed

"Does, does that seem OK to you guys?" Bentley asked.

"Sounds fine to me," Greco said.

11:10 P.M.

It was time to call Jeri again. Greco didn't want to say too much on the phone. He told her that he'd been talking to Dana and that if they wanted to talk to her they could come to the station. Jeri said they'd be there in about half an hour.

James McElvain took Jim out so he could have a cigarette, then led him to the report-writing room. Jason was next. A female officer had been keeping him busy, feeding him a Happy Meal from McDonald's and letting him play with the toys they kept at the station to entertain children who were victims or witnesses. Out of courtesy, Greco and

Bentley mentioned to Jim that they were going to speak briefly with Jason, and Jim agreed. The officer who had been entertaining Jason brought him into the interview room. She asked him to spit out his gum and then sat him in the same chair that Dana and Jim had been using. Greco's objective was to capture on tape the fact that Jason remembered the name of the woman who had cut his hair at Esthetiques Salon and could give a basic description of her. Greco got that out of the way fairly quickly using child-friendly descriptions such as hair "dark like mine" and eyes "the same color as yours."

Pointing to a Band-Aid on Jason's leg, Greco asked whether he'd ever seen Dana with a boo-boo, or if he'd ever seen blood on her. Jason said Dana had had blood on her when Bossy, Dana's brown labrador retriever, bit her after getting "bumped" by a car.

Greco ran down the list of shopping sprees that Jason had been on with Dana—buying cowboy boots, eating cheesecake at Baily's Wine Country Café, getting a boogie board and new clothes.

"So, uh, those shoes, who bought those shoes?" Greco said, pointing to the new athletic shoes Jason was wearing.

"Dana," Jason said.

"Dana bought you those shoes?"

"They're magic shoes."

"They're magic shoes?" Greco asked.

"Yeah."

"Oh, they make you jump high, huh? What about these jeans? Who bought you these jeans?"

"Dana."

"Dana bought you the jeans, too, huh? Wow! Dana's very nice, huh? Buying you clothes, what else does Dana buy you?"

"A lot of stuff."

"What else does she buy you? What other stuff?"

"Like toys and stuff."

"Toys and stuff. What was the best thing she ever bought you?"

"She buys me candy, too."

After the interview, Greco walked Jason back to the report-writing room where Jim was waiting and told them

they were free to leave. An officer would drive them to a
friend's house because the police were still going through
the house. Jim nodded. Greco thanked Jim for his time and
cooperation and escorted them to the door.

He didn't ask about Dana.

11:40 P.M.

Russell and Jeri were waiting for Greco in the lobby. They
looked worried and anxious. Greco could see the sadness in
Russell's face. Greco shook their hands and walked them
back to the report-writing room.

"I'm sorry to have to break this to you," Greco said.

"What's going to happen to her?" Russell asked.

"She'll be arrested and she'll be held overnight," Greco
said softly. "Then she'll be arraigned in court within forty-
eight hours and it'll go to a preliminary hearing and then
it'll go to trial."

"What is she . . . what's the charge?" Russell asked.

"Well, it'll be murder," Greco said quietly. There was no
way to cushion the impact. "It's for the murder of June and
there was another woman in Sun City who was killed. That
happened today."

Greco didn't mention Norma. He didn't have enough evidence at the moment to charge Dana with her murder. After
a moment, he added that it she wouldn't be going home
tonight because it was a no-bail, special circumstances murder case. Greco didn't explain that "special circumstance"
was a legal eupheumism for a possible death penalty case.
Multiple murders is one cause the legal system has to send
a defendant to the gas chamber or to sentence him or her to
life in prison without parole. But all of that would be explained later. He just didn't want to get Russell's hopes up
that Dana would be going home anytime soon.

Russell cleared his throat, fighting for composure.

"How do you know for sure that it's my daughter?" he
asked in a hoarse voice. "How do you know?"

Greco told them the evidence was pretty compelling: the
information they'd picked up during serveillence, the description of her from storeclerks, the fact that the card was
used within an hour of June's murder. He told them that

Dana had been followed to the bank that day and that she'd
already admitted using the bankbook of the woman who had
been murdered hours before. As he spoke, looking at both
Russell and Jeri, he could see the heartbreak and incredulity
on Russell's face. But Jeri knew the truth.

"I can't believe this," Russell said. "It must be, there
must be someone else. This can't be my daughter."

It had taken weeks for Jeri to come to the horrifying
realization that it *was* Dana. It took a couple of days of silent
denial and gradual realization before she decided to tell
Greco. Now Russell would need time to do the same thing.
It would take him a long time to comprehend the gravity of
what was happening and to understand his wife's involvement. Even though Jeri had told him, Greco knew that she
hadn't told him everything. Russell had a right to be in
shock, and as a father, it would have been very unusual for
him to turn his back on his daughter and agree with detectives that she was a killer.

Russell and Jeri were victims twice over. Through
Norma's murder, they were victims. They were also the immediate relatives of a homicide suspect. It was unusual for
Greco to be comforting the relatives of someone he had
arrested and interrogated. The parents of his suspects never
had a good relationship with him because he was trying to
put their sons and daughters behind bars. And here he was
trying to comfort the parents. It felt weird that they were
being nice to him, particularly since June's son-in-law had
not been very cordial.

"You'll have to trust me on this one," Greco said. For
the time being, he would preserve Russell's belief that Dana
wasn't the only one involved in the murders. It would come
in handy shortly.

"Can I see her now?" Russell asked.

"Yes, you can see her in a few minutes. I'm going to
have you wait here and then I'll come and get you," he said.
Greco didn't want to tell them that Dana was sitting in a
cell down the hallway. He and McElvain wanted a few more
minutes with her before letting Russell in. He didn't want
them to see one another unless it was on tape. There was
no telling if Dana would admit anything to her father. But
Greco thought Russell might be motivated to get some an-

swers from Dana if he knew this would be his last chance
to talk with her before she went to jail. He knew he was
manipulating Russell when the man was at his most vulnerable. And recording it on tape. But Greco had seen
Dana's handiwork. He had smelled the blood spilled from
her victims and spent hours at the crime scenes where she'd
slaughtered two innocent women. Notwithstanding his loyalty to Jeri, Greco had a higher calling to the victims of
Dana's crimes.

"She's not going home tonight," Greco said, watching
Russell's face. "She's not going to be getting out. She'll
spend the night here and then she'll be transported to the
Riverside County Jail, so this is a chance to talk to her. You
might want to ask her some of these things yourself.

"In a day or two, she'll be arraigned and a lawyer will
be appointed for her, unless . . ." Greco paused.

"I can't afford a lawyer," Russell said quickly.

Greco nodded and turned away, saying he'd come back
in a few minutes. On his way back to the interview room,
Russell's comment struck him as odd, given the healthy
state of their finances. He wondered if he'd just heard the
sound of Russell's wallet slamming shut.

CHAPTER TEN

Greco brought Dana back to the interview room. He told her that she could talk to her dad in a few minutes. They also told her that they'd spoken with Jim, who'd said that she had come into some money earlier that day.

"Yeah. When I got the cash from the, from that savings book, uh, that's what I, that's what my story was," Dana said. "I didn't want him to know."

"What was your story?"

"That my aunt had sent me some money, that's all."

"OK. There's a, there's a lot of stuff that still points in your direction. And it's, it's time for you to come clean," McElvain said.

"I've given you all of the information I have," Dana said, sounding annoyed.

"No, you, you haven't. And, and just like earlier, it's, it's time for you to clean the slate and start your life over again. You can't get past this point in your life until this is done.

"All we're asking you is complete honesty."

Dana's expression hardened, like a businesswoman trying to negotiate a deal. She dug in her heels.

"Well, I want a lawyer to say anything more. I've given you everything I can give. You know, I was scared and it was stupid for me to try to spend a credit card, it was even stupider . . ."

Dana kept talking, so Greco picked up the questioning. He wanted a confession, even if it wasn't admissible in court. Let the lawyers fight it out later.

"It's just that we don't feel that you've given us everything . . . because of the circumstances . . ."

"It looks bad," Dana said, finishing his sentence.

"Look at the circumstances, OK? Look at our position," Greco said.

"I do look at your position. I know that's why you're hammering me so . . . But I'm tellin' you, it's . . ." she stammered, breaking down again. "All I wanted to do is get some cash and some things."

In a way, Greco felt that they'd hit the real core. She was a long way from admitting the murders. But she probably *was* telling them everything about her motivations—as much as she wanted them to believe.

Greco pushed on. If she was about to break, it was now or never.

"There's a lot of unanswered questions about victims here. It's not just about cash. It's not about credit cards. It's about people's lives that were taken."

"Well, I don't know," Dana said, reaching for a tissue.

Greco saw that, for some reason, talking about her own desire to shop, to acquire material possessions, triggered Dana's tears. But talking about the loss of human life was like a cork for her tears. She stopped crying immediately.

"It's very important."

"I don't know what to tell you," Dana sounded annoyed. "I've told you everything I could tell you. Now that I know that it's your job to keep asking me over and over again, but I don't know what else to tell you. I really don't.

"I lied," Dana said, breaking down again. "I was scared."

"I understand, and you may still be scared about what else is, is behind that."

"Today," Dana said, now so fully engulfed in tears that she had trouble speaking, is the biggest fuck-up I think I've ever done in my life. I don't have any criminal history. I don't steal.

"And I've been under stress. I just wanted to *have* something," she said, raising both fists and bringing them down hard, "have some cash, some clothes for Jason, you know. That's, that's really all I really wanted.

"I can't have kids . . . I tried like hell to get it to work and it's just . . ." she said, pausing to sniff. "You know, I saw that wallet and I went, 'W-O-W!' And I lost my head . . . I lost my sense. You know, but you find something, you know, and you look and it's there and you just think, well, should I do it, can I get away with it?

"Obviously I didn't, I'm not a, I never did it, I fucked up. Don't you understand?"

Greco later realized that this may have been the closest she'd ever get to a confession. She was telling him that she did it—without saying she did it. She was basically explaining that she killed these ladies so she could shop.

Dana had already asked for her lawyer, but they wanted to see how far she would go.

"I don't know what to tell you . . . I'm lucky because it's, it's not, I just got lucky and it's bad. I wish I wasn't there to find the card . . . to find that purse."

Dana was holding fast to her story. Now was the time to see if she would change her story if she thought someone saw her.

But the more they tried, the harder Dana clung to her version of events. Only after 20 minutes of painstaking questioning would Dana admit that she'd been in Sun City on the morning of the murder. But she insisted that she'd been lost and only got out of her car to smoke a cigarette.

THURSDAY, MARCH 17, 1994, 12:25 A.M.

Greco and McElvain got up to leave, saying they were going to let Russell into the room. Greco wanted to prep him for a few minutes before bringing him in. McElvain would keep an eye on Dana via the hidden camera. She shifted positions often, laid her head on the back of the seat, picked at her tissue, burped and blew her nose. Greco walked back to the report-writing room, the hours of interviews swirling around his brain. Her callousness disgusted him. He had no doubt that she'd killed Norma, June and Dora, and had attacked Dorinda in the antique store. But every time they tried to push her, she backed off. Chipping away at her lies was taking a long time. It was eerie the way she turned the tears on and off. And she seemed to cry at odd times. Greco had a feeling that her reluctant admission, that she had stopped in Sun City for a cigarette, would probably never see the inside of any court because she kept asking for a lawyer.

The past few hours of trying to wear Dana down had

worn on him as well. He didn't get the full confession that he wanted, but they got her to admit to using the credit cards, which put her in striking distance of the murders. It was still worth a try to see if she would admit anything to her father. It was important that Russell believe that perhaps Dana hadn't acted alone, that maybe Jim had some hand in the murders.

He saw them in the report-writing room.

"How're you two doing in here?" he said.

Russell nodded and Jeri tried to smile.

"OK, we're done talking to her. She's admitted to using the cards, but we're thinking that maybe Dana wasn't the one that did it," Greco said.

Russell looked up at him sharply.

"If she wasn't the one who committed the murders, then she was there and knows who did," Greco said slowly. If Russell had any hope left, he would be motivated to ask Dana for some answers.

"Just get her to tell you the truth about what happened," Greco said. "There are, um, people who were killed. People whose mothers and sisters and grandmothers are dead and they need some peace, too. And it'll be better for her to come clean about it and tell you what she knows." He didn't tell Russell that their conversation would be taped.

Russell looked determined. He stood up and Greco walked him back to the interview room where Dana was waiting. Jeri stayed behind.

When Greco returned, James told him that he had a phone call from Jim, who was furious that his dark green pick-up truck, as well as Dana's Cadillac, had been seized as evidence. The vehicles had been towed to the county yard, where they would be processed for blood and trace evidence. Greco tried to reassure Jim that he'd get his truck back once the lab technicians were done with it, and took down the phone number of a friend's house where Jim was staying. Jim appeared to care more about his truck than he did about Dana.

Greco put down the phone to watch the monitor with James McElvain. As soon as Russell entered the room, Dana let out a loud shriek and ran to the door to hug him. Dana and her dad walked arm in arm to the interview side of the room. The police had full audio, but only the tops of their heads were picked up by the hidden camera.

"What is it, honey, what is it?" Russell said, holding Dana by the shoulders.

"I saw a man at the Ready Teller using this credit card trying to get some money out. And it wouldn't work, so he threw it in the trash," Dana said quickly, the words spilling out as she was sobbing.

"Credit card?"

"A credit, two credit cards and a little purse. Not looking at the name, I just, oh I've been just so devastated by this. I took 'em and I charged on 'em and looked later and the name was June, but I didn't know it was June Roberts."

Russell asked Dana questions in rapid-fire fashion: How did you get the cards? What did the man look like? How long have you had the cards? Did you go to work Monday? What about the woman in Sun City?

Gone was the smug arrogance. This was Daddy's girl, alternating her sorrowful baby voice with sobs and shrieks and curses, giving her father the same phony story she told the police. She was desperate for money, she'd wanted to buy things for Jason, she'd lost her head—now she wanted Daddy to bail her out of trouble.

Russell persisted as the detectives had asked him to, asking questions and pressing her for details, like whether she had borrowed Jim's truck, but Dana resisted.

A clerk at one of the shops said they believed the female suspect using June's credit cards was driving a dark sport utility vehicle or pick-up truck. Dana insisted that she never drove the truck, except to deliver lasagne to them after Susie's death.

". . . Dad, you have to get me out of here," said Dana.

"Um-hum," Russell said. "We're gonna do everything we can, honey. I'll do everything I can."

"Oh God!" Dana said, shrieking and crying. "I got so desperate, Dad, I just did this stupid thing, but I never hurt anybody, I never hurt anybody, Dad," Dana said, her hand over her nose and mouth.

Russell hesitated.

"I wanna believe you, darling. I wanna believe you."

"Do you?"

He hesitated slightly.

"Yea. Yes."

He paused.

"Because there's so much evidence against you, honey. That's why I've got to know everything. . . ."

Russell continued with the questions, asking Dana if she was on medication, whether Jim knew about any of the credit cards. Dana insisted that Jim knew nothing and that she'd lied to him that her aunt gave her some money.

Dana continued to ask if he would get her out.

"Can't you get a lawyer and get me out tonight?!"

"I can't get you out tonight, honey. It's midnight, it's one o'clock, almost."

"Is it?"

"Twelve-thirty."

"Oh God."

"I'll see if I can do it tomorrow. So long as you tell the truth, honey."

"I did, I did."

"That's all you have to do is tell the truth."

"I did, I did. And they kept badgering me because I initially lied. I initially lied because I was scared!" Dana said, her voice rising to a squeal. "I'm not gonna commit, ah, confess right away, you know. You know I was scared 'cause I know I had done something morally bad."

"That's why I've got to know everything."

Greco briefly popped his head into the room to ask if they wanted a few more minutes. Dana's wails increased at learning that her father was about to leave. She insisted that he call a 24-hour bondsman, asked him to "be hard on" the detectives to release her and begged him to bail her out first thing in the morning.

Russell said he'd try, but in the meantime, said she should "try to hold up."

"I love you, Dad," Dana said, starting to wail again.

"I love you, too."

"I'm so soooooooorreeeee," Dana wailed. "Please talk to Jason."

"I will, OK? I love you, sweetheart," Russell said as he left the room.

"Oh my God, Dad! Oh my head," she said, sobbing heavily. "Is anyone out there? Hello! Do you have any aspirin?"

As her father was leaving, she tearfully asked for a cigarette, but her father said no one there smoked.

Dana laid her head on the table and sobbed heavily for
several minutes, loudly wailing, "Oh God! My head. Oh
God, can you help me?"

12:49 A.M.

After they'd watched her wailing for a while, Greco went
back in to give her water and aspirin. They were still waiting
for Antoniadas to drive up from the Beebe crime scene.
She'd been so tight, Greco doubted that she'd say anything,
but you never knew. So far, she'd admitted using the cards,
which would corroborate what the clerks had told them and
what the handwriting comparisons suggested. What bothered Greco was that Russell and Jeri had never admitted that
anything of Norma's was missing. He suspected that Dana
had taken something belonging to Norma, for the simple
reason that she never seemed to leave empty-handed. She
had stashed items from her post-murder spending binges all
over her house like trophies. She surrounded herself with
them or, like Dora's credit cards, hid them somewhere. They
could be looking squarely at something and not know it
belonged to Norma. He'd have to work on that later.

Greco gave her the water and the aspirin and sat down.
She gulped the pills and looked at him.

"Feeling better?"

"Yeah, thanks," Dana said.

He asked her about her visit with Russell and she started
crying again, because her father had said that things "didn't
look good."

Greco seized the opportunity.

"Well," he said, "it would be better if you could explain,
you know, this can't all be a coincidence. It just doesn't
make sense. Is it possible you were in the area at the time?"

"Yeah, I was driving around," Dana said. "I was driving
and I pulled off to the side of the road to smoke a cigarette
and I look over and, um, I see this house with the screen

door that's closed, but the front door was open, so I think, well, maybe there's something.

"I walked up to the house and opened the door and looked inside and I see, um, there's this lady, this woman on the ground and she's obviously dead. So I went inside and saw this purse and it, um, it was just too tempting. I needed the money and it was too tempting, so I took the purse and I left."

Greco couldn't believe what she'd just told him. The problem was, he didn't know the Beebe crime scene. It wasn't his case and he didn't know exactly what to ask her.

"Where was the purse?"

"Right there. I just grabbed it and left," Dana said.

"Did you think about calling an ambulance for the woman?"

"No, no, you could tell she was beyond help. There was nothing anyone could do for her."

Greco was shocked: Dana had finally admitted that she was at a crime scene after hours and hours of going nowhere. He knew that if he could get a chance to talk to her alone, she might admit more, but he knew Antoniadas wanted to interview her, and he didn't want to mess with that case.

"OK, well, is there anything you think might be important that we missed?" Greco asked.

Dana shook her head.

"OK, I need to go check on something."

Greco practically ran out of the interview room to check the tape. When he got back to the office, he saw Bentley talking to Antoniadas. James was sitting nearby. No one was watching the monitor.

"Did you get that?" Greco asked.

"Get what?" James said. Bentley and Antoniadas were still talking.

"You didn't get that?" Greco wanted to shout, but if he did, Dana would be able to hear him. The walls were pretty thin. Greco took a step over to the machine and felt his face grow hot. The tape machine had been turned off, probably to save tape.

"Get what?" James asked.

1:18 A.M.

Antoniadas used to get so many pedophiles to cop out to him that he'd earned a reputation at the station. It started to bother him that these sick men trusted him so much that they would almost always end up confessing to him. But it was the same old thing. He'd bring them into the interview room, talk to them for a little while, size them up, be their friend, confide in them, and then he would casually mention that sometimes little girls—and he'd fill in the approximate age of the victim in that particular case—looked good to him. He would "confide" in the suspect that he also had those feelings. They'd get to talking about that and the suspect would confess. Antoniadas hated pedophiles, but he knew what to say to them. You have to size up your suspect, figure out their weakness and use that to get them to talk to you. A confession usually saves the taxpayers money. By the time the guy hired a defense attorney, who would quickly learn his client had copped out, there would be little else to do but plea his guy out. Saves the taxpayers another expensive trial.

Antoniadas knew a lot of ways to talk to criminals. A lot of times, he just started talking about how good it feels to get something off your chest: clear it up, get it out, you feel better, you get on with your life. Some crooks had pride, so you insulted them a little—told them they did a sloppy, amateur job. When they started protesting, you got 'em. Macho guys hated it when you insulted their manhood. Antoniadas took advantage of that by telling them that if they had the guts, they'd be man enough to say exactly what they did. He wasn't allowed to use the religious angle anymore. If he had a guy who was real religious, Antoniadas used to be able to ask whether he believed in God, whether he thought God was looking down on him, and if he thought God would want him to confess his sins and cleanse his soul. The DAs told him he couldn't use that anymore, so he stopped.

He didn't know what he was going to use on Dana. The interrogation was already underway and he was getting sloppy seconds. That wasn't how he preferred to work. Ideally, you got one person in there and they questioned the suspect for all cases. You never tag-teamed it. But he wasn't running the show.

When he and his partner, Mark Cordova, got to the Perris station, the detectives there were taking a break. McElvain briefed him about what Dana had said about finding credit cards at an ATM machine. Their last attempt centered on telling her that a witness saw her come out of Dora's house. Antoniadas nodded.

Bentley took him aside and complained about how the interview was going. He didn't like the way McElvain and Greco were interviewing her and didn't think they had the experience to handle her. Dana was controlling these guys, running them around in circles. He needed someone with experience who could handle a hard case.

"I want you to push her," he said. "Push her real hard."

Antoniadas had no problem with that, but the problem was, he hadn't been there for the past four hours to know how to push her, so he was going to have to start slow and easy like everyone else had. He and Mark Cordova walked in, introduced themselves and picked up where McElvain and Greco left off, telling Dana that a woman had positively identified her coming out of Dora's house.

"Maybe I stopped there, but I didn't go into the house that I remember," Dana said.

"Well, she saw you come out of the house and you ended up with this woman's property," Antoniadas said. "And this woman is dead. Did that woman, did you just steal the, the checkbook and her, uh, credit cards from her while she was alive and somebody else came and killed her after you left? Is that possible?"

Antoniadas was doing the same thing—offering a chance to minimize, lock her into a lie and proceed from there. But Dana didn't bite.

"I don't know," Dana said, her head down. "I don't know what's possible."

"I know you got it from the house, OK, Dana? At least be, have enough inside your heart to be enough of a person to admit that. If you don't remember killing her or something, that's fine, but at least don't sit there and insult my intelligence and . . ."

"I'm not trying to insult you."

"Yeah. But we know you got it out of the house. I've got the woman sitting here telling me this, telling me that you came out of the house."

"I stopped! That's three times . . . But I don't remember walking into anyone's house."

"Well, you were in there. And you ended up with her property. She's dead now. Can you explain that to me?"

"No, I can't."

"Well it's not that you can't, it's that you don't want to. Don't you feel . . . remorse at all?"

"I feel, I feel like shit, yes. I feel terrible," Dana was twisting a tissue.

"No, not about the woman, you feel shit because things haven't gone right for you."

"I feel terrible about everything that I've heard and I really feel terrible about stealing her money and from her . . ." Dana said, breaking into heavy sobbing, "from her bankbook, you know. It's just, I feel terrible."

"You feel bad about killing her?"

"I didn't kill her." Dana's hands were to her face again. Antoniadas wasn't going to let her slide.

"Yeah, you did."

"No, I didn't. I didn't kill her," Dana said, raising her voice. Every time she denied the killing, her hand was either on her nose or trying to cover her mouth or her face.

"You were in the house. Was there somebody else with you?" He paused, waiting for her to answer, then he continued. "She didn't see anybody else with you, said you're the only one who came out."

"I did not kill her," Dana said. She couldn't look him in the eye.

"You know what, Dana? You can sit there and you can tell me that, you can tell the other officers that. It's not what I think, it's, it's that I know. And all's I want to know is, why? Maybe you had a problem. Obviously you had a problem.

"Is that why you killed her?"

"I did not kill her." Dana twisted in her seat, crossing her legs and turning away.

Antoniadas continued as if he hadn't heard her. By now, Dana was crying freely.

"Is that what made you do what you did, then? You were in the house, you took her property. I'll grant you that, maybe someone else killed her, maybe you went in and took her property and somebody else came. It's a possibility, but you can't even admit that you were in the house. Even though I can put you in the house with that eyewitness. Even though you ended up with her property."

"Yes, I ended up with her property. . . . I might have stopped near her house. But I did not . . ."

"You ended up with some property from somebody else at Canyon Lake who was killed also. All right. . . . And that, how did you end up with that property, Dana?"

"Because I was going to the Ready Teller to get some cash out. There was a man in front of me, he was in a car and he said several times . . ."

"Yeah, I've heard that story, but I want to ask you something . . ."

"I'm talk—can I finish!"

"Sure. I'm sorry, go ahead."

Dana insisted on telling the same story with the same excitement about shopping with someone else's credit card, claiming that she hadn't noticed that it belonged to a friend of her father's.

"Do you think it's kind of weird or unusual that you end up with credit cards from two different ladies in that same area and that both of them happened to get murdered? In the same way, almost? Not in the exact same way, but some things were consistent from one murder scene to the other. You find that kind of unusual? How unusual do you think a jury is going to find that?"

The stark reality of this odd circumstance didn't faze Dana one bit.

"I don't know. I guess it depends on how well the prosecutor prosecutes it," she said defiantly.

"Real well. Real well."

"What's gonna happen now?"

This was enough for Antoniadas to size up what he had to deal with. This woman didn't believe she was going to get nailed for killing these old ladies. No one was going to touch her. She was strong-willed and cocky. She was smarter than the cops. She thought she was going to beat this case.

Antoniadas wanted to see what would happen when he tried to elicit some kind of remorse from her, but she acted like he'd never said a word: "I feel sick. My head aches."

"I feel so bad for this family," he said. "I had to sit up there and clean up that scene and deal with it , . . and I feel sorry for you because I know you have a lot of problems. And I can sympathize with you. And I really feel sorry for you because you're making it worse by lying. And it breaks my heart to see somebody like you that has these problems that need some help in order to give yourself the chance and then throw away your whole life.

"Because you can't look at me and tell me the truth. And that's your choice, you know. I'm not mad at you about it, I feel sorry for you. Because you know what, that could be me sitting there. Sometimes I get stressed out. I know when I get stressed out, I don't do the things I should sometimes. Stress causes people to do weird things sometimes."

He wanted to give her an out, an excuse, some kind of a reason, but she cut to the chase.

"I never killed anybody." Her hand was on her face again.

"Maybe not, maybe not knowingly." Antoniadas still wanted to give her a graceful way to admit to the crimes.

Suddenly Dana burst into tears.

"But I've been a nurse for thirteen years," Dana said, her voice becoming distorted from sobbing. "I didn't kill anybody."

Antoniadas figured that by bringing up a noble profession, she'd hoped to make him think highly of her. It wasn't going to work.

Since she was sobbing so heavily, he tried a variety of questions to bring her back to the Dora Beebe crime scene, asking what time she was out there and whether she wandered around before shopping and why she was in Sun City in the first place. Dana said she wasn't sure of the time and talked about needing a calendar insert to keep track of job interviews.

After a pause, Antoniadas asked, "You feel pretty angry about this happening to you?"

Dana didn't hesitate.

"I'm angry, I'm hurt, I'm pissed and I just don't know what to think. I feel . . ." she sighed heavily. "I feel exhausted."

"You've got to start doing something constructive. You've got to start getting your shit together, Dana. 'Cause, you know, you can lie to us, you can lie to the court. The truth is going to come out. And you'll sit there and lie the rest of your life until you sit down and decide you're gonna tell the truth.

"What you did was a horrible thing and I think maybe with all the problems you have, nobody's really ever gonna know 'cause you're never gonna give anybody a chance, 'cause you're never gonna be truthful with anybody and you're going to court and they'll probably convict you or whatever and you're gonna sit there and lie. You're gonna sit there and hurt yourself. . . ."

Dana was openly sobbing. Antoniadas was trying to give her another outlet to confess. By talking about a conviction, he wanted her to know that this was her opportunity to tell her story in a favorable light, one that would come across as a lot more human here than it would at trial.

"The thing is, you're never gonna get any better until you own up to it. I know you're scared, I know you're tired, but it's got to start somewhere, Dana—the healing process— and it's got to start with you being truthful to yourself at least. Am I right or wrong?"

She didn't buy it. Crying heavily, Dana asked if she would be booked and what would happen after that. Antoniadas explained the rudiments of the court process. She thought she was in control. He started to understand what he needed to do—he needed to break her down, make her feel that she was not the one running the show and take away her feeling that she was in control. She had no idea that she was burning herself by telling him this, Antoniadas thought. No jury was going to buy the fact that she'd simply found the cards.

Antoniadas tried to pin her down to a time, but Dana

again said she didn't know. He switched directions suddenly.

Dana said she wanted a lawyer, and "some psychiatric counsel. I think with the stuff I've been through, the depression I'm in and the anti-depressant, I think . . ."

Antoniadas was not about to stop questioning Dana just because she'd asked for an attorney.

"You can sit there and cry if you want, but you can't fool yourself."

"I can't fool anybody," Dana said.

"Yeah. Just like you aren't going to fool those twelve people up there."

"Can you please stop? I need to rest my head. I haven't eaten." She was crying again.

"Dana, you have children, right?"

Antoniadas, unaware of Dana's two previous miscarriages, unleashed another heavy bout of sobbing.

Finally, she stammered, "I can't . . . I can't have a kid," her words barely discernible. "I just keep miscarrying them."

Unmoved, Antoniadas was nevertheless patient. He waited a moment, then asked Dana whether she'd found a wallet or a purse. He just wanted her to admit that she had Dora's belongings.

Answering his question dowsed the crying jag and she went into a detailed explanation about how she'd found a billfold, but it had been stripped of cash and major credit cards.

1:40 A.M.

That was round one. Now Antoniadas had something to work with. He had found out where she was vulnerable and now he knew how to attack her. Remorse didn't work; she was too goddamned cold. He had wanted to see if she had a soft side—she didn't. Antoniadas thought he would use her need for control and superiority against her. She liked being in control. Antoniadas was going to take that away from her. He and Cordova went back in. If Bentley wanted him to push her hard, he was going to push hard.

"I'm not taking any of your bullshit," Antoniadas said.

Dana looked surprised.

"We know you did it, you know you did it—"

When Dana shook her head and tried to speak, he cut her off.

"You're going to listen to me now!" Antoniadas said, shouting. "I don't want you to talk now. I'm not taking any more of your shit, Dana. We know you murdered these people. We know you did it—"

"I want a lawye—"

"Shut up!"

Antoniadas got up from his chair and screamed in her face.

"We're tired of your bullshit! We're tired of your lies! We're done with that. You tell us the truth, Dana—"

"You can't yell—"

"Shut up!"

"I want a lawye—"

"Shut up, Dana! We're in charge here, not you. You're not getting a lawyer right now," Antoniadas said. He was standing over her. Dana cowered in her chair and covered her face with her hands. She was sobbing.

"I can't . . ."

"Shut up! You do this heinous thing and you can't even admit it. All you're doing is hanging yourself and making it worse. You're gonna go to court and go to trial and get in front of a jury and no jury in the world is going to believe you, Dana."

"You have to get me a lawyer—"

"No, Dana, you don't get what you want. We're not taking your bullshit anymore. You're gonna start telling us the truth and you're gonna start telling us the truth right now.

"Right now, Dana!" Antoniadas was yelling in her face. She was sobbing hysterically, turning her face away, but Antoniadas was moving, literally getting in her face. "You're going to tell us the truth, Dana!"

"I want—"

"We don't care what you want! You're going to do what I want and I want you to start telling the truth, Dana. No more of your shit. All you're doing is hurting yourself by lying. You're wasting your time and you're wasting our time.

"We have a witness, Dana. A witness IDs you coming out of the house. Start talking, Dana."

Dana was a mass of tears; her face was red and distorted from crying.

"I—I went up to the door," Dana said, her voice quavering. She swallowed. "I went to the door and I looked inside."

"What else?" Antoniadas said harshly.

"Nothing else," Dana said. "I didn't do anything else. I didn't see anybody and I left. I just poked my head in the door."

"We'll be talking to you later," Antoniadas said darkly. "You aren't going anywhere."

CHAPTER ELEVEN

THURSDAY, MARCH 17, 1994, 2 A.M.

Greco was dead tired, but he didn't know it yet. He was in "the zone," the Zen-like state that cops get into after staying up for 36 hours straight. They don't feel the cold, can't smell the corpse at a crime scene, and they're immune to fatigue. All they know is they gotta collar their suspect and they don't stop until they do. Even though he was done interviewing Dana, his night was far from over.

He was thrilled to finally, formally arrest and book Dana for murder. She was curled up in her chair, clutching a tissue. For all the bluster from Antoniadas, she got away with telling him less than she told Greco. The hours of interrogation left Dana subdued and a little irritated. When Greco stood in front of her, she barely looked up.

"You know you're not going home tonight," he said, the words seeming less threatening in his soft-spoken voice. "You're under arrest. I need you to stand up and turn around and put your hands behind your back."

Once the handcuffs were on, he talked to her back.

"You're under arrest for the murder of June Roberts," he said. "You'll be transported to Riverside County Jail tomorrow and arraigned in forty-eight hours. After the arraignment, you'll have a preliminary hearing.

"Do you have any questions?"

"When do I get a lawyer?" Dana asked.

"One will be appointed unless you want to hire one," Greco said, gently pushing her elbow to steer her out the door. "Come on."

All night, he had been escorting Dana back and forth down the hallway. This time, it was different. Starting tonight, her life was going to consist mostly of being led in handcuffs from one place to another, wearing ugly blue jail jumpsuits and eating crappy food. If everything went right, she would never see her home or sleep in her own bed again.

The tears that had flowed freely during the interview were gone. Greco was intrigued with how she could turn them on and off. When she wanted them off, they stayed off. He was also impressed with her ability to hold them at bay and extract information from them while they were trying to get information from her. Greco was a little frustrated that he hadn't obtained a full confession to make the case airtight. Other than Dorinda, they had no live witnesses, which meant that the case would rest on a jury's ability to piece together circumstantial evidence. No one saw her going into Norma's house, June's house, or Dora's house. As far as they knew, she left no fingerprints, blood or hair, although the evidence gathered at the crime scenes would be examined and tested. Their case consisted of showing jurors that Dana had spent June's credit cards and used Dora's bankbook less than an hour after each of them was murdered. Greco hoped that Dorinda would identify Dana. There were no credit cards or checks with Norma's murder. He hoped the search of Dana's house turned up the shoe that had left the shoeprint. Greco thought that the June and Dora murder cases were strong, but he wanted something indestructible.

Getting a confession could have been instructive. She could have told them how she chose her victims, how she killed her victims, why she so brutally slaughtered them and why she used household items, like the iron and the wine bottle. In the case of Dorinda, he wanted to know why she attacked a woman in a retail store during business hours.

Greco walked behind Dana, as he did with every other prisoner he arrested, guiding her by the elbow out of the carpeted, softly lit interview room and down the hallway past the detective bureau and the report-writing room.

They turned a corner past the dispatch center, to the hard linoleum floors and bright lights of the lock-up area. Dana squinted slightly, her red-rimmed eyes swollen, her sandals making a soft noise on the hard floor. Greco paused by the office where the on-duty watch commander sat at his desk behind a row of video monitors. Video cameras were aimed at prisoners in each cell for two reasons—so they wouldn't hurt their officers, and wouldn't hurt themselves. If they were busy trying to make some kind of a weapon or using something to hang themselves with, the police could intervene. Over the years, Perris had lost two prisoners to suicide.

"I have a prisoner," Greco said to the watch commander, who wrote the information in the station's jail logbook. "Dana. Sue. Gray, with an 'a.' 187," he said, giving the penal code section for murder. The watch commander also wrote down the time—2:08 a.m.

"This is going to be a no-bail, special circumstances case," Greco said. He wanted that entered into the logbook so no one would make a mistake and release her in the morning. After she was booked, the watch commander would come by to see if she wanted to eat. At this time of the morning, it would be breakfast. Greco thought the food was putrid, although it was the same stuff supermarkets sold in the frozen food section. Eggs, sausages and pancakes in a cardboard box, plus a little tin of maple syrup.

They passed the cluster of six cells where Dana had been kept off and on during her interrogation. One of those cells was the drunk tank: no bunk, no blankets, just a cold floor with a drain in the middle. The smell permeated the lockup and booking areas. Every time Greco had to go back there for a prisoner or to book someone, he was glad he'd never been arrested. The stench alone was enough to keep him out of jail.

When she hesitated, Greco said, "Just keep walking straight. Now turn right."

Once they turned the corner, they entered the booking room, an open area consisting of a computer on a counter and a wooden bench secured to a wall about eight feet away. A Breathalyzer was in an adjoining room. For some reason, the booking area was a lot colder than the rest of the station. It was always colder in there. That and the smell spilled over from the drunk tank.

Greco sat Dana on a bench and cuffed one hand to a solid steel eyebolt on the seat while he pulled out the booking forms and grabbed a Polaroid camera. She gave him a blank face for her booking photo and, in contrast to hours of cat-and-mouse interrogation, Dana obediently answered

all of his questions regarding her vital statistics, employment
history and next-of-kin. Greco took his time and double
checked all of the information, including the murder
charges, and making certain it was clear that she was a "no
bail" case. Her booking information would accompany her
to the Riverside County Jail, which would be her home
while she was arraigned and awaiting trial. Because she'd
killed more than one person, Greco expected Bentley to file
special circumstance allegations, California's legal gateway
to the death penalty or a sentence of life in prison without
parole.

Greco called a twenty-four-hour nursing service to take
blood and saliva samples and scrape underneath her fingernails in hopes of collecting evidence linking her to the murder of Dora Beebe hours before. He also arranged to have
a community service officer take photos of Dana without
clothing to see if she had any bruises or cuts, particularly
on her arms and hands. He unhandcuffed Dana and fingerprinted her. Even though James had taken a set that night,
he needed additional sets for regional, state and national law
enforcement databases. As Greco rolled her fingers, he examined her hands and fingers for cuts and saw nothing.

By the time he was finished, Julie, the community service
officer, had arrived to take pictures. He walked Dana back
to her cell and went back to the detective bureau to do paperwork.

He picked up the phone and called Wyatt to see how the
search was going at her house. Wyatt briefed him about the
merchandise they found from Mervyn's, Nike and the other
mall stores. They'd also found some credit card slips as well
as the receipts for the massage from Murrieta Hot Springs,
Baily's Wine Country Café and the Ferrari Bistro. Greco
asked about the Nike shoes and Wyatt said there were
plenty. They were taking all of the Nikes. Greco said he'd
be out there soon and hung up, satisfied that the search
seemed to be going well. He was happy that he and Wyatt
were working well together. With Dana in custody, they
knew the importance of the case took priority over personalities.

At 3:20 a.m., Dispatch rang his desk to let him know the

nurse was there. He escorted the nurse to the lock-up and stood by as he took fingernail scrapings and clippings, a saliva sample and a vial of blood.

The nurse gathered up his equipment, packed away the vials and left Greco with the evidence samples of Dana's genetic material. Dana stood there for a moment surveying her surroundings. The bars were about six inches apart with heavy-gauge mesh between them. A cot built into the wall had a wafer-thin plastic mat with an olive-green wool blanket folded on top. The rimless, stainless-steel toilet had a sink and drinking fountain built into the tank portion of the toilet. A window, too high to look out of, had double-paned glass and was covered with bars and the heavy steel mesh. The concrete floor and walls, painted a faint peach hue, were unadorned except for stains left by prior occupants. Dana had been bagged and tagged and was now an official prisoner with no control over when she would eat, when she would sleep and when she could make phone calls. Every half-hour, the watch commander would come by her cell to see what she was doing and make a note in the logbook. If Dana was hungry, the watch commander would feed her. Unlike the severe emotional outbursts Dana had displayed during her interviews, she hadn't even sniveled.

Greco slammed the door shut and turned away. He was glad she was behind bars, but it wasn't his style to pat himself on the back. Arresting and booking Dana at 2 a.m. that morning had triggered the forty-eight-hour time limit within which the system had to file charges and arraign her. They had a little leeway because the time would technically run out Saturday at 2 a.m., so she wouldn't have to be in court until Monday. Greco had to pull the paperwork together and present the case to the DA's office later that day. A committee of DAs would review the case, decide what charges to file and do their own paperwork so she could be arraigned. Even though arresting Dana was the slam dunk to a successful investigation, the game wasn't over. Now they had to prove it.

Greco yelled into the microphone for someone in Dispatch to let him out. A second later, he heard the buzzer, pushed open the door and left.

THURSDAY, MARCH 17, 1994, 6:45 A.M.

As Greco was driving home, the rosy sunrise cast a warm glow on the large "M" marking the entrance to Moreno Valley, where he lived. He felt happy, satisfied, and a little numb from fatigue. He'd solved a high-profile case—and the case seemed pretty tight—all in one month. It was only his second homicide case and the experience had been overwhelming. But within that month, he'd come a long way from the near-crippling feeling of self-doubt.

He'd gone by Dana's house again to take a longer look at her environment and see how she lived her life and what magazines she read. When the police had asked Jim whether he and Dana had been reading any newspaper articles about the murders, he said that Dana had been buying papers recently to look at the want ads. Now Greco picked up the Canyon Lake paper and thumbed through it. The front-page article was about the murders, but the little paper carried no classified ads.

Wyatt and the ID techs had also made another discovery. They'd found a coiled plastic ring with keys that seemed to match those described by Dorinda Hawkins, hanging from a hook on Dana's entertainment center. That, along with Dorinda's description of Dana—provided that she identified Dana as her attacker—would solidify that charge. They'd also found one of Dora's credit cards in Dana's sock drawer, where she said it would be. Dana's purse held two bundles of cash: $1,900, just short of the $2,000 she withdrew from Dora's account, and $170 in her wallet, which came from writing checks for $50 over her grocery store purchases. They'd also found six pairs of gloves in her room, an unusually large assortment for a dry, desert climate where winter temperatures rarely dip below 50 degrees in the daytime. Another pair of gloves and several hanks of rope, including water-ski tow rope, were taken from the laundry area. More rope was found in the kitchen cabinet and several lengths of rope were found in the hallway, including new water-ski tow rope still wrapped in plastic. Outside, more rope turned up in the garage, and in a small tool shed. A pair of white latex gloves were found in the trash.

That was about 4 a.m. Greco came back to the station to do the paperwork that the DA's office would need to file charges. Wyatt closed the search at 4:40 a.m. and they hauled 86 bags of evidence back to the department. One of the community service officers who had assisted on the search organized the evidence into piles all over the detective bureau so she could categorize everything while she booked it into evidence. It looked like a yard sale.

Greco sat down with the bags of Nikes at his desk and started going through them, examining the soles. Between Jim and Dana, they had a lot of Nikes, particularly Dana. He had pulled his own copy of the one-to-one picture of the dusty shoeprint from his file cabinet and compared shoe after shoe to the imprint. Each matching pair had been strung together with plastic ties. He didn't know there were so many different patterns on the soles of athletic shoes. About halfway through the bags of shoes he found a white pair of Nike Air athletic shoes, size 6½, that seemed to match. The shoe obviously belonged to Dana, whose smaller sneakers were dwarfed by Jim's size 11s. He placed the shoe over the photo of the imprint. It looked good to Greco, but a forensic shoeprint expert would have to render an expert opinion. Greco was satisfied, though. He didn't have any credit cards, checks, cash withdrawals, key rings or any other evidence directly linking Dana to Norma's murder. Dana said she hadn't been in Norma's house in two years. There's no way that shoeprint should have been in Norma's house. This would do it.

Greco was still excited about the arrest. Discovering the shoe gave him a renewed burst of adrenaline. He returned the remaining shoes to the bag, took the pair that he thought matched to the community service officer and told her to send them to the DOJ for comparison, then he tackled the DA paperwork. He was so excited, he couldn't stop working. Those shoes would definitely place Dana at the scene, he kept saying to himself. With his paperwork just about done, he decided to book the videos of the interviews. It only took a few minutes.

The drive home wound him down somewhat, but a million thoughts were jumping around in his head. Later that day, he would have to go to the DA's office and brief a committee of prosecutors that decides which criminal charges will be filed in murder cases. For example, if Dana had taken credit cards out of the house after killing someone, they could file one count of murder and one count of burglary for that incident. They could also file charges of forgery and credit card fraud.

Something else struck Greco as he was driving. He rifled through his notes to find the phone number and reached for his cell phone.

"Mr. Owens?" Greco said. "This is Joe Greco. I thought you might want to know that I have a suspect in custody who's going to be charged with your mother-in-law's murder.

"I think we have a pretty strong case against her."

Greco waited a moment. He could hear Owens sighing, as if he was emotional.

"I'm, I'm really relieved," Owens said, stammering somewhat. "I just want you to know, well, uh, I really appreciate your, everything you've done in this investigation. I have to say, well, I really didn't think you could do it."

Greco listened.

"I just want you to know, if you ever need a job in Nevada, just let me know."

THURSDAY, MARCH 17, 1:30 P.M.

The new, modern-looking Robert Presley Detention Center in downtown Riverside doesn't even look like a jail. Its smooth, sculpted concrete curves and lines resemble an attractive office building instead of housing for hundreds of inmates. The telltale difference is that there is very little foot traffic through the front doors. Prisoners enter the building through a secure rear entrance and the guards, all sheriff's deputies and a few civilian employees of the sheriff's department have a separate, secure entrance. Inmates are transported to and from the nearby courthouses via underground tunnels to reduce the potential for escape. Very few people ever enter by the front door except on visiting days, when the lines of mostly women and squalling children line up for hours to visit their husbands, boyfriends, sons, nephews and fathers. The inmate receiving center processes upwards of 100 men and women a day. Some are just getting arrested and others are being released after spending a weekend, a few days, a few months or a few years inside. They get interviewed by the staff about gang affiliation, sexual orientation and experience in the jail system to determine where they will be housed. All inmates are screened by medical personnel, and by psychiactric personnel if they're suicidal, clearly psychotic or schizophrenic. Their housing can be determined by type of offense, sexual orientation or gang affiliation alone. Members of known rival gangs are not housed together. Male transvestites are housed separately from the rest of the male inmate population. High-profile, violent offenders will not be housed with an inmate arrested over the weekend on a traffic warrant.

It takes a couple of hours for deputies to process each inmate through the jail's receiving center. Dana, like the other women in her holding tank, had removed her "civilian" clothing, shoes and underwear and was physically searched and given jail-issue underwear, a blue jumpsuit with "RCJ"—for Riverside County Jail—stamped in huge black letters on the back, and brown plastic sandals. Her clothes would be stored either until her release or until they were retrieved by a relative. Greco had already taken her earrings as evidence. Dana was taken from the holding tank and again fingerprinted, photographed and formally booked, having to spell her name, her date of birth and other vital information. Dana was assigned a booking number— #9408779—and placed in a holding cell while a clerk ran her name and fingerprints through separate state and national law enforcement databases to determine if she had any other wants, holds or warrants for her arrest. A deputy asked her questions about her gang affiliation, sexual orientation and experience in the jail system. He took a look at the murder charge and determined that she should be housed in protective custody, with other women who do not mix with the rest of the inmate population, and sent her to medical screening.

A nurse took her blood pressure, her temperature and pulse. Dana told the nurse her height was five feet, two inches and her weight was 136 pounds. She told the nurse about a dog bite to her hand the previous July and that she'd had four miscarriages, two more than she'd told her friends, her husband, her boyfriend and her father. She denied having problems with seizures, heart problems, TB, diabetes, hepatitis and AIDS. She answered "no" when asked about crabs, lice and venereal diseases. She was experiencing menses at that time and asked for an ob-gyn exam due to menstrul pain as well as a mammogram. She admitted drinking two alcoholic drinks a day. She complained of weakness, lethargy, weight loss, night sweats, loss of appetite, and chronic diarrhea after "slowing down on drinking," claiming that her "symptoms have increased since incarceration. Wants vegetarian diet." She said she was suicidal and wanted to see a counselor.

Dana was handed a bedroll consisting of a gray wool blanket, two white sheets, a towel, a pillowcase and a small cardboard box, known as a "welfare pack," containing a toothbrush, toothpaste, soap and a razor. A second empty cardboard box was to be used to store her own belongings: books, magazines, mail, pencils and personal hygiene items. Dana was probably the only inmate at the county jail who'd traveled to Germany and Sweden, windsurfed in Australia and New Zealand, partied in New Orleans, gone to Hawaii three times a year to sail and play golf, had pedicures religiously every month and was so meticulous about her hair that she never let her roots show. Dana didn't find any shampoo in the welfare pack. One of the guards told her that if she didn't have money on her books to buy shampoo from the commissary, she could use soap, and she was shown to her new home, a concrete cinderblock cell.

Dana was hungry, having not eaten since lunch the day before. She hungrily eyed the trustee, in a white jumpsuit, making the rounds with food trays stacked on a cart. The trustee shoved the tray through the horizontal slot. Dana took one look at the tray and shoved it back.

"This is moldy!" she said to the trustee. "What is this, some kind of microwave crap? I'm not going to eat this! Can't you give me something else!"

The trustee gave her a blank stare.

THURSDAY, MARCH 17, 2:57 P.M.

The criminalists were going through Dana's Cadillac at the impound yard, listing the evidence they were removing. They took photos of the interior, the exterior and the tire tread. Strands of hair were removed from the driver's seat, the seat belt, the head rest, handwritten directions, a pager from the front passenger floor, a cassette labeled "Dana's tape," a box of latex surgical gloves and a variety of lengths of rope from under the rear driver's side floor mat, a bath towel, three boxes of women's hair coloring—in blonde and brown—and a Von's receipt.

The trunk held some interesting items: a black plastic bag containing fossil bones, legal divorce paperwork involving Tom Gray, and an assortment of ropes and straps. The last thing the criminalists did was cut out a sample patch of vinyl material from the front passenger seat.

The criminalists also photographed and took material from the front bench seat of Jim's truck. They confiscated hairs and fibers from inside the car and from the floor mats as well as some ropes from the small compartment under the driver's seat.

THURSDAY, MARCH 17, 6:20 P.M.

Dana recited her history to the intake psychologist: four miscarriages, divorce, fired from her nursing job just before Thanksgiving. She had gone to marriage counseling during the divorce last year, but that was it. She told the counselor she was very fearful, depressed, distraught and unable to cope. She said she had experienced suicidal thoughts during the last several months. She admitted a history of alcohol-abuse as well as marijuana and cocaine use. She said she was on anti-depressant medication.

The psychologist noted that she was oriented as to time and place, was not delusional, and was not experiencing hallucinations. Dana said she was not suicidal at that moment, but the counselor decided to take precautions anyway and place her on observation status. She would be briefly interviewed in follow-up exams and evaluated, possibly medicated. She would have one hour of free time out of her cell each day and she'd be locked up the rest of the time. The interview lasted less than 15 minutes.

She was allowed a phone call a few minutes after that. By 8 p.m., she was back in her cell.

FRIDAY, MARCH 18, 6 A.M.

The deputy showed Dana to a holding tank where she would await her arraignment sometime later in the day. They got her up at 4:30 a.m. for transport to court, which was across the street. Dana looked around at her temporary environs.

"Hey!" Dana shouted. "The toilet in here is grossly clogged!

"Hey!"

The deputy was long gone.

FRIDAY, MARCH 18, 11 A.M.

The phone was ringing as soon as he got home.

Tom Gray, his long, narrow legs clad in jeans, raced across the studio to get it.

"Tom, what's Dana's middle name?"

"Why?"

"Just tell me!"

"It's Sue."

"Oh my God, you're not going to believe this!"

"What's the matter?"

"Well, Dana . . . Did you see the paper this morning? She's been arrested."

"What?"

"For murder."

"What are you talking about? You mean . . . Dana?"

"Yes, Dana! Can you believe it?"

Tom hung up the phone, stunned. His entire body felt numb, as if he had been struck. It was the weirdest thing he'd ever felt.

He thought, *Are we still married?*

FRIDAY, MARCH 18, 1 P.M.

It was Jim again on the phone and he wanted to know when the hell he was getting his truck back. Greco had talked to him the day before—twice. Jim was upset and he had a right to be. Greco sympathized with him: it was a real inconvenience, he said, but some of the store clerks said that Dana had driven away in a dark sport utility vehicle or a dark pick-up truck, and they had to process his car. He told Jim he should have it by Monday at the latest, and that he'd call the criminalists again. They had a lot of evidence to process from four different crime scenes as well as a truckload of evidence from his house. Greco wasn't about to rush them, but he didn't tell Jim that.

He hung up the phone, finding it revealing that every time Jim called about his truck, he never asked about Dana. She'd barely spent two hours in the Perris jail until the watch commander shipped her off to Riverside County Jail. She arrived at the Riverside jail at 5:45 a.m., about two hours after the nurse had taken her blood, saliva and fingernail scrapings. Greco hadn't realized that until he came into work early Thursday afternoon. Her purple dress, her pristine off-white leather Birkenstocks and the contents of her purse were now in a storage locker at the Riverside jail. There was something satisfying about knowing that she was now clad in a baggy blue jail jumpsuit with "RCJ" stamped across the back.

When he saw Julie Bennett, she said she'd taken photos of the front and back of each hand, each side of her forearms as well as full-length shots from the front, back and sides. Julie told Greco that it was unusual to have a murder suspect with manicure-perfect nails. Knowing that Dana had committed a homicide earlier in the day, Julie noticed that Dana hadn't even broken or chipped a nail.

Greco chuckled to himself at this. He also wanted to know how she went shopping in public without blood all over her clothes minutes after committing extremely violent murders. Julie said she was submitting the photos for processing and that they'd be ready next week. Dana's arraignment was scheduled for Monday. He had presented the paperwork involving the murders of Norma and June to the committee of district attorneys on Thursday, but Rich told him they didn't have enough evidence to file charges for Norma's murder. Greco was disappointed, but he knew they were reluctant to file charges until there was more evidence linking Dana to that crime scene. Like the shoeprint. They needed a positive match, and that would take time. Antoniadas had presented his evidence about Dora and Riverside sheriff's detectives had presented evidence regarding the attack on Dorinda. They had filed charges of murder for the June Roberts and Dora Beebe slayings, one count of attempted murder for the attack on Dorinda Hawkins, and a robbery charge for stealing money from Dorinda's purse.

"Hey, have you seen this?"

James McElvain was holding up the front page of the *Press–Enterprise*. Greco scanned the headline: "Nurse, 36, Is Prime Suspect in Three Slayings and Assault." The front-page story had a map of the region and the locations of the murders, like the pin map that Greco still had up behind his desk. There was a second story quoting neighbors and friends of Dana, including her father-in-law, expressing shock over her arrest.

"Thanks," he said. He took the newspaper and said he'd read it later.

Greco was curious to know what the papers had said about his case. The reporters had called yesterday, but he'd been buried in reports, then had to rush off to the DA's office to present his case. Not that he shunned the press, he simply didn't have time to talk to them. Even that afternoon, he knew there was a press conference about Dana's arrest scheduled at Canyon Lake. Wyatt would be the center of attention there and that was fine. If Wyatt wanted the glory, he could have it. Wyatt hadn't even asked Greco to go. Greco probably wouldn't have gone anyway, not when he had reports to write. A couple of Perris officers had stopped by his desk to congratulate him on his work and he appreciated that. It chafed at him that none of his supervisors had even said a word to him.

FRIDAY, MARCH 18, 3 P.M.

Why did Dora let Dana into her house?
   Why did Dana use an iron?
   Did she strangle Dora first and then hit her?
   How did Dana choose Dora in the first place?
   Antoniadas was sitting on Dora's bed, just thinking. After everyone had cleared the crime scene, he usually returned a day or two later to sit by himself and let everything sink in and let ideas come to him. What he had seen seemed cold and calculating. There was an element of deliberation in the attack: the suspect had grabbed the phone cord ahead of time. But there had also been a bit of spontaneity: she seemed to have grabbed whatever was handy to hit them with. She was a very physical person who overpowered her victims. The attacks were definitely overkill, showing that she was expressing a lot of rage and hostility. This was not about credit cards and bankbooks. When he'd talked to her, he could easily see her doing this. The crime fit her personality. She didn't care about anyone but herself.
   He'd attended Dora's autopsy that morning. He'd attended more than 100 autopsies, including a few elderly victims of homicides. The frailty and vulnerability of elderly victims never failed to make an impression on him.
   Antoniadas figured the findings of Dora's autopsy would be similar to those of June and Norma's autopsies. Multiple modes of death linked all of the victims. Dora, like June, was killed by manual strangulation, ligature strangulation, and multiple blunt force trauma to the head. The blows to her skull were so hard, they had literally split her head open, which explained why chunks of hair were strewn on the carpet. When they brought the body in, she was virtually unrecognizable, she was so swollen and bloody. Like June, one eye was hugely purple and swollen shut. An ID tech took pictures from multiple angles, her head still turned to one side and her right hand still raised in a protective posture, even though she was on a gurney. She had defensive cuts and bruises on her hands and her right thumb as well as bruises on her right shoulder and on her chest. A criminalist took tape lifts from her clothing, even though it had

also been done at the crime scene. Once the autopsy atten-
dant swabbed the blood from Dora's face and hands, the
ligature mark around her neck emerged and the skin on her
face was stippled with red dots, the result of the hemor-
rhaging during strangulation. There were five blows on the
left, rear side of the head.

That was the same conclusion drawn by criminalist Ric
Cooksey, who'd just spent a few hours diagramming the
blood splatter marks in the hallway. Antoniadas was amazed
that Cooksey made the same finding as the coronor just by
looking at blood dots on the walls. The ID techs had taken
photos of the splatter the night of the murder, but Cooksey
plotted the marks on graph paper, transferring the gruesome
blood splats so they looked like some sort of hyperkinetic
graph. Cooksey was good. From the arc, angle and direction
of the splatter marks, he surmised there were five blows and
was able to approximate the source of the splatter: the location of the victim's head when each blow was struck.
Because small drops don't travel far, he could tell the head
was very close to the wall when certain blows were struck,
but he didn't theorize which blows came first. Splatter marks
near the floor by the bathroom and the oblique angle of
splatter in the door jamb indicated that the victim's head
was near the floor several inches away from the jamb. Cooksey noted that some of the drops had demarcated edges and
were very low, leaving open the possibility that two or three
of the blows occurred with the head between the attacker's
legs. Given the location of the head when the blows were
struck and the angle and arc of the splatter, Cooksey also
suggested that a left-handed attacker might have produced
the blows.

Dana was so goddamned cold. She was smart, but she was
also stupid in the way that criminals are stupid. Smart criminals don't talk to cops. Dana had never been arrested and
had never been through the system. She'd thought she was
smart enough to control the interview and for the most part,
she had. But she was not smart enough to express sympathy
for the victims. Antoniadas had been around more clever
killers who were conniving enough to say, "I have no idea

who did this, but I sure feel terrible about what happened to those poor ladies."

Dana thought she was smarter than the cops, felt superior to the cops and wasn't afraid of the cops. She had a controlling attitude and a lack of sensitivity. It was those qualities that made her a killer. What was he missing? What else did he need? What was he leaving out?

He tried to look at his cases from the standpoint of a defense attorney to see where the holes were and how they were going to attack. Like Bentley, Antoniadas also saw an insanity defense emerging. Right now, he had a paper case. He knew the taped statements would never see the inside of any courtroom since she was screaming for a lawyer. He just wanted to make sure she was working alone so they didn't have to try finding someone else. Now he had to build a profile on her, talk to her friends, find out what she was like and get as much information as possible about her work habits, her finances, her relationships.

Antoniadas didn't feel like his case was weak, but he knew the second you say you're done, some defense attorney down the road will try to poke holes in your case by filing motions to ban items of evidence or statements made by his client. If the judge agrees with any of it, your case has the potential of biting the dust, in which case the defendant walks. You can never have too much evidence. That's one reason he liked to pick up everything at a crime scene, even if it seems superfluous, because you can't collect it three or four years later when the case is in trial. There was one murder case where some woman was stabbed to death and they found what looked like candy at the crime scene. When Antoniadas asked the criminalist to pick it up, they found that it was Tic Tac breath mints and Excedrin. While they were at the crime scene, some guy kept riding by on a bicycle again and again, staring. Antoniadas got a funny feeling and sent a unit to talk to the guy. When they shook him down, he had Tic Tac and Excedrin in his pockets. Apparently, some had fallen out while he was stabbing the victim. At another crime scene, it looked like someone had taken a bite out of a big chocolate bar and left it in the bathroom. The criminalist didn't want to pick it up, but Antoniadas wanted it. It turned out to be a bar of soap. When they went to talk to the victim's son, Antoniadas went to the bathroom and saw the other half of the bar of soap. He arrested the guy. Antoniadas had no idea why the guy had left a half a bar of soap at the crime scene.

He knew they would not use all the blood, all the fibers, the carpet exemplars, every single blood smear, the hair chunks, the hair combings from the autopsy, the tape lifts from the body and the blood splatter patterns in this case. The most pressing matter was to get a documents examiner to compare the signature on the checks Dana passed at the grocery stores, the stationery store, and the health food store against the handwriting from her own checks and checkbook and the exemplars she wrote out during the interrogation. He wanted the same checks compared to Dora's signature in her own checkbook. He'd also coordinate with Greco and get the examiner to compare Dana's handwriting to the signature on the credit card slips where she signed June Roberts' name. There was no doubt in Antoniadas' mind about what the examiner would say about who had signed those checks.

There was something else. Antoniadas pulled out his cell phone and dialed a familiar number.

"Yeah, Detective Antoniadas, Elsinore station. I want to put a mail cover on this inmate. I want everything sent to me."

He waited a moment.

"Dana. Sue. Gray. G-R-A-Y. 187. She was arrested on the sixteenth. She'll probably be in P.C.," he said, the shorthand for protective custody. Antoniadas asked that everything be sent to the Southwest station of the Riverside County Sheriff's Department in Temecula, which covered Sun City.

From now on, every piece of mail Dana sent and every piece of mail coming to her would be copied and sent to Antoniadas. They would also conduct periodic sweeps of her cell, common for many inmates, and collect any unfinished letters and anything else she had written, copy it, return the originals to her and send the copies to Antoniadas. Her phone calls would be monitored and her jail visits would be monitored and taped. What they could not review or copy were incoming and outgoing letters marked "legal."

Other than legal mail, prisoners have no right and no expectation of privacy. If she was going to confess or describe her crimes to someone in a letter, he wanted it. He also wanted to protect the only living witness, Dorinda Hawkins, in case Dana had worked with a partner.

FRIDAY, MARCH 18, 3 P.M.

Tom fished the yearbook out of the box. There were still a few unpacked boxes from when they'd moved out of their home in Canyon Lake. The little house they'd bought on Ketch Drive for $108,000 several years ago was ratcheted up in value by the real estate market, but they had taken a second and a third mortgage to pay off the credit card bills that Dana had run up. When they'd split up, they moved out of the house and Tom had moved to a small studio, his personal belongings taking a back seat to his drum set and his recording equipment.

Music had always been a big part of his life. Even though he drove a backhoe to make a buck, he dressed like a hard rock musician—ripped jeans, long, wild, wiry blonde hair and lizard-skin boots, black leather jacket. He'd been playing drums since he won a talent contest in junior high in Covina, a suburb of Los Angeles about fifty miles northwest of Riverside County. It was in junior high that he first laid eyes on Dana. She was so beautiful, he had a hard time breathing when she was around. He couldn't help but look at her and stare. She was a little blonde spitfire, full of energy and sassy attitude, a free spirit.

From that moment, he was head-over-heels in love with Dana. But for all he knew, she had no idea he existed. His boyhood crush never went away and he continued to worship her from afar in high school until she moved away after her freshman year. Ten years passed and when he ran into her at a grocery store, his knees felt weak. He took her to his tenth high school reunion and a little more than a year later, they married. Tom was the happiest man in the world and knew that with the golden-haired, athletic goddess of his dreams, they could tackle anything together. But after he and Dana got married, everything changed.

CHAPTER TWELVE

"Woo-woo!"

The guys unloading boxes from a truck at the dock behind the May Company department store stopped in their tracks and looked up at the two teenaged girls speeding around the docks on a moped.

Dana, her blonde hair flying, and her dark-haired best friend Carrie Ann on the seat behind her, buzzed the guys on the docks at the local outdoor mall, catcalling over the sound of the moped's whiney engine.

"Woo-woo!"

They zipped around town a bit before speeding home. But the young girls caught the eye of a patrol officer who stopped them and cited Dana for driving the moped without a license. He also didn't like her flippant attitude. He sat Dana and her friend in his black-and-white, loaded the motorized bike into his trunk and carted them home.

"Watch out for her," he told Dana's mother. "If you're not careful, she's going to lead a life of crime."

Beverly, Dana's mother, let Dana have her moped back with a warning: "Next time, don't get caught."

At 13, Dana was more than a handful. She was developing into a beautiful girl, but she couldn't take "no" for an answer. A simple request to do household chores would result in a screaming match because she wanted to go to the movies or do something with her friends. All Beverly wanted was to instill a little discipline and responsibility, but Dana would have none of it. Dana was temperamental and demonstrative.

Sometimes she acted more like a teenaged boy. One year Dana had gotten her mother a snake for Christmas. Afterward, Dana said that her first choice had been an iguana, but it had died under her bed, so she went back to the store and got a ribbon snake. On Christmas Eve, it got out of its box and Beverly finally found her Christmas present slithering around the bathtub. Beverly's little lecture to Dana about gift-giving—it's for the person you're giving it to, not for yourself—fell on deaf ears. Dana had simply expected to get in trouble.

Once when they were getting ready for dinner, Dana asked if she could start the car and Beverly said no because Dana was still rather petite and the driveway was on an incline. Dana didn't argue, but a few minutes later, there was a crash in the front yard. When Beverly ran out of the house to look, Dana had crashed the car trying to get it started.

Beverly was an ex–beauty queen and still tried to play the part. She liked being made-up and dressed. She had been a Rose Princess in the Tournament of Roses Parade in the 1930s, modeled at Bullock's and was the model in the Hamilton watch ads. She had the drop-dead looks that attracted men in numbers. A would-be actress, her Hollywood career never quite took off, and she drifted from job to job and eventually had two sons by two different fathers.

Ten years later, she met Russell, Dana's father, a women's hairstylist, and she charmed him with her outgoing personality and bubbling sense of humor. People who knew her well said she'd never met a stranger because she immediately put people at ease as if they were old friends. Russell and Beverly married. Russell bought a house in Covina and worked at being a father to Dana as well as to Beverly's sons, Rick, 10, and Craig, 8. Beverly and Russell tried many times to have another baby and Beverly suffered several miscarriages until she finally became pregnant. By the time Dana was born, their little family was ecstatic and Dana was the cherished new addition. Beverly, who worked at a beauty supply shop Russell owned, soon began using an assortment of medications. Russell thought the house resembled a drug store, with bottles of pills all over the house. He didn't like it. He also didn't like the fact that she charged his credit cards to the limit. He could not get her to stop spending money. Beverly was aggressive and liked being the queen bee of her own home as well as the small block where they lived, but she didn't get along with one of their neighbors. One day he came home to find Beverly outside the house wrestling with the woman in the gutter. He left her soon after that. Dana was not quite 2 years old.

As Dana was growing up, Russell visited once or twice a month, sometimes more, sometimes less. Early on, Dana exhibited daredevil and destructive antics to get attention, from dying her hair green to recklessness in sports. Dana thought her mother paid more attention to her older stepbrothers because Rick had appeared in a sky-diving television commercial for Marlboro cigarettes and Craig, a musician, had played a big gig at Disneyland, caught the eye of a record producer and cut an album. Dana tried to play Craig's guitar and would sing in the driveway of their home where she thought no one could hear, but resented that her mother never gave her the praise she gave her older half-brothers. She felt that her mother didn't pay enough attention to her and that she was too young to compete for her mother's affections. Feeling rejected, she retaliated by using pinking shears to cut a hole in one of her mother's dresses. At 5 years old, she knew she'd get punished and didn't try to hide what she had done. With her eldest half-brother, Craig, out of the house playing gigs with his band, Dana retaliated against Rick by crawling into his bed to take a nap, and wet his bed. He was furious at her, but she kept doing it because she thought it was funny. She finally stopped wetting his bed when she was 8 years old. Rick moved out of the house to live with his great aunt, Beverly's mother's sister, who agreed to take him in.

Beverly tried to discipline Dana, and at the same time pay more attention to her, by laying out clothes for her to wear and fixing food for her to eat. But Dana interpreted that as a form of control. Whenever Beverly disciplined her, Dana would rebel by stealing money from Beverly's purse to buy candy, sometimes as much as $10 and $15. She liked Jolly Rancher and Pixy Sticks, and stashed it in her room. If Dana didn't have any money, she would steal candy or other food and hide it in her room to eat later.

When Beverly thought she was tucked away in bed, Dana would read Grimm's Fairy Tales, her favorite book, from cover to cover. Later, she fell in love with horror movies. She'd get up in the middle of the night to catch the 2-to-4 a.m. movies, preferring older movies that relied on suspense to slasher flicks. She liked good, scary stuff: monsters and sci-fi with genetically altered mutants. Her favorite was the werewolf, a powerful person you didn't want to piss off, because it could change into a fearsome beast and rip your lungs out. She saw every werewolf movie she could.

Dana's destructive behavior continued and, although she was bright, she didn't do well in school. She always thought the teachers were looking down their noses at her or trying to put her down. When she was in sixth grade, Dana and a friend defaced the homeroom of a teacher she didn't like. She got caught and spent weeks cleaning classrooms. Seventh grade brought more teachers that Dana didn't like. She thought they didn't like her either, so she ditched class. She became a banner carrier, one of the uniformed girls who walks in front of the marching band carrying the school's name on a banner, but was dismissed because she couldn't work with the rest of the team. She was suspended from school several times for forging notes to get out of class. With Rick, a young sky diver, Dana created a contraption to catapult neighborhood cats—outfitted with tiny parachutes—off the roof, so they would splash-land in their pool. They built their own makeshift high-dive platform from stacked orange crate boxes. One of the more dangerous stunts was to climb to the top of the rickety platform and kick off the top crate on the dive into the pool. Sometimes Dana got hurt, but she liked playing rough. Dana became an expert swimmer and excelled at softball. She got into a fight with another girl in sixth grade, claiming it was retaliation for a beating by the same girl. Dana admitted she'd cold-cocked her classmate, and said afterward, "It sure felt good. She beat the shit out of me and I got her, but I knew I would get in trouble." Dana was suspended again. She said her mother took her to Baskin-Robbins, an ice cream parlor, to celebrate standing up to a bully.

Beverly was into Scientology and had a big poster in the kitchen listing the stages of development, with "apathy" at the bottom of the chart and "clear" at the top. She occasionally took Dana to meetings. Beverly was spending so much money for Scientology classes, which were required to progress in the organization, that she had to take in boarders to make some money. A man going through a divorce moved into a bedroom vacated by Craig, on tour with his band, and a couple of guys lived in a camper in their driveway.

Beverly didn't set the best example for an adolescent Dana. Threatened by her daughter's emerging beauty, she dressed in attention-getting outfits, dated aggressively and didn't shield her daughter from her private life. Beverly often skinny-dipped in their pool and stayed out all night dancing with girlfriends. One night, Dana and her best friend found Dana's mother and a local cop in the pool, with his boots, hoster, uniform and badge strewn around the house. Upset, Dana flipped on the harsh, bright pool and outside spotlights full blast and left them on. At 12 years old, Dana lost her virginity to one of the men living in the camper.

Craig's success in the band was paying off. He became the primary breadwinner for the family. In between gigs, he came home to mow the lawn, do repairs and help around the house. He tried to tie up the funds to ensure that the money was spent on household expenses, not Scientology courses.

Despite meager finances, they always had food in the house and Beverly's comedic, upbeat attitude lifted the household spirits. The divorced boarder, Michael Carpenter, was delighted by Dana's spirit. She dyed his undershorts purple and put a "For Sale—This Week's Special" sign on his car as a prank. He grew very attached to Dana and she regarded him as a surrogate father. Carpenter was delighted with Dana's antics and thought she was "full of the devil." Beverly lifted Carpenter's spirits with her natural gift of comedy and inadvertently helped him get through a difficult divorce by showing him another side of life. She laughed away their unusual living arrangements and celebrated holidays like a patched-together family. Beverly tried to make Christmas and Halloween special by decorating the house and doing special things. On Christmas Eve, she would run a long thread of brightly colored yarn from their Christmas stockings to some gift in another part of the house or outside. One year, Dana got a redwood playhouse with windowboxes.

In seventh grade, Dana tried stealing earrings and perfume at the May Company department store, but she was caught immediately, and the store called her mother. Dana's activity skyrocketed when she got the moped. She and Carrie Ann would ride for fun after school, zipping up and down alleys and backstreets, being careful not to get caught again. They loved high-energy and edgy rock music—David Bowie, Frank Zappa, the Rolling Stones and Spirit. Sometimes Dana, Carrie Ann and Beverly would spend hours in the kitchen cooking sauteed mushrooms and French toast, talking and eating. When no one else was around, Beverly would give them each a glass of Champale, an inexpensive brand of wine. Dana and Carrie Ann became fast friends. They would run up to the mountains and hike around with Dana's dog. Carrie Ann's parents were more restrictive and she envied Dana because she had so much freedom. Dana craved independence and wanted to live life on the wild side. She resented being told what to do. When her mother tried to keep her in line and give her chores to do after school, Dana would explode in anger and there would be a high-pitched screaming match. Punishment didn't seem to work. If Dana was grounded, she would simply slip out of her bedroom window at night and return when she pleased.

Raising a teenaged girl with high spirits gave Beverly plenty of stress, but she had another problem—she'd found a lump in her breast. For some reason, Beverly interpreted the teachings of her new-found religion as reason to ignore the lump, but her health began to deteriorate and she quickly began to fade. Out of vanity, Beverly rejected getting a biopsy and, when her condition worsened, a mastectomy, but she eventually agreed to undergo chemotherapy. Her health was on a roller coaster. She would periodically improve and then deteriorate to the point of being bedridden. Then she would be up and around again. Craig hired a maid to take care of the household finances, buy groceries and clean the house.

The reality of having a terminally ill mother was beyond young Dana's ability to cope. Michael Carpenter had to drive them to the emergency room one evening. As her pale, weak mother awaited treatment, Dana raced up and down the hallway of the hospital with the wheelchair. When her mother entered a treatment room, Carpenter gathered Dana in his arms and told her to prepare herself for her mother's eventual death. Dana sobbed and they both cried together. To relieve the stress, he took Dana to dinner at a nice restaurant and Dana proceeded to order a cocktail. The waiter never flinched or asked her age, but Dana could pass for 18 at the time. Dana thought it was a big joke, but Michael was mortified. He knew that Dana liked putting him on the spot.

When Beverly was very ill, Dana would try to take care of her mother, getting her food and drinks and pills. Beverly suffered mood swings from the chemotheraphy and the abject horror of cancer. As a reasonably attractive and robust woman in her middle years, she shrank and shriveled into a shell of her former self as the cancer spread to her lungs and liver.

Beverly clung to life until Dana was 14. It was the summer between her freshman and sophomore high school years. Dana spent the evening in the hospital with her mother and asked Carrie Ann to go with her.

Carrie Ann thought Beverly was already dead. She was struggling to breathe. Dana sat by her bedside for a while to comfort her.

"Let go, Mom. It's OK. I will be all right. Let go. Just let go."

Dana didn't last two years at her father's house. Russell had married again, to a woman named Yvonne, but Dana didn't like her new step-mother, nor did she like Yvonne's daughter, Cathy, with whom she had to share a room. Russell and Yvonne had plenty of money and a beautiful, spacious home in Dana Point, an upper-class beach city. Dana spent a year in a depression. Losing her mother was a combination of extreme pain and relief, and she struggled with her feelings, alternately loving and hating Beverly. Dana thought her mother was an asshole for being promiscuous and not paying enough attention to her.

Because of the move to Dana Point, Dana had changed high schools and now attended Newport Harbor High School—when she felt like it. Her brother Rick saw his little sister having trouble and introduced her to his hobby of skydiving. He took her up in an airplane for a spectator ride.

Thousands of feet in the air, Dana looked down from the plane, her eyes wide, and he asked her what she thought. She said she wanted to jump. And when she did, she outjumped him. Dana was hooked. At 16, Dana had disarmingly light blue eyes, sun-kissed good looks and a figure that turned heads, but she preferred sky-diving to dating. Dana had some hair-raising experiences with sky-diving, but she considered the possibility of losing her life part of the adventure. Months after she took up the sport, she collided with another sky-diver and their gear became tangled in a free fall, thousands of feet in the air. As the seconds ticked away, they frantically tried to get their equipment to open up. Finally, about 400 feet from the ground, her reserve chute suddenly opened and she drifted slowly down to earth. Dana didn't regret the collision. At that young age, she was so absorbed with the sport that she didn't mind dying her way, on her own terms. She had skipped school that day and that experience intoxicated her with being in charge of her destiny.

At the same time, she and her new-found sky-diving friends were experimenting with drugs. When Yvonne discovered marijuana in the room that Dana and Cathy shared, Russell confronted both of them and told them that they were forbidden to bring drugs into the house. But by this time, Dana had her own life. She moved out of her father's house and moved in with Rob Beaudry, her 23-year-old jumpmaster. She managed to graduate from Newport Harbor High School in 1976. In the yearbook, she answered a question about her favorite pastime with "Getting into trouble." Her favorite place to be? "In free fall."

The relationship with Rob centered around sports, primarily sky-diving. With the stamina, coordination and fiercely competitive drive of an athlete, Dana quickly mastered windsurfing, wave sailing, hang-gliding, water skiing and scuba diving. A year after moving out of the house, she invited her father to dinner for his birthday. Before dinner, she and Rob drove him to the airport, outfitted him with an emergency parachute and stuck him in the jumpmaster seat of the plane, and up they went. Dana and Rob clambered out under the wing of the plane and leaped off, did a few stunts and landed smack on the target in the drop zone. Dana felt happy to see the look of pride and admiration on her father's face—she was able to share her adventurous lifestyle with him and get his approval. She was particularly happy that her "evil stepmother," Yvonne, was left at home.

Rob helped Dana through nursing school at Saddleback College in Mission Viejo. She had hated the way the nurses at the hospital treated her when her mother was dying and wanted to become a nurse so that she could demonstrate kindness to patients and their relatives. It took her five years to get her associate of arts degree in nursing.

She and Rob stayed together for several years and became engaged, but Dana decided she didn't want to rush into marriage when she was still so young. She had become pregnant twice and he convinced her to end the pregnancies, even though Dana wanted children. She loved him, but she knew that she would always resent him for that.

In 1981, just after she'd received her nursing degree, a group of sky-divers decided to take the ultimate challenge: sky-dive into the Grand Canyon, a spectacular—and illegal—thrill. They plotted and planned and took practice jumps for months before flying to Colorado for the secret jump. Because conditions were dangerous and volatile, many of the divers missed the drop zone, including Dana and two others, who were arrested and hauled off to court. Their gear was confiscated and they had to pay a fine, but Dana looked back on that as one of the greatest moments in her life.

For the next five years, she was in a volatile, on-again, off-again relationship with Chris Dodson, an excellent windsurfer. Sports kept them together. They would go to Hawaii three times a year just to go sailing and play golf and traveled to Oregon for sailing competitions. Though they were great at sports, they were crummy at having a relationship. Both hot-headed and competitive, neither one would back down during a fight. Inevitably, Dana moved out and, while she was dating a paramedic, met Evan Campbell, a Scotsman, who also was involved with someone else. Smitten with Dana, he took her to Hawaii for three weeks of hanggliding, sky-diving and golfing. He returned to his girlfriend, but he and Dana remained friends and stayed in touch.

In 1986, Russell married Jeri. Shortly after, Dana moved

into their house with them in Canyon Lake for several months to figure out her next move. She had been working as a nurse at the nearby Corona Community Hospital since 1981, a few weeks after getting her state nursing license. Over the years, she had held down positions in obstetrics and the emergency room, and had assisted in the operating room, which she preferred.

It didn't take long for Tom Gray to find out that Dana was in the area. An ultra-light aircraft pilot, Tom was lucky to have a hobby that generated income. Local businesses and car dealers would pay him to pull advertising banners in the air above weekend festivals and over freeways during rush hour. When he heard through mutual friends that Dana was living in the area, he would look for her car whenever he was up in the air. It took him a while, but he spotted it, parked at a house in Canyon Lake. He found out that she was living with her father and wasn't dating anyone, but he didn't know how to approach her.

Starting as a drummer in grade school, Tom had been in rock bands during his entire adolescence and into adulthood; he had his share of groupies, but they didn't appeal to him as serious girlfriend material. His band, Longshot, played at Disneyland, Magic Mountain, Gazzari's, the Starwood and other kingmaker venues that were popular during the hard-rock glory days of Los Angeles in the late 1970s and early 1980s. The band hadn't had a big gig for a while—they were doing midnight shows at local bars—but they were OK with that. No one in the band had ever wanted a record deal—they were just in it to have fun.

Tom's passions for music and flying came together by way of informal weekend picnics in the local foothills off Ortega Highway, the windy, hilly road that links the Inland Empire to Orange County. The word-of-mouth get-togethers had no corporate sponsors and no admission fees and consisted of people drinking beer, firing up the barbecue and riding dirt bikes. At night, they'd build a big bonfire and everyone would dance and party with Longshot. One weekend, some sport flyers who flew battery-operated remote-control toy airplanes decided to get their group together to check out the ultra-light scene. News of the mega-gathering grew and by the time the weekend rolled around, Tom heard that both ultra-light pilots and sport flyers were driving in from around the state. Someone pulled together a banner saying "Welcome to the Fly-In" and Tom agreed to pull the banner over the festival as people were arriving in the afternoon.

Although it was still springtime, the temperatures had climbed to the 90s. Tom was up in the air and he was looking for Dana. He'd heard she was coming with friends and possibly a date. As he scanned the crowd, he saw another pilot take to the air in his ultralight, so Tom flew higher to give him lots of airspace. The daredevil pilot started to wow the crowd by buzzing them at low altitude at high speed, then shooting upward and doing other tricks. On his next fly-by, he soared upward to execute a risky maneuver and took a turn, but his wings folded up like a big butterfly. He went into a death spiral and the crowd roared its approval, thinking it was a wonderful trick. It wasn't. He hit the ground at high velocity and was killed on impact.

Dana's nursing instinct kicked into gear and she ran over to help, but she was a long way from the site of the accident. By the time she got there, she was suffering from a slight case of heat stroke. In the meantime, Tom was still up in the air with the "Welcome to the Fly-In" banner behind him, thinking, "Oh, this is just great." He began his descent right after the crash. He thought the accident must have been fatal, but didn't know for certain until after he landed. Tom didn't get to talk to Dana that day, but Dana later joked that his banner should have read, "Welcome to the Die-In."

A few weeks later, Tom spotted Dana at the grocery store. She took his breath away. He thought his heart had stopped. Blonde and athletic with a cute little sunburnt nose, as sassy and wise-cracking as he remembered from junior high. They exchanged numbers and Dana told him she was working at the hospital in Corona. Tom started driving out there to leave little notes on her car. She dismissed them, but Tom didn't give up.

Tom was on the quiet side and had never before been aggressive about having a girlfriend. Sometimes he went for months without dating, and that was fine with him. He found that women usually approached him most of the time anyway, but he shrugged off contacts from women who only knew him onstage. He wanted to get married someday, but not to anyone he'd met in a bar.

One night, he decided to surprise Dana by showing up in the emergency room of the hospital where she worked. Tom drew a few looks with long, wiry blonde hair to his hips, black leather jacket, shredded Levi's and snakeskin boots. Dana took one look at him and hurried him off to a waiting room. Tom thought it was funny that she needed to hide him from her professional colleagues, but he didn't care. He wanted to ask her to go to his high school reunion and she agreed. He picked her up in a limo.

They had a great time. She wore a Hawaiian print dress with a mid-summer tan—but it wasn't just her good looks that attracted Tom. He loved her adventurous spirit and prowess in sports. He loved the fact that she was a great windsurfer and was into riding bikes and sky-diving. They started dating just as Dana was preparing to leave the country. She had been planning to hit Hawaii in early January, travel through New Zealand, then zip through Australia to catch the last week of the America's Cup yacht race, and possibly relocate. She had been scouting nursing jobs there. Tom helped her sell everything she had for her trip as she made plans to live there. He didn't think she was coming back, but he didn't discourage her from going—he didn't want to feel like he was stifling her. As it turned out, one of Tom's brothers lived in Australia and he offered to put her up for a few weeks. Tom drove her to the airport and she called him periodically with reports about the dismal job hunt. Employers didn't want to hire a foreigner, and even if she found a job, she would start at the lowest level of the pay scale. Dana had a good work history and didn't like that. But she had fun playing sports there.

Tom picked her up from the airport and, having nowhere to live, she temporarily moved in with him. About a week after she got back, he surprised himself by proposing to her, and she surprised herself by accepting. Tom was overjoyed. His mother was a nurse and his father worked in construction. They got married young and were still married and had a fantastic relationship. Tom wanted the same dynamic team with Dana. In August 1987, the couple bought a house in

Canyon Lake for $108,000 and moved in right after the deal closed. They had an elaborate wedding in October 1987 with 200 guests and five stunt sky-divers. Tom's parents fell in love with Dana too after she and Tom had invited them over for dinner and served them wine brought back from Australia. She and Tom delayed their honeymoon for six months because they were both working so hard, and Dana wanted to take some time to plan it. They decided on Maui.

Shortly after they were married, they bought bikes, but Tom, more of a musician than an athlete, had trouble keeping up with Dana, mentally and physically. She had the hard-driving temperament of a competitive athlete and that clashed with Tom's easygoing attitude when it came to sports and exercise. They drove down to Ensenada, Mexico, for a 50-kilometer bike ride and Tom suffered mightily keeping up with Dana. She didn't stop or slow down and always rode just a little ahead of him. He jokingly complained later that she just about killed him on that ride. Both of them were certified scuba divers, and Tom surfed occasionally, but Dana was a much stronger swimmer than Tom. There didn't seem to be any sport in which she didn't excel. On a ski trip to Utah with Tom's brother, she skied circles around them both, even though the brothers had been skiing longer.

Tom considered that part of Dana's charm—she was a hardcore athlete. After a bike ride, she would cook dinner for him, and make jokes over a glass of wine at dinner. He was head-over-heels in love. He was so much in love, he didn't even care about music any longer. She had been bugging him about playing in the band and he agreed to give up the band scene for married life. He was tired of playing the same songs every night year after year with only two weekends off. Now, the band was just for fun. They performed at weddings and messed around at parties. Tom taught Dana how to play some instruments and she had a natural gift for singing. Their partnership was electric. Together, Tom thought, we can do anything. Dana, the little blonde spitfire he had fantasized about since he was in junior high, was everything he ever wanted.

*   *   *

"Dana!"

Tom's head was bobbing up and down in the waves. He was getting tired.

"Dana!"

Tom was trying to get her attention. But it looked like she was already looking straight at him.

"Dana!"

Tom was hanging onto the windsurfboard, but it was hard because the wind was whipping the waves. The Maui sea was rough and the wind was blowing hard. Tom was tired after taking windsurfing lessons all day. That was part of their pact: Tom wanted Dana to learn some of the things he liked, like music and flying ultra-lights and remote-control model airplanes. For Tom, it meant learning how to golf and water ski and windsurf. He'd had windsurfing lessons earlier that day and he was tired. He didn't have any floatation—no lifejacket, no wetsuit. He was very tired.

"DANA!"

Tom could swear she was looking straight at him. That was weird. They were on their honeymoon. He wanted to come back in, soak his aching muscles in a hot bath and take his sunkissed, newlywed wife to dinner on their honeymoon. Bobbing around in wind-whipped surf wasn't what he'd planned. After the lesson, Dana had taken him to a remote part of the island where the waves were bigger and rougher to practice in more challenging waters, but it had been too much for him. He was about a half-mile from shore when he tried taking a turn, and the windsurfboard tipped over, and he couldn't get it back up. He'd struggled with it for the better part of an hour and he was exhausted. He wasn't a strong swimmer. Now it was all he could do to hold onto the board. He knew that Dana could hop on her board and get out there to help him in a heartbeat.

"DANA!"

He was getting tired of yelling. She was just sitting there on the beach, looking at him. Finally, he saw her get up and get her board. She didn't look concerned at all. Well, maybe she couldn't hear him over the wind and the pounding surf. The waves were getting high.

He watched gratefully as Dana hopped on her board, jumped in the surf and came out to get him within a minute.

Finally! he thought. He thought he was gonna drown out there. But when she got closer, she leaned over, grabbed the haul rope of his board, tied it to her board and took off. Tom held on, thinking she was going to pull him out of the surf, but she hadn't said a word. She just tied up his board and sailed back to the beach. Tom, already exhausted, could not hold on, with the wind gusting her sails powerfully. He yelled at her to come back, but if she heard him, his cries were ignored. When she got to the shore, she sat down again on the sand with both boards and continued to watch him.

Tom was as bewildered as he was panicked. He couldn't understand what she was doing and why she didn't help him. She knew he was a poor swimmer. She'd been looking at him when he fell off the board. Tom knew that Dana knew what was going on. If he had thought he was going to drown with the board to hang onto, he knew he was doomed without it. He could feel the cross-currents tug at him and knew that trying to swim was futile, but he had no other choice. Already exhausted, he tried to get back to shore, but the current kept driving him back. He continued fighting, his tired arms slapping at the choppy waters, knowing that he couldn't last much longer. An occasional wave slapped him in the face and he swallowed a lot of water, which was making him feel sick. He tried resting by floating on his back, but the water was too choppy. Fear set in as he struggled. He tried not to panic. Tom wondered if he was going to die. He was so exhausted, his muscles were aching and he didn't think he was going to make it to shore. He could see Dana; he knew she could see him. She was just staring into space, not moving, not saying a word.

Finally, Tom saw that he was making some progress. He spotted a buoy and thought it was his only chance. He channeled all of his energy into reaching it. He finally got to it and was so taxed, he lay over it. After he rested for a while and got some energy back, he started yelling at Dana. She was still just sitting there watching him. Tom finally worked his way to shore by pulling himself along the buoy line and literally crawled up onto the beach. He was drained and his muscles were so tight, he just lay there a while. Finally, he walked unsteadily over to where she was sitting.

"Couldn't you see me? Why did you leave me out there?

What the hell were you doing? Why didn't you help me?"

Tom, standing over Dana, was so angry, he shook his fist at her. Dana flinched slightly, but didn't answer him. She never said a word. She just sat there with a distant, blank stare. Tom was angry enough to hit her, but he was too tired and he wasn't the kind of guy to hit women anyway. He didn't know what to do, so he just lay back down on the beach to rest and stayed there for about an hour without talking. Finally, he said, "Let's get out of here," and they left.

At dinner that night, Tom never brought it up and they never talked about it. They both acted like it had never happened. Tom wondered if she'd been hit before, given the way she'd winced when he raised his fist. He wondered if she'd been in some kind of a blackout, but neither of them had been drinking that day. Tom couldn't explain her behavior, but he began to watch his back around Dana.

Married life with Dana soon became a contest of wills. After spending thousands of dollars on their wedding and thousands more on the Hawaiian honeymoon, Tom wanted to cut back a little on their spending. Dana didn't. Each of them was making around $45,000 a year, Dana as a nurse and Tom as a heavy equipment operator driving a backhoe for a construction company. Even though the economy was booming, they soon found themselves in debt. Fortunately, the couple's choice in real estate had been a wise one. Their $108,000 Canyon Lake home spiked in value to $170,000. Tom and Dana decided to exploit their good fortune and get a one-time, $40,000 equity loan to get themselves out of debt. But the money didn't last long. In May 1988, eight months after their marriage, they were still drowning in debt and took out a $27,000 second mortgage.

Tom and Dana liked the good life—going to nice Italian restaurants, ordering appetizers and several glasses of wine, and buying things for the house. After their storybook wedding, Tom was mortified at being in debt, but took it in stride as part of a package deal: marriage and the "I owe, I owe, it's off to work I go" philosophy. He put the near-death experience on his honeymoon in the back of his mind and concentrated on enjoying life. With Tom retired from playing bar gigs, she suggested they build an in-home studio. Dana began to act jealous around his friends—even his male friends—as if she resented the fact that he had fun without her. She would make comments about them and felt uncomfortable when they were around. Tom didn't see anything wrong with his gorgeous newlywed wife wanting to be around him and only him. After all, Dana had long ago put her sky-diving days behind her. The couple worked on turning their house into a home, painting one room lavender with white trim, installing oak blinds instead of curtains and turning the garage into a studio. They spent upwards of $26,000 on music equipment—amplifiers, guitars, recording equipment, keyboards, drum sets, microphones, monitors. With the home equipment, Tom laid down tracks to one of Dana's favorite songs, "These Boots Were Made for Walking," and Dana sang and pranced around in high-heeled boots as Tom recorded the whole song on video.

Dana, always a good cook, took a classes at a local college, and was soon creating Italian dishes better than those some restaurants served. She excelled at veal picatta, spaghetti, and filet mignon with bernaise sauce, Tom's favorite. Not everything turned out. A chicken dish with lemon turned out so lemony, she dubbed it, "Lemon Pledge chicken." When she got home from work, she would shoo Tom out of the kitchen and sip three or four glasses of wine while she fixed dinner. She'd have more wine with her meal. Gradually, Dana's athletic physique rounded out. Drinking became a pastime and weekends dissolved in a haze of bourbon, 7Up and tequila shooters.

Dana took a job as the night nurse at a 12-bed hospital on Catalina Island off the coast of Southern California from Thursday through Sunday. The hospital provided a small cottage for her to live in during the week and she would scuba dive in the pristine waters off Catalina in the afternoons before work.

Change was rippling through Dana's family, as well. Craig had given up his life as an itinerant musician and become a born-again Christian minister in the mid-1970s. He'd moved to Virginia and was studying to become a pastor. Craig, who had never been as close to Dana as Rick had been, had a major falling-out with her. When their mother died, her meager estate was split equally in thirds, but Dana complained that she should have more because she had spent more time with Beverly when she was ill. Rick bowed out by giving up his third for Dana and Craig to split. Then Dana was angry at Craig for taking a larger share because he had fixed up the house to sell. Dana had become furious that Beverly's car was not given to her. Relations between them had been rocky ever since. Now the problem was with the great aunt with whom Rick was living.

Dana made annual visits to see her great aunt, sometimes with her brothers. She was upset that her aunt had not included Dana in her will, reasoning that Dana's father would leave her a handsome estate, which she did not have to share with her brothers because they were no relation to Russell. Rick, who was living on his aunt's property, tried to convince her to create a living trust under which Dana, Craig and Rick could equally share, but she didn't understand that concept. All Tom knew was that any mention of Craig or her aunt reduced Dana to hysterical tears.

Though he was in his later 30s, Rick was experiencing severe arthritis in his knees, spine and hips. He was attempting to get his master's degree and moved to Alhambra, a suburb in Los Angeles County about 55 miles from Riverside County. To help his little sister and her new husband get a leg up on putting their home together, Rick gave Dana and Tom a number of things to keep for him while he was in school—a complete dining room set, a dresser, chairs, two TV sets, a complete stereo set, and a truckload of music and film equipment, including several of his acoustic guitars, a bass guitar, his cache of record albums, a lawnmower and a set of family silverware monogrammed with "W," for Ward, Rick's father. He also wanted Dana to hold for safekeeping the family Bible, and slides, 8mm film and pictures of their family and his sky-diving adventures. Dana thanked him for loaning them the "all the goodies" with a cute card, a cartoon of a grossly heavyset couple about which she commented, "Hey bro—I hope Tom and I never look like this! I think the trick is to eat less and fuck more as you get older. What do you think?" She wrote another note thanking him for his love and support and apologizing for being "a big turd" and "wigging out," and signed the note, "Your sister, fartblossom Gray and Tom-the-black-hippie Gray."

About two months after they were married, Tom and Dana had a big New Year's Eve bash for their friends and family. Afterwards, Rick got a perplexing letter from Dana accusing him of trying to manipulate her marriage. Rick wrote a five-page letter back saying that if she didn't appreciate his brotherly advice, then they no longer had to share their personal life with one another. Rick thought Dana was hyper-sensitive and would interpret anything he said or wrote as criticism. "I guarantee, this will be the last time you ever send me a snippy little, 'shove it up your ass and let me live my own life' letter and get a civil response back. Sometimes I don't know who the hell you think you are. You seem to think you can just dash off a quick line to someone in regards to a major issue in the relationship and the recipient is just supposed to roll over and take your shit lying down. I used to make exceptions for your behavior because you were young, but I'm through with that now. You're old enough to get that you're not the center of the universe like you've been coming across lately." Rick cut down on correspondence with Dana and continued through school as his health worsened. He developed a thyroid condition and his arthritis was threatening his mobility. Eventually, he was declared legally disabled and received checks from the state every month.

Tom and Dana found creative hobbies to do together. Tom had obtained a mail-order ministry from the Universal Life Church and had performed marriages for friends before he and Dana were married. When Russell and Jeri decided to renew their vows, they asked Tom to perform the ceremony. Dana went wild with the preparations. When the ceremony was held in Russ and Jeri's backyard, it was such a success that they launched a side business, Graymatter Matrimony, performing weddings, complete with a band in which Dana sometimes sang. Tom had taught her to play electric guitar, which she learned rapidly. Dana designed the business cards, featuring an anatomical sketch of a brain with a wedding veil on it. Dana had also learned to do screen-printing and purchased thousands of dollars' worth of equipment. She soon had several business accounts for T-shirts, hats and posters.

Dana and Rick tried to patch up their sibling squabbles and create some kind of family for themselves. Despite their "insane family situation," Dana wrote, "the object is not to use that as a justification, but figure out how to deal with it and quit putting so much attention on it and go on making our lives as happy as possible . . .

"You're the only one in our family that I feel I have a chance to have the family relationship with, so now that I feel secure in my personal life, I feel I can safely put some energy into our relationship . . . maybe now we can be more trusting with the feelings and viewpoints that we have and will share down the line."

A couple of years into Tom and Dana's marriage, the economy took a downturn, hitting the construction industry in the pocketbook. Tom was reduced to working part-time and picking up jobs where he could. As their income dipped dramatically, Dana tried to pick up the slack by working double shifts, but she continued to spend. Tom came home from work one day and found a new lawnmower in the garage. They already had a lawnmower, but Dana had wanted a new one. She charged the credit cards up to the limit and they had a hard time making the payments. Tom implored Dana to cut back on the cards and she told him that she would, but then she'd just get another credit card and do the same thing. Despite the reduction in their income, Dana still wanted to eat out at her favorite restaurants and keep up her standard of living: a weekly manicure, monthly pedicure, eyebrow, lip and bikini waxes and keeping her hair cut, permed and colored. Tom knew these little luxuries, combined with the other more frivolous expenditures, were important to Dana, but were also driving them deeper in debt.

They fought over money and Tom's inability to get work. Tom knew Dana was fatigued from working extra shifts for both of them, so he backed down. He wasn't fond of arguing anyway, and Dana had a talent for delivering particularly stinging rebukes that her brother Rick called "castrating zingers," so he tried to avoid fights. Tom had faith in their relationship and he knew that despite the temporary rough times, everything would ultimately work out. He found contentment in being married and having a good relationship, but he noticed that Dana needed to buy things to be happy. He got the impression that she rarely felt good about herself, even when he told her that she looked good. "Yeah, what do *you* want?" she would snap back.

The longer Tom was out of work, and the more the bills piled up, the worse their fights became. Dana resorted to the door-slamming screaming matches she'd engaged in during her adolescence, a part of her that Tom had never seen. She would rage at him, blaming him for the crisis of the moment, then screech out of the house in her Cadillac or go for a long bike ride. Tom accepted that behavior in part because he felt responsible for not bringing in his share of income and felt bad about constantly being the one to put his foot down about the credit cards. Dana had staked her claim to handle their finances at the start of the marriage and Tom had no problem with that until he discovered that she was driving them into debt. He had no idea how to handle her volatile temper. Shrinking back in the face of her anger seemed to fuel her eruptions. Tom was relieved when she stormed out of the house to take a drive or do something physical. It seemed like a better way for her to channel her anger.

As their income dropped, Dana stepped up the pressure on her aunt, nearing 90, to the point of waltzing through her home and staking claims to valuables, even saying, "When you die, I want this cup, this Chinese cup," on one visit. Craig was incensed at Dana's callousness and ruthless pursuit of money, and didn't hesitate to confront her about her behavior, causing Dana to fly into tantrums. Any phone call from Craig would cause a fight with Dana as well as with Tom, who got so frustrated, he tossed a photograph of Craig in the trash.

Craig had seen the change in Dana from the time she started sky-diving, which was around the time that he became a born-again Christian. After she started running with that crowd, she no longer shared the same values with him, and in his mind, she ceased being his baby sister. He was frustrated that any confrontation about her behavior resulted in a screaming match in which she would claim to be the victim. He came to believe that Dana was out for whatever

Dana could get. He disliked having contact with her, but felt obligated to send birthday and Christmas cards. He was also inclined to write or phone when Auntie complained of visits from Dana.

Despite the family turmoil, Dana's biological clock was ticking and she decided it was time to have a baby. In March 1989, she went off birth control pills, and went on the "no party program" for several months to clean the alcohol out of her system. Her goal was to become pregnant by summertime. In a note to Rick, she was upbeat and irreverent about impending motherhood. "Does that scare you? Me as a mother?" She and Tom picked out Melody May if the baby was a girl and Marshall if it was a boy. She signed the note, "Love you, dorkface, my fartblossom."

By summertime, they were working on the house, making planters out of halved whiskey barrels, and planting lime and lemon trees, herbs and strawberries, as well as a vegetable garden with eggplant, tomatoes and cucumbers. Dana was finding solace in Tom's parents, who were a good example of a long-term married couple. Tom was building remote-controlled planes for Dana and teaching her how to fly them, but "Tom builds 'em, I smash 'em," she joked in a note to Rick. Dana liked the two-cycle engines and the grease and decided to organize a contest among model plane enthusiasts called "Graymatter Splatter" with prizes and T-shirts. She took two months off work to organize their fall contest, which she said would "slip by like goose shit on a muggy day."

Dana's relationship with her brothers waxed and waned. She bought a ten-gallon fish tank with an eight-inch rubber eel that she named "Cedric Eel," a send-up of Rick's formal name, Cedric Erle. When Rick visited, Dana was delighted to see him. She wrote a quick note to Rick about completely disconnecting from Craig and was happy that he was sticking with the grind through grad school. She addressed her note: Dearest Sir Cedric Erle of Alhambrashire," and signed it, "Love ya and all of that, Lady Fartblossom & Lord Tom."

That summer, when Rick came out to see Tom and Dana, Dana confided in him that she had lost her virginity to one of their boarders when she was 12 years old, When Rick suggested that she get some counseling, Dana said she was deeply insulted, didn't need a shrink, and would never consult one because she already knew what made her tick. Besides, she told Tom about it and when he responded with "love, understanding and support," Dana said that that was more than a shrink could do. She wrote Rick a note that included a poem called "Age of Reason," about moving forward. "Why can't we love each other, is kindness an ancient skill buried by our blindness?"

By December, Dana had received another painful letter from Craig decrying her continued badgering of their aunt. Dana had gone to the nursing home and persuaded her to sign a will splitting the estate three ways. Craig said that their great aunt, who was so senile she believed she was living in the 1920s, condemned Dana for her greediness. Dana denied forcing her to do anything and said she would abide by whatever Auntie decided. But at that point, the will had been changed. Craig's wife, Jini, thought Dana had a frozen heart, and wanted very little to do with her.

Dana felt Craig was truly responsible for creating the vulture-like atmosphere around their aunt and never really asked for anything—other than the china cabinet. "I only asked her for that china cabinet as a child and did it innocently . . . I'm not worried about who gets what . . . I will be grateful for whatever (if anything) that is left."

During the holidays, Dana thoroughly enjoyed fixing up the house with lights and decorations, but she didn't often make it over to Russell and Jeri's house for family get-togethers. Everyone knew that Dana and Jeri's ex-mother-in-law, Norma, didn't get along, and they figured that was the reason. She and Tom usually spent holidays with Tom's family.

Despite their best efforts, Dana had not yet conceived by springtime and it was putting a strain on the couple's relationship. She was 33 and desperate for a baby. She continued to spend lavishly, though Tom pleaded with her to keep their finances under control. Their fights were getting bigger and more serious. Tom believed that Dana was just taking her frustrations out on him. He felt that she treated her dog better than she treated him, and she told him that he was right. Tom thought that Dana was never happy with what she had and seemed always to be searching for something else. She would bounce from project to project, the way she'd bounced between continents before they were married, but nothing seemed to make her happy.

On the Saturday before Easter, Dana took her brother, Rick, and Tom's brother, Gerald, for a day of boating and water skiing on Canyon Lake. Rick told Dana that she was being bossy and thought she seemed upset that no one was jumping at her commands. She retaliated by pouring a beer on Tom's head as he piloted the boat. He responded by pouring a beer on her head. The whole afternoon, Dana hounded Tom about whether he still loved her, asking him over and over again. After they got home, she became upset and stormed out of the house, but came back in and demanded that Rick take Gerald to a Mexican restaurant around the corner and wait for them while she talked to Tom. When Tom said he couldn't understand why Dana was acting so irresponsibly, she unleashed her fury on him. Rick phoned both of them the next day and called Dana a "goddamned, fucking, ball-busting bitch" for acting like a child and having such a ridiculous temper tantrum. "You have little consideration for anyone else's feelings or comfort," he said in a note, adding that he disliked "the tension that surrounds you, Dana, when you don't feel that you're being obeyed . . ." Rick didn't speak to Dana for six months. It wasn't the first time that she had cleared the house. Dana would snap for apparently little reason and explode at Tom, make a scene, clear their friends out of the house, and then leave herself. Whatever friends Tom had left stopped coming over. Tom allowed Dana to hit him in the shoulder— and she could pack a punch for a woman. Tom was said he felt "beat up" and isolated.

Their playtimes were also getting rough-and-tumble. Dana liked rough-housing and would sprint at Tom and tackle him, knocking him down. One time, she punched him hard in the face while they were wrestling around. Tom was hurt, but he didn't get mad because Dana said it was an accident.

In August 1990, Dana got a new job as an operating room nurse at the Inland Valley Regional Medical Center in Wildomar, making $46,000 a year. The construction industry was still in a slump, and Tom was earning less than $16,000 a year. Still facing down credit card bills, they borrowed $2,200 from a relative and asked Russell and Jeri for help in refinancing their Canyon Lake home. They declined because Tom and Dana owed more on the house than it was worth.

In November, Rick wrote a three-page letter to Dana warning her that he did not want to resume their relationship until she conducted herself responsibly, referring to the Easter incident earlier in the year. He expressed appreciation for Tom, who he thought was "busting his ass to love and serve you. His only frailty so far is probably his tendency to remain soft-spoken and being afraid to tell you what his true feelings are at any time because he is afraid of hurting your feelings."

Rick's physical condition had deteriorated considerably and he was in a great deal of physical pain, as well as mental anguish and stress over trying to create some semblance of a family. "I have seriously considered that if I become much more physically disabled or have to suffer much more physical or mental pain that I'm just going to go up on some high peak somewhere with a majestic view of what's left of this poor planet, lay my serape down, and let my life cease."

Dana responded by sending him a humorous Christmas card with a note saying that his letter wasn't pleasant or fair. "Do you think we could ever cut out the bullshit and just get along? Ya know, family, love, etc?"

In another three-page letter, Rick wrote that he was bowing out of his relationship with her because it was "upsetting and painful to contribute to you what little I have and then be told that I am not working in your best interest."

He also wrote about Dana's requests for money from their aunt. "I have asked you repeatedly to let me handle it, but you just don't get it that she doesn't see things the way they are. Now that she's so old and senile, trying to make sense out of anything with her is an incredibly frustrating experience. She is in no financial position to help any of us. What she has is hers to do with as she wishes regardless of what anybody thinks."

He recommended that Dana look at a video series on family interaction by author and psychologist John Bradshaw, and said that she needn't respond to his letter. He asked her only to leave him out of her life and to stop being an irritant. He was tired of the fights, the conflicts, the upsets. "I bear no animosity toward you or Tom . . . I no longer want to confront our relationship nor do I want to attempt to have anything remotely resembling a family."

A year later, in November 1991, Dana sent Rick an irreverent, funny birthday card with a note, "Wishing you a happy b-day despite your total disgust with us and all of your family."

Rick wrote Tom a six-page letter one month later, bitter about Dana's "poor little Dana, nobody loves me" routine, her profound disregard for other people's feelings and her thirst for things, not people. Rick said the emotional and physical pain and exhaustion that came with his increasingly debilitating arthritis, and the unsuccessful history of trying to create something of a family with Dana, led him to the conclusion that was forcing him to have no more contact with her. He asked Tom to return his photo albums, his guitars and the silverware with the monogrammed "W." Rich again referred to the Easter debacle, criticizing Dana for refusing to apologize for or acknowledge her behavior in being oblivious to anything but herself . . . "She doesn't give a shit about anything but having everyone else fall into line with her dreams and wishes even if they don't begin to approximate reality. So, it's reality be damned, Dana's dreams however impractical or neurotic, will prevail."

Dana wrote back immediately, saying that she will never "live up to your expectations and [I] have finally stopped trying." Dana insisted that she "truly cared" for her aunt because she loved her and wanted to share "precious moments" with her, and "all I hope is that when she goes, she goes happy and in her own home . . . Whatever her will says I really don't know. I can only hope whatever decision is made, it comes from her heart."

She asked Rick to "let go of all the hate and disgust you have for me and quit insisting I apologize to you for my entire life. If I really seem like a ball buster [sic] bitch then most likely I am. I am also your sister, your only sister so can we ever be civil? . . . Let's just drop all the past shit and go on, OK?

Dana promised to stop sending Rick her hard-bitten remarks if he promised to "quit persecuting my existence and turn off the spotlight shinned [sic] on all my mistakes . . . I love you anyway, fuckhead!"

Tom didn't care whether he lived or died. Dana had alienated him from his friends, put them thousands of dollars in debt, and was getting more violent. She was constantly hurting him, verbally, physically and emotionally. She even threatened to run him down with his own truck. Tom was afraid and told her that he was afraid. The fear and the psychological torment rendered Tom emotionally paralyzed, which drove Dana into a frenzy. She hounded Tom for affection, to make him say he loved her. He tried to reassure her often, but it was never enough. He began to realize that whatever he did would never be enough for Dana. He realized he had been clinging to what their relationship used to be and what it could be instead of what it was. Like any relationship, there were good times and bad times, but it was difficult for him to step back and recognize that he was being abused. He'd never minded Dana "wearing the pants" in the family, but he decided that he should start living life more for himself instead of for her. He began taking time for himself to fly planes more often and thought about getting back into music. He began practicing his drums and started getting another band together.

Dana was angry at his new-found focus, particularly because the focus was not on her. She was still trying to get pregnant and in late January 1991, she realized she had succeeded. She was overjoyed. She happily gained weight and their relationship took on a rosy glow. Both Dana and Tom believed having a baby could save their marriage. The relationship settled into a period of normalcy until Dana had a miscarriage in March. She became deeply depressed and started drinking more.

Still desperate to have a baby, Dana began to take fertility drugs. The drugs, consisting of female hormones, contributed to Dana's extreme mood swings and she resumed her rampages. Tom was torn between wanting to assist his wife through a difficult period that, with all due fairness, was partially the result of the hormone imbalance brought upon by fertility drugs. But he also realized he needed time for himself. When Dana was pregnant, he realized he had been walking on tenterhooks waiting for Dana to combust. Tom put a band together and started having practice sessions.

He began to stand up to Dana, and let her know when she was out of line. Dana would call her outbursts "speaking up for herself" and "speaking her mind." Tom had another name for them: "insta-bitch." He would also say that "the bitch notch was going up to ten," which was his way of telling Dana that she could have handled something better. Tom tried that as a way of stopping tempers from escalating. Sometimes it worked; sometimes it didn't. Since he was working with a band again, he had an outlet and somewhere constructive to put his energy and attention.

Dana threw herself into her different ventures—the wedding business, silk-screening and her hospital work. She had a need to organize everything and be in control. She had an excellent work history and was diligent with her patients, all of whom seemed satisfied with her care. But her domineering attitude made her co-workers' lives miserable. She would become friends with a co-worker and then, six months later, something would happen and they were no longer friends. She didn't get along with most of her co-workers because she was highly critical of their work. Dana had no tolerance for what she saw as people's stupidity; she had a low boiling point, and was known for "getting into people's faces and giving them the business" because they irritated her, just to "shock them into reality." Dana had no problem being called a bitch. She prided herself on earning the title.

Dana was still working extra hours but the financial problems continued to build. They missed house payments and were sometimes broke. Somehow, Dana always found a credit card. She managed to keep up her monthly pedicures and weekly manicures, and always looked neat, clean and professional. She also started hanging around with the band and watching their practices, particularly their guitar player, Jim Wilkins. He often brought Jason, a tow-headed toddler, along with him. Dana would take Jason and play with him while they practiced and that lifted her spirits.

Soon, Jim and Jason became a part of Tom and Dana's social life. They flew planes, picnicked, partied, drank and made music together. One night just before the holidays, the band was booked for a party. Tom and Dana had been fighting again and Dana that night decided to go home with Jim. She arrived back at her Canyon Lake home at 6 a.m. the next morning and told Tom that she was going to leave him for Jim.

Dana and Tom reconciled and she came home, but they had a restless holiday season. Soon after, Dana found that she was pregnant again. Tom wondered whether he or Jim was the father, but it didn't matter—in March 1992, Dana suffered another miscarriage. This time, she didn't seem as depressed as she had been after the first one, and within weeks, Dana made plans to go to Sweden to visit some friends. She was there three weeks. When she got back, Tom picked her up at the airport and told her that he was leaving her. Dana was so devastated, she started seeing a psychiatrist, who prescribed Paxil, an anti-depressant.

That summer, she went back and forth between Jim and Tom. It seemed as though she was using Jim as a tool to get Tom back, because as soon as she went to live with Jim, she would desperately try to get back with Tom. But Tom didn't want to discuss reconciliation unless she had finished her business with Jim. Dana would insist that she was having nothing to do with him, but Tom would fly over Jim's house in his ultra-light and find her car parked there every night and every morning.

Tom and Dana vacillated for months. Their financial situation went from precarious to dire, and they missed mortgage payments. Dana was still bringing home most of the income and she resented having to deplete her paycheck for the mortgage, leaving little to spend on herself. They continued to miss mortgage and loan payments on the second trust deed.

At the start of 1993, around the time she decided to move in with Jim for good, Dana's abuse of alcohol increased. She kept the prescription for Paxil and sought out another psychiatrist who prescribed different medication. In April, she started stealing painkillers from work and tried to hide the drug use by reporting that glass vials containing medication had broken. Controlled substances at a hospital are strictly inventoried and accounted for when they are administered to a patient or wasted, which usually has to be witnessed by another employee and documented. Dana tried to hide the thefts of medication by reporting that she had dropped and destroyed glass vials or had administered it to a patient via verbal order from a doctor, though that medication had not been prescribed. Every time Dana stole painkillers or other medication, her nursing supervisor was making a note of it. Dana had barely avoided getting fired months earlier because she was unable to get along with other nurses in the obstetrics department, but she had been transferred to post-op recovery and seemed much happier. She had been talking about leaving nursing to go into silkscreening full-time.

The summer of 1993 was a difficult one for Dana. Her drug and alcohol use intensified and in June she filed for divorce from Tom. In August, Tom moved out of the Canyon Lake home and back to his parents' house in Covina, and Dana moved the rest of her things to Jim's house in Lake Elsinore. To stave off foreclosure proceedings on the Canyon Lake house, Dana and Tom filed for bankruptcy in September. They owed $177,400 on a house that, at that time, was worth $125,000. They also listed their parents as creditors for their loans of $2,200 and $3,000. Dana was netting $2,500 a month and Tom was clearing about $600 a month. They claimed their musical instruments as assets worth $3,500, but Dana didn't claim her silk-screening equipment.

In September and October, Dana was stealing drugs from the hospital regularly, sometimes twice or three times a week. She took a four-day trip to New Orleans in October for a silk-screening convention at the Hilton in the French Quarter using Jim's credit cards. Dana said she attended the conference during the day and partied up and down Bourbon Street at night. Jim was now paying for most of her bills, and helping her settle some debts and pay back her parents.

On November 18, Dana was called into a meeting with the hospital supervisors and confronted with details of four separate incidents in which wasted medication was improperly documented or medication not prescribed was recorded as being administered to a patient. The missing medications were Demerol, Sublimaze and Astramorph, all opiate-derivative painkillers that are administered intravenously. Dana stated that she could not remember certain incidents and in other instances, explained that the doctors had asked for the additional medication. The doctors recalled differently. At the end of the meeting, the supervisors decided to suspend Dana for three days.

Dana was called into another meeting on November 24 and given another opportunity to respond to the same allegations as well as a string of 34 additional incidents. Some of the amounts she claimed to have administered were so high that if she had given the patient that much, it might have been fatal. Dana referred to nurses or doctors who witnessed her wasting medication or who had verbally ordered a change in medication. Each of those nurses and doctors said they hadn't spoken with her. When asked if she had anything else to say, Dana said she was upset that everyone knew about her suspension. Dana's supervisor reminded her that she herself had announced her suspension at a staff meeting. At the end of the meeting, she was fired.

Dana sank into a deeper depression, but brushed off the loss of her job to friends and family as "incomplete documentation." She never acknowledged pilfering drugs, but said she was the victim of backstabbing and made a scapegoat because she had the "biggest mouth." To quell her feelings, Jim took Dana away for Thanksgiving, to the family cabin in Mammoth Mountain, an upscale ski resort in Northern California. Although there was some snow on the ground, they spent their days fishing and biking around the lakes. Dana cooked a turkey and the fish they caught for an intimate Thanksgiving dinner.

In December, Dana plunged into decorating the house for the holidays and put her energy into her silk-screening business, exercise and trying to find another job. She made Christmas stockings for Jim and Jason. On her birthday, December 6, they all went to Disneyland, where Jason went wild. She applied for unemployment. Because she was not working, she tried to establish a schedule for herself. She picked out a $1,000 Trek mountain bike and put it on layaway. She would take Jason to daycare and go for a bike ride or do some other kind of exercise in the mornings, scan the classifieds, make phone calls and go on job interviews.

Dana told her manicurist that she was putting a woman's touch on Jim and Jason's bachelor pad. She scrubbed the place from top to bottom, lined all the cupboards, bought new curtains, got Jason a computer and a new monitor for his games, went through Jason's closet and got rid of old clothes, bought him new ones, replaced the headboard on his bed, bought curtains and bed and kitchen linens. She pulled Jason out of daycare and put him in a private preschool. Dana spent a lot of time with the boy and took him to the beach a couple of times, on the warmer winter days, to teach him how to swim. They would take their bikes and run by the lake with the dogs. She seemed determined to give him what his biological mother, whom Jim characterized as a drug user, could not. She talked about Jason incessantly and her friends and family began to wonder whether it was Jason, not Jim, that she had fallen in love with. Even Jim seemed a little jealous that Dana had so much time with Jason and was bonding with him. Jeri warned Dana not to get too close to Jason, just in case the relationship with Jim didn't work out.

Jeri and Russell saw Dana infrequently—they didn't have a close relationship with her. They weren't invited to her parties, and she didn't introduce them to her friends, but she would drop in on occasion, or all three would come by for a visit.

On Thanksgiving and Christmas, like each year before, Dana was invited but did not go to Russ and Jeri's house. For Christmas, Jim paid the balance on the mountain bike so she would have it for Christmas. On New Year's Day 1994, she and Jim took Jason to the Tournament of Roses Parade in Pasadena.

On Jan. 2, 1994, Dana received another long letter from Rick, who had not communicated with her since his last letter in 1991. He called Tom and Dana "spoiled little brats" for acting irresponsibly during the break-up of their marriage and demanded the return of his belongings. He included copies of Dana's previous notes thanking him for the loan, so she could not later claim they were gifts. Now living on food stamps and Medi-Cal, Rick said he was about to undergo major surgery after breaking his back in an accident on Memorial Day that had left him completely disabled. Rick was angry that Dana hadn't returned his phone calls. When he did get her on the phone, she was angry with him because he wanted his microwave back, "and that's fucked!" Rick railed at Dana for that remark because he never mentioned his microwave, but Dana was compelled to assume what he was thinking, making herself a victim again. Rick's reply seemed to cut to the heart of one of Dana's most troubling personality traits, that of perceived slights by others and her desire for revenge. "I never had the intention to play nasty tricks on you the way you seem to need to do to others ... I have seen you in action and have heard you tell me in conversations how you planned to get even with various people for supposed indiscretions that you assume have been perpetrated against you."

Rick also cut to the heart of Dana's empty soul that seemed never to be filled. "Anything you personally have done for me I feel has been done with a selfish motive beneath it. You think because you have done someone a kindness they must tell you how much they love you, and love you, and love you ...

"Eventually, whether you want to or not, you will have to face the truth of your life, even if it's with the last breath you take ..."

Rick called Dana again on Sunday, January 30, two weeks after his back surgery, and said he would "come unglued" if she didn't return his call. She called a couple of hours later, saying, "Do us both a favor, fuck off and die." Rick said he just wanted his stuff back and Dana hung up on him. She called him several times that day, letting the phone ring 10 or 15 times, knowing that it would take him that long to get to the phone because of his back surgery, and hung up once he answered the phone. She called one last time and shouted, "Are you so pissed off you could stroke out and die? I hope so!"

Rick had had enough. He called his local police department in Alhambra to report a threatening phone call. The detective got ahold of Dana the next day and she agreed never again to call and harass him. Dana later said, "Yeah, I was a bitch. He deserved it."

Dana had the post-holiday blues and sank into another round of depression and vodka-drinking. She tried a couple of part-time jobs, but found them demeaning. She tried to put time into silk-screening, but was restless and bored. Things weren't working out with Jim. If she was going to move out, she'd need a place to live. She went over and asked her parents about moving in with them. They said it would be OK, but they were already starved for closet space. It would be tight.

Jeri had another suggestion.

"Why don't you move in with Norma? The condo has tons of room."

MONDAY, FEBRUARY 14, 1994, 9:30 A.M.

Tom had a funny feeling. Dana had called his parents' house and asked to meet with him. He didn't want Dana to have his phone number or know where he was living. If she needed to reach him, she called his parents' house. He agreed but, at the last minute, got a bad feeling in the pit of his stomach. It was unmistakable. He hadn't felt that way since their honeymoon.

Tom didn't call to cancel, he just didn't show up.

CHAPTER THIRTEEN

SUNDAY, MARCH 20, 1994, 3:30 P.M.

"How are you doing today?"

"Well, I've been vomiting all day, but other than that, fine," Dana told the counselor. Clad in a medium blue jail jumpsuit, Dana's collar-length reddish hair was fluffy and soft. A white plastic wristband indicated her housing status in the mental health observation unit.

"I can't eat the food in here. The only thing I've been able to keep down is an orange and some Kool-Aid. I *really* need a vegetarian diet."

Her daily mental health follow-up had taken on a familiar quality. Every day since her arrival at county jail, she had been pulled out of her cell by a sheriff's deputy and escorted to an hour-long interview with a psychological counselor. Except for the first day, she denied having any suicidal thoughts. She said she had been depressed and suicidal before she was arrested, but didn't have those feelings anymore. She replayed the events of the past year, her crummy marriage, the loss of her job, foreclosure, bankruptcy and alcohol abuse, and she recounted the death of her mother when she was a young teenager. When asked about her primary fear, she said she hated being alone. The boilerplate interview for a new inmate included questions about her support structure upon being incarcerated. Dana said that she'd been in regular contact with her father since her arrest. After declaring herself suicidal, she was placed alone in an observation cell with twenty-four-hour video monitoring. Every half hour, a deputy strolled by and wrote down what she was doing. Food trays get shoved through the slot in the cell and she got an hour or so a day in the communal day room where she had contact with other female inmates. Dana didn't like this arrangement anymore, didn't want to be interviewed by a counselor every day and didn't want to take any medication.

"I need to get out of this cell with the camera on you the whole time," Dana said. "I need to get out more—how can I get more time in the day room?"

Dana sat quietly and cooperated as the counselor asked the standard questions about her family, her marriage, her job. She complained about her poor appetite and said she was using sleep as an escape mechanism and trying to make friends with the trustees. Dana answered all of the questions in great detail and in a loud voice, complete with exaggerated hand gestures. When talking about her parents, she was reduced to tears, but the tears disappeared when a "superficial" subject was raised, the counselor noted. The counselor wrote that Dana's mood was "anxious, labile, histrionic and hyperverbal. Main energy is devoted to learning about her environment and how she can get her needs met. Urgent to learn jail system." She also noted that Dana was very observant, noticing that Dana scanned her hand to see if she was wearing any rings.

The deputy who had escorted Dana, standing watch nearby, mentioned that there was some discussion of her case in the day room because there was a newspaper article about it.

"There was an article about me?" she asked excitedly.

The deputy said the article had created quite a stir in the day room and that the other inmates and some of the sheriffs were talking about it.

Dana nodded her head and proceeded to quiz the guard about the vegetarian diet, changing her housing status, and getting more day room time.

MONDAY, MARCH 21, 1994, 12:57 P.M.

"What can you tell me about Dora's social life? Did she have a lot of friends, or . . . ?"

Helen Carlson paused for a bit. It had been just a few days since her friend of twenty-one years had died. She wiped away a tear and spoke slowly.

"No," she said in a quavering voice. "She did not have

a lot of friends. She had friends, but, I mean, she didn't have a lot of callers."

Despite having a suspect in custody, Antoniadas wanted to tighten up his case. Detective Mark Cordova, Antoniadas' partner, had interviewed Dora's boyfriend, Louis. If they needed to, they could talk to him again. He was pretty broken up. Antoniadas had assigned Detective Mason Yeo to track down the paper—the bank records, the store receipts, the original checks from the bank—and to interview the clerks to nail down the times, see if they recognized Dana's picture from a six-pack of mug shots. Antoniadas wanted to profile Dana as well as Dora and find out something about their personalities and their habits. He also wanted to know how Dana had gotten into the house.

"OK. In reference to Dora's habits, was she pretty outgoing?"

"No, she was a very retiring person. Very much to herself."

"OK. How would she behave with strangers if somebody came to the house? I don't know how to put this any other way, but was she gullible or was she pretty sharp if somebody came to the house and wanted to go in—was she suspicious of people?"

"She never let anybody in. She was very cautious," Helen said. "That's why I can't understand this, because I can't see how she'd let anybody in."

"OK," Antoniadas said. "Is there anything else you can tell me about Dora that you think is important? Any of her habits? Anywhere she frequented?"

Helen paused again.

"Well, she was a very religious person," she said. "She sang in the choir. She's the one that got me into the choir. Her husband is the one that got my husband into ushering and we used to go to church together all the time."

2:06 P.M.

"She was a very caring person," said Darlene Addison, the nursing supervisor who had fired Dana. "She was the first person to go when someone was down and out. The flood victims—she gathered clothes; the dog shelter—she gathered cans. She organized everybody's life as well as her own. I had no contact with her after I terminated her because, of course, she hated me and let it be known to everyone in surgery that she hated me.

"I have letters from her. Many cards from her. You know, stating life was getting rough. She was having a hard time . . . dealing with the bankruptcy, the divorce, the loss of her house, the foreclosure . . . the world was closing in on her."

Darlene said that Dana had a lot of "idiosyncrasies," but didn't think she was capable of committing murder. Antoniadas wanted to know how well she fit in with the other nurses at the hospital.

"One of the girls summed it up in that our surgery is like a family and it's probably the best home life Dana ever had," Darlene said. "She had a hard time fitting into situations and we made a lot of allowances for her and she did seem to function very well there."

Darlene said that Dana was hard to work with because she always had to be in control and organize everything around her—her own life and everyone else's. She was domineering and critical and made her co-workers' lives miserable until they let Dana take the reins. When she first started in obstetrics, no one got along with her and the hospital considered terminating her. Dana asked to be moved to post-op recovery, and fit in there a little better. Darlene decided to give her a chance and moved Dana to surgery, where she worked up to the point that she was fired for stealing drugs.

Antoniadas had expected Dana to be controlling in her work life like she was in her personal life. But he had to know something else.

"I know this is a strange question, but I have obvious reasons for asking. Did she ever have any problems with any of the elderly people?"

"None at all," Darlene said. "She took excellent care of people. As far as patient care, I've never had a complaint. I've had a complaint about other co-workers against her, but never a patient complaint . . .

"She is sarcastic. She does get her point across if she's crossed, or doesn't get her way. But I mean, that's something that we all knew and accepted."

3 P.M.

The clanking from the thick shackles around Dana's ankles cut through the buzz of casual conversation. The bored photographers and reporters sprang into action as she entered the courtroom, escorted by two sheriff's deputies. The press had been waiting most of the day for her arraignment. Dana's cuffed hands were awkwardly linked to a thick chain slung around her hips. She nervously scanned the courtroom, stone silent except for the whirring of motor-driven cameras. She spotted a few familiar faces. She pretended not to see her brother Rick, who was sitting with the cluster of reporters. She saw Lisa Sloan, a nurse she'd worked with at Inland Valley Regional Medical Center. She knew Russell and Jeri would not attend her arraignment, but would visit with her later. Rich Bentley was seated at the prosecution side of the counsel table, next to the defense table facing the judge. Dana sat down next to her court-appointed lawyer, Deputy Public Defender Stuart Sachs, trying to ignore murmurs from the crew of news photographers and reporters and the drone of high-speed cameras. While the press was waiting, Bentley fed reporters a few quotes about nabbing the county's first and only known female serial killer. He told them that getting a chance to prosecute a female serial killer "is rare."

The purpose of an arraignment is to formally read the accused the charges they are facing and allow them to enter a plea of guilty or not guilty. It is typically a very brief, pro forma procedure—a legal necessity lacking the glamour of a trial, live witnesses or the dramatic presentation evidence. In this case, though, it was the media's first look at the comely serial killer who had been terrorizing the region's elderly population. The judge had acquiesced to requests to photograph the defendant and was allowing a few minutes for pictures before he took the bench and started the proceedings. Dana was like a caged, feral animal. She was forced to sit and have her picture taken whether she liked it or not.

A bailiff uncuffed Dana's hands while she sat hunched with Stuart Sachs. The defense had opposed photographers in the courtroom, but it was a losing battle. The law allows the media to cover news stories in the third branch of government—the judiciary. Stuart explained to Dana what was going to happen, how he thought they should proceed and what to expect from the prosecution. Stuart told Dana that he wasn't ready to have her enter a plea. He wanted to delay her arraignment until they had received more police reports and investigative results from the DA's office. It was the prosecution's job to turn over all material they planned to use at trial to the defense, a process called "discovery" that usually drags on much longer than a day or two after the initial arrest, especially with large, comprehensive investigations. In this case, there were two agencies that had investigated four different crime scenes and seized mountains of evidence from those scenes as well as from the defendant's home. It would take months to get all the reports. Dana wasn't thrilled with delaying anything. She was in a hurry to get to trial and get out, but she went along with Stuart's suggestion.

When they finished talking, Rick tried to get her attention, but he found he was competing for her attention with Lisa Sloan, who was blowing kisses to Dana. The press went wild, taking pictures of the beautiful blonde nurse blowing kisses to an accused female serial killer. If Dana and Lisa were lovers, or if the slayings were part of a lesbian love triangle, they wanted photos. Dana didn't return the kisses, but simply turned and smiled at Lisa. Dana saw Rick and ignored him. He finally went up to the bailiff to see if he could have a word with her, but the bailiff said he could not. Rick then asked if he could ask Dana to sign something and pulled a sheet of paper out of a folder. It was a form Dana needed to sign before the police could release the contents of the storage unit containing his belongings. The bailiff took the paper over to Dana. Rick could see from where he was standing at the rail that she refused to sign it. Rick got his paper back and returned to his seat in the courtroom.

The proceeding took just a few minutes. Dana never said a word. Sachs asked for a continuance and the judge agreed, setting a return date for April 8. Still chained, Dana was led out of the courtroom as Lisa continued to blow kisses.

Afterward, Rick Ward courted the press, revealing his

theory of why his half-sister had become a serial killer who
went on post-murder shopping binges. He recounted how he
had raised his younger half-sister from the age of 13 and
said she had always been a spendthrift with budget problems
who was constantly asking friends and relatives for money.
Rick told reporters that he had been generous with emotional support and had even loaned Dana his furniture and
other personal belongings, which he was now trying to get
back. Rick told the reporters the last thing his half-sister had
said to him: "Are you pissed off enough to stroke off and
die? I hope so."

6 P.M.

"Do you think I did it?"

Dana's voice was quiet. She was looking at her father
through the glass in the visiting room of the county jail. On
one side of the glass was a long row of inmates seated at
shallow carrels facing their husbands, boyfriends, children,
parents and friends on the other side of the glass. Each side
had a row of big, black phones. It was very noisy. Children
were squealing as they played around the chairs, visitors
shouted over the din and the noises reverberated off the hard
linoleum floor.

Russell hesitated a bit.

"Th–the evidence is very damaging, honey," he said carefully. "I don't think—I think a lot of it's circumstantial."

"You know, we're not supposed to talk about the case
over the phone, but I needed to ask you face-to-face," Dana
said, her voice quavering slightly, "because I need your love
and support, Dad."

"You've got that," Russell said quickly. "You'll always
have that, whether you did it or didn't do it. You know that."

"OK, that's all I wanted to hear."

Dana and Russell had been talking about the mess left
by police after the search, which had left Jim's house looking as if it had been tossed upside down. Jim was incensed
about the hole—about the size of a newborn's fist—that
criminalists had cut in the driver's seat of his truck. Police
had taken his checkbook, his bankbook, and several sets of

keys, including those to a storage shed out back. Dana said she wanted to compensate Jim for his loss.

"As soon as they release my Cadillac, I want you to sell it and I want you to give the money to Jim to fix his truck," Dana said.

Dana also wanted her father to pick up some pictures of her mother that she had left at an art and framing store. She spelled out the name of the store and the location. But Russell was still curious about his daughter's culpability.

"What do you think, do you think you did it, honey?"

"No," Dana said flatly.

"Hm?"

"I did use June's credit card."

". . . I know that," Russell said.

"And I did write checks and take some money out of a lady's account I didn't know. But I did not kill June. I did not, Dad."

"What about the lady in Sun City?"

"No. I'm not supposed to talk about it—"

"Well, we won't—"

"—over the phone, but I'm telling you no."

"OK, we'll go through the attorney," Russ said.

Dana said she wrote out an explanation for Stuart that she wanted Russ to read. She also read him a portion of a letter she had written to Jim about keeping Jason in his private preschool, which brought Dana to tears. She said she was concerned that Jason would be traumatized by the events. Russell said he was too young to really understand what was going on, but Dana insisted that he was being harmed. She said she had been trying to give Jason a stable mother to come home to every day, something Dana's own mother could not provide her because she had worked during the day.

"But with Jason now, what's going to happen if the worst happens to me? I want Jason to have as much love and support when he comes home," she said, crying. "What does he have to come home to? There's no Dana there to give him a bath and cook his meals!"

Dana turned her anguish from Jason to her dire straits behind bars. She pleaded hysterically with her father to help her get a vegetarian diet and medical attention for her "terrible" bleeding. Even though Russell had just placed $100 in her jail account, she asked for more, tried to play on his sympathy, claimed she was vomiting every day, and told him that the jail psychiatrist wanted to medicate her.

"Every single meal I have thrown up," she said with surprising vigor for anyone who was truly ill. "I'm real weak, Dad. I can't eat. It's been six, seven days since I've eaten . . .

"I need to get some help [for] my female problems at a *real* doctor at a *real* hospital . . . This is a butcher place."

Russell reminded her that he was having knee surgery and would be "laid up for a few days," but Dana was unable to consider her father's needs.

"Well, I hope someone comes out to see me, Dad, because it's, it's *hell*."

Monday
3/21
Jim, I [sic] sitting here waiting at 8:00 P.M. at Night to take a fucking shower!

Her first letter to Jim was more than 20 pages, scrawled in pencil and giving him a snapshot of the indignities of living life in a 6-foot-by-12-foot cinder-block cell where privacy is nonexistent. "I had a day-crew of pod officers (they oversee us) that acted like it was too much that I needed extra peripads just 'cause I'm bleeding my brains out!" Her fear of abandonment was so acute, she immediately started to question Jim's loyalty and even discussed their relationship with her father before even speaking to Jim. "I talked to my dad and he assures me even more how you won't ditch me." She promised that her parents would "watch over him" and told him that despite the nasty stories in the press, ". . . I see our live as a hot summer blast against all the shame, finger-pointing and crap we both endure. We can come out about this. We must do it together as a family . . ."

TUESDAY, MARCH 22, 1994, 2 P.M.

By this time, Dana had just about had it with the same questions from the mental health counselor every day. Although there were different counselors on different days, the questions were the same. Dana was getting to the point where she was answering questions before they were asked. RN, accused of murder, history of alcohol abuse and depression, divorce, foreclosure, bankruptcy, miscarriages. She claimed to be eating and sleeping well, didn't want any medication and wanted to get out of the fish tank, get away from the video trained on her every movement, twenty-four hours a day.

The counselor recommended that she stay in the observation unit.

In a letter to Jim laced liberally with Biblical references, Dana tried to wrap the apron strings of her family around Jim and Jason, including having her parents pay for Jason's kindergarten tuition. She groused about the horrors of jail life, playing the part of the wrongly accused inmate ingenue terrified at being housed with real criminals. Dana said she was finding solace in God from reading the New Testament—which she'd first picked up the day before. Although it was the only reading material she had access to as a prisoner at that point, she asked Jim not to be negative about her "getting religion in prison." Dana demonstrated her overnight spiritual awakening by explaining what drove her to "do what she did," although Dana steadfastly maintained she was not a murderer.

"Negativity and self-pity take a lot of energy. I know, I spent a lot of time there lately." While Dana said she had done some soul-searching, she divulged no real insight. Dana admitted that she "held a lot in" before her arrest and had spent hours talking with her father in his visits to the jail. While she said she was not blaming anyone, she pointed the finger at Tom Gray for messing her up and saying she was "too weak to see what I was letting happen to myself. I see how it helped get me here."

3:30 P.M.

Tom stood in line at the police impound yard. He'd gotten the phone call to pick up the Cadillac, but he was scared shitless about going down there. As the co-owner of the

Cadillac on the DMV records, he got the call from the police to retrieve it. He thought he was going to be questioned. When it was his turn, he showed them his driver's license and they made a photocopy of it, checked the paperwork, and handed him the keys. He couldn't help but ask a few questions about what was going to happen to Dana.

It's in the hands of the courts, the clerk told him, handing him a form to sign.

When he went to get the car, he saw that a big hole had been cut out of the driver's side seat and the floor mats. No big deal. He got in, kicked on the engine and drove away. It had been painful for him to come in, but now he felt good.

7:30 P.M.

"I'm OK. I don't have anything to say."

Another day, another mental health interview. Dana had very short answers for the jail's mental health counselor.

"I feel good. Can I get out of observation status now?"

Dana said her depression was gone, she had no suicidal thoughts and didn't want to see a psychological counselor in jail anymore.

"I have my own who will see me," she told the counselor.

WEDNESDAY, MARCH 23, 1994

Dana not only wrote one or two letters to Jim each day, she also phoned him every night. Her emotions swung wildly from hope to despair. When the previous night's phone call yielded a cold shoulder from Jim, Dana used a mixed bag of anger, religion, self-pity and outright emotional manipulation to win reassurance from Jim to stand by her. She claimed to be fearful of his "chills and coldness" and anger that she found so "violent in tone" that it made her "quake in [her] boots," and said she was afraid of losing him—then attacked him for not figuring out what was wrong with her.

"You always said you couldn't tell me what to do, but

you could! And you still can. You just always expected me to figure it out for myself and I couldn't . . . ! I was weak and mixed up and trying desperately to be in control and appear normal . . .

"We both have much mental healing ahead of us. I hope we can lighten each other's load and do it together.

"I LOVE YOU right through your fucking COLD ASSED ARMOUR. DEAL WITH IT!"

8 P.M.

While Dana wrestled with her relationship with Jim, Antoniadas was building a picture of Dana from her sky-diving friends Jeff and Lynn Fogleman, brother and sister, who had watched her grow up as a young teenager. With his partner, Mark Cordova, Antoniadas talked to the Foglemans separately. Jeff wholeheartedly agreed that Dana was an intense and vindictive person who wanted things done her way and would embarrass people in public. Their relationship sank when it appeared that friendship worked one way with Dana—her way.

"My wife and Dana were supposed to be friends, but then my wife would tell me how, you know, she was only a friend when she wanted to be and when it was convenient for her, but if my wife needed something, or help or support or somebody to talk to, [Dana] didn't really concern herself much about it."

Even though they were still friends, Lynn called Dana a bitch.

If Dana was angry, "she'll get right back in their face . . . She'd make sure that you knew she was upset about something."

SUNDAY, MARCH 27, 1994, 3 P.M.

Dana's mood toward Jim turned conciliatory as she experienced the long days and lonely nights without her live-in companion, expressing an intense desire to become pregnant with his child: "My hormones are wiggin' big time. If I was home and feeling like I do now—you'd never leave that bedroom til I was pregnant—that's how overwhelming this drive is."

Ever the organizer, Dana compiled numerous "to do" lists for Jim, including the dispersal of her belongings, ordering books to be delivered to the jail, and maintaining a web of support that she expected would become useful in her defense. As details of her crimes reached the newspaper, Dana countered by accusing the district attorney's office of sensationalizing her case because it was an election year, and attacked the press: ". . . as we know, the paper is 99% bullshit. . . ."

In the next breath, she leaned on the Holy Spirit to lend a hand in her defense and closed with a hope that Jim can "feel the love I'm sending you every moment. It's alot Babe. I love you. God Bless."

Dana was moved out of the observation tank and into protective custody, a wing of the county jail, separating certain inmates from the rest of the general population. Protective custody (PC) was reserved for inmates whose release into the general jail population could cause a disruption because of their notoriety, like police officers accused of crimes, or the type of offense, such as baby killing or child molestation. Being accused of killing helpless, elderly ladies in a high-profile serial murder case more than qualified Dana for PC status.

As she sought to regain control of her surroundings, Dana mounted an intensive campaign to establish a network of friends on the outside, convincing her supporters to believe in her innocence and directing her parents to collect and dispose of her belongings as she liked. Unable to shop, drive or phone, and without direct contact with family or friends, Dana was desperate to have her needs met. Not only did she ask for books and crossword puzzles to stave off boredom, she tried to fill the constant, aching emptiness within her. In the same way that she had continually badgered Tom to say he loved her, Dana solicited visits, phone calls and letters, attempting to whip up enthusiasm for what amounted to a "Support Dana" committee. She dispersed phone numbers and addresses to her friends and relatives, all with the focus on keeping her spirits up, and helping with whatever errands she needed, including being character witnesses at her trial.

Nursing buddy Lisa Sloan took charge of dog duties, bringing "Penny," Dana's white, black and brown Queensland Healer, home to live with her. She acted as Dana's spiritual compass, visiting and providing Bibles and religious passages to assist Dana, who insisted to Lisa that she was no "jailhouse convert . . . Pray for me Lisa to get out and get on with my life."

She asked another nursing buddy to call Jim, gave her his phone number and his work schedule, and described her life behind bars in contrast to the wretched conditions she was moaning about to Jim and her parents.

"Tonite was a real up nite! I got to exercise in the exercise rm! I smelled real nite air and got to see the beautiful full moon. I went on the exercise bike, used the weights . . . played basketball and had a great time. On the way out the door I made 3 one handed basketball dunks in a row! Then got to hang out for 3 hrs with the girls watching TV, taking showers, and getting to know some of them better.

"The one girl I've been wanting to know was extra sweet to me and 3 of us held hands and did a prayer out loud (It was super special.) . . ."

Despite her hatred of Tom Gray, Dana kept in touch with his father, tried to enlist his support and supplied him with a phone list. "I have always loved you DAD, you've been the best to me . . . Just one letter from you, from your heart, would mean the most to me . . ."

At the same time, Rick was also mounting a campaign to get his things back. He wrote a seven-page letter to Russell on March 29 apologizing for "blowing up" at him when Rick called him to enlist his assistance in getting the furniture and other items returned. Rick recounted how he had loaned Dana his possessions all the way up to Dana's ugly phone call on January 30.

Rick told Russell he was not shocked at her arrest and, with insight, honesty, and a stunning lack of sensitivity, offered him some insight as to why his only daughter was a killer. "I had warned her on many occasions in the last seven

years that her behavior was not going to get her where she
wanted to be. But she never listened, she just became more
set in her ways. I still never dreamed it would come to
this . . ."

CHAPTER FOURTEEN

WEDNESDAY, MARCH 30, 1994, 3:30 P.M.

After two weeks in custody, Dana, still adjusting to the routine of jail life, was starting to discuss her actions with friends. Jail breakfast was served at an eye-opening 5:30 a.m., lunch at 10:30 a.m. and dinner at 3:30 p.m. She was in a cell with cream-colored concrete cinderblocks with a small, mesh-covered window. There were two bunks, each adorned with a gray blanket and white sheets. Every Saturday, the inmates got clean jumpsuits and a change of bedding. Fresh underwear came twice a week. Vending machines supplied snacks, candy bars, chips and instant noodle soups as well as some personal hygiene items. Inmates could also fill out a commissary slip to purchase shampoo, tampons and pads, and deodorant. The commissary didn't sell make-up, hair spray or perfume. A book cart, functioning like a library on wheels containing primarily paperback fiction, circulated occasionally. No inmate carried cash. Any money furnished by relatives was recorded under their names and booking numbers. The amount of money in the account, along with name and booking information, was placed on an ID card bearing the prisoner's booking photo. If the prisoner wanted to purchase something, the card was either swiped at the vending machine or the guards could swipe it for commissary items.

The jail building was tall enough for fourteen floors, but the jail actually had seven fully contained, two-tiered floors. All female inmates were on the sixth floor. The seventh floor was for inmates requiring medical care. Each two-tiered floor contained bank of cells, a day room with a TV set, a rec room with minimal exercise equipment and a "pod," a bulletproof, glass-walled booth from which one deputy—the "pod officer"—electronically controlled the doors and gates

within that two-tiered section. None of the elevators had
buttons to push. If an inmate needed to be moved, a guard
made a hand signal, holding up four fingers for the fourth
floor. The pod officer opened and closed the elevator doors
and the inmate rode alone. Within each two-tiered section
was a set of stairs the inmates could use to go from one's
cell to the day room or the rec room. Each of the sections
contained a bank of phones where inmates could make collect calls. No other types of phone calls were allowed: no
toll-free calls, no phone cards, and no incoming calls.

Rules and discipline were enforced by granting and removing privileges. If an inmate misbehaved, a guard would
verbally warn her or write a "marker," a written complaint
against her for a rule violation. A serious assault on a guard
could be handled either by placing the inmate responsible
in solitary confinement or by sending an incident report to
the DA's office so they could consider filing charges. For
inmates accused of extremely serious offenses, jail authorities knew the DA's office would brush aside a relatively
minor assault, so they handled the discipline themselves.
Inmates usually got an opportunity to explain their behavior
to an upper-level jail authority before punishment was administered or privileges were removed.

To pass the time, inmates read, wrote letters, chatted,
played games, watched TV and exercised, though time in
the recreation room was limited. Verbal spats were common
and erupted over something as minor as a snide remark,
hogging a phone or removing a favorite section of the newspaper.

The contents of Dana's letters show a growing hysteria
over Tom picking up her Cadillac from the impound yard,
a major blow to Dana's ironfisted control over her possessions. Two strange themes emerged: Despite her denials that
she was a jailhouse convert to Christianity, she plunged into
Bible study. True to form, Dana kept the focus on herself,
arriving at the conclusion that her confinement was a bless-
ing in disguise that would allow her to strengthen her relationship with Jim and give her a chance to straighten out
her life. Dana still seemed to think that if she could only
get someone to sit down and listen to her rather than the
corrupt DA or the sensational newspapers, she could explain

everything and walk out of jail. Instead of taking the time to do some serious soul-searching, Dana was consumed with retaliating against Tom, mustering support from her friends and mastering jailhouse beauty tricks.

At learning that not everyone was convinced of her innocence, Dana cast herself as the virtuous inmate in a letter to Lisa Sloan about a mutual friend. "I need to forgive those who will turn against me, so I can go on and not hold bitterness in me. George is another Judas Iscariot, Lisa . . . The rest will catch up to him, so I worry not. I'm curious who is and who is not on my side." She enlisted Lisa's help in convincing others of her innocence, sent them messages and told her what to say on her behalf.

Dana called a longtime nursing friend early in the morning to rant about Tom picking up her Cadillac, then wrote a letter apologizing, ranting some more and asking her to make some phone calls. She threatened to have Tom arrested, either forgetting or ignoring the fact that she and Tom owned the car jointly: "If [Tom] doesn't cooperate, he will be picked up and I will press charges . . . I can make trouble for him and I will if he fucks with me. I am done with him. . . . Snake!"

Aware that she had been in custody for two weeks, Dana made the bizarre observation that jail had been good for her and she had metamorphosed into a healthy, self-actualized being.

"This solitude in many ways has been good for me. I truly needed to take a look at my life and set priorities. It's 2 weeks today. I thank Jesus every day for my new self; for my ever increasing awareness of the beauty around me . . ."

Dana's next priority was maintaining her beauty regimen, particularly during her appearance in court for her preliminary hearing, which was scheduled for July. The other inmates helped Dana with jailhouse beauty secrets.

"Tonite I learned how to pluck my eyebrows by rolling them onto a new pencil eraser head, then you yank 'em," she wrote, then expressed dismay at the effect the harsh shampoo was having on her perm. She said she would have to experiment with sponge rollers and setting gel to handle her "fright wig hair." For court appearances, Dana learned she would wear her own clothes in front of the jury. She wanted to look good.

She humorously described the indignities of jail life, calling the weekly searches Toga Day because the inmates had to strip to their underwear, wrap themselves in the scratchy wool blankets and sit down while the deputies searched their cells, then they gave inmates cleaning materials to mop and scrub down their own toilets.

Once Dana got ahold of some lipstick, she planted lipstick kisses on her letters to Jim and scanned the Bible for romantic passages: "I slept but my heart was awake. Listen! My lover is knocking . . ." On April 1, her mother's birthday, Dana told Jim that she used to celebrate it even after she died by going out and doing something fun. Because her mother died when Dana was a young teenager, she was never able to establish an adult relationship with her as she was able to do with her father. Beverly's charisma and a bit of a wild streak put verve in Dana's growing years, "camping, clamming at Pismo, best Halloween parties and best Xmases a poor family could have. She could make fun time out of just about anything."

Despite her Bible study, Dana ranted about Tom: "FUCK FUCK FUCK HIM! In the Bible you're supposed to forgive those despite all reasons you should not. Well I'll forgive and forget him after the car is back!"

As more time passed, Dana's contact with the outside world slipped as she sank deeper into the doldrums and crudity of jail and learned to bottle her emotions. Dana revealed to Jim a heated exchange with another inmate, "a mouth, a self-centered manipulative & heartless little Bitch with a 'C' This smartass bitch whips off with a real zinger comment . . . I felt stupid let such an immature, fuck for bucks bitch get my goat . . . Guess I have to get a prison mask . . . and act tough." In still another incident, she described how the distribution of the newspaper was enough to spark an argument between twenty "hormonal women" in the day room.

It wasn't long before news of the female serial killer attracted attention among the thousands of male inmates in custody who sought to establish contact with a good-looking—and maybe dangerous—female compadre in a jail jumpsuit. A TV reporter who attended the proceedings reported speculation that the woman blowing kisses to Dana was her lesbian lover.

Dana's tone with Jim shifted noticeably as his refusal to visit her behind bars took its toll. She openly doubted whether he was as interested in a relationship as she was, but it appaved that she was primarily looking to see if he was still on her team. Never shy about asking for money, Dana started using her support system as a source of cash contributions to hire a private defense attorney and she continued to lean on her father and Jeri to help sell off her belongings, including the Cadillac. Despite the fact that she'd already promised proceeds from the sale of the Cadillac to pay for the damage to Jim's upholstery, Dana revealed just how far she was from reality, having no concept of how offended her victims' relatives would be at the idea of starting a defense fund for her.

> Dear Dave [Dave Dresseker, a friend and realtor who sold Dana and Tom their Canyon Lake home]—
> I just wanted to say thank you for the support you gave me in the press after my arrest. It *means alot!* Although I am not allowed to discuss my case, I will ask you to judge me from your heart. You know me pretty well and know I may have been depressed but not *that* depressed . . .

Dave later turned over excerpts of Dana's letter to the local newspaper, which printed excerpts. Outside of combatting sheer boredom, Dana's intention was clearly to continue accumulating supporters and keep them apprised, wisely keeping a human face on what the newspapers were calling a "rare" female serial killer. But she had no idea that she had unintentionally sabotaged a potential defense—perhaps her only defense—of her crimes by self-evaluating her mental state at the time of the crimes by telling Dresseker she was "not *that* depressed."

As the days passed, Dana's emotions rode roller-coaster

highs and lows. She expressed her undying love for Jim and
demanded that he do the same, allowing him scant time to
absorb the shocking news that she had secretly been committing crimes. Although he accepted her collect calls from
jail, Jim had not written to Dana and couldn't bring himself
to visit her. While Dana had quickly adapted to her surroundings, Jim needed some space in their relationship, but
his distant behavior triggered her panic button. "I've never
felt so desperate in my life . . . [Jim's failure to visit her]
fucking hurts." In letter after letter, Dana pushed Jim, demanded affection, insisted that he help her find a lawyer,
asked him to decide—now—whether he loved her and be-
rated him for not somehow divining her distress signals before her arrest.

With her emotions in high gear, Dana offered Jim a variety of reasons why he couldn't, wouldn't, or didn't want
to visit: He was angry and didn't want to come to jail and
have an argument; he was avoiding her because it was painful; he blamed himself for not "seeing her distress signals.
Is this a slow painful break-up or are you really trying to
heal yourself so that you can help me, too?"

Dana created a questionnaire—like a relationship quiz in
a women's magazine—that included an indirect marriage
proposal. But instead of waiting for Jim's answers, she answered her own questions the way she believed that he
would, claiming that she was refraining from "pushing" him.

Dissatisfied with Sachs, her county-supplied attorney,
Dana's other obsession was to hire a lawyer. She wielded a
multi-pronged hammer—whining, familial guilt, personal
expressions of innocence, and outright begging—to convince her father and Jeri to fund a "real" lawyer. While she
was insistent and demanding, the reality that she was headed
for prison appeared to be settling in. But first, she asked that
the financial arrangements be adjusted. She put a copy of
the commissary rules into the same envelope.

"Mom + Dad—I CANNOT handle this place for years!"
Dana pleaded, acknowledging that the sooner she went to
prison, the sooner she could take courses, exercise, and see
visitors without a glass partition. Her desperation climbed

and assumed an adolescent whine, reminding her father that she would work to pay him back and that she always kept her word. The tone changed again, as Dana pulled out the stops and used her last argument—that she was innocent.

"Please don't let me rot here, please . . . I won't last long here . . . I am not a murderer! HELP ME DAD And Jeri. I'm flat out begging you both . . ."

As her father and Jeri chewed over a response, Dana delivered more "to do" lists to Jim over the disposition of the Cadillac and other possessions as her moods went sharply up and down and up again. After Dana talked to Jason on the phone, her feelings soared, but sank into dark anger after Jim finally unloaded his anger on her, blaming her for not even considering how her actions would hurt him and, particularly, Jason. In letters scrawled with giant letters and peppered with Bible quotes, Dana blared that she was "FUCKIN SORRY!!!" blamed the bankruptcy, being fired, her marriage with Tom—all of the usual suspects— and begged for reconciliation. "Don't ditch me, Jim, please. I'm fucking begging you on my hands + knees." But in her next letter, she pointed a finger at Jim for being so "self centered" that he didn't see she was troubled. "I needed YOUR help—you didn't see it, so I fucked up in a way I'll regret the rest of my life . . . Was I just a housekeeper— cook—babysitter—occasional fuck or what? You tell me. Yes you say you love me—now show it. I hope your balls get bigger than your anger and you come face me. WELL . . . ?"

By the next day, her anger apparently exorcised, Dana returned to the saucy flirt Jim fell in love with. Writing as she sat and patiently waited for the twice-weekly underwear, sock N shirt delivery and playfully criticizing the delivery of new jail jumpsuits once a week. "Rank—Oh! You know what a trauma that is to this laundry queen." . . .

Dana primly noted she turned up her nose on the carbo-heavy jail chow in favor of noodles, fruits, and vegetables, but sorely missed smoking cigarettes. And sex. She whisked away the angst and anxiety of her previous letters with a light-hearted proposal, making it clear that a marriage of

convenience would satisfy her—as long as they made use
of the conjugal visit trailer. "You don't have to love me, I
just want your body. I had to ask. You think I'm joking,
don't you? NOT!"

CHAPTER FIFTEEN

THURSDAY, APRIL 7, 1994

As Dana faced arraignment, her anxiety increased over her desire to have a personal attorney, her relationship with Jim, support from her former friends and the disposition of her property. When Dana's hysterical letter did not convince her father and Jeri to open their pocketbooks to fund a personal attorney, Dana wrote to Jeri on April 8, the day of her arraignment, hoping to convince her to sell the condo that Norma lived in and use the proceeds for the private attorney's fee, using the argument that "we are all family." But Dana's efforts more closely resemble that of a brazen killer taunting a grieving relative, coupled by an ineffective stab in using guilt over Dana's inability to get along with her former step-mother, Yvonne, whom she only lived with for a scant two years.

At this point, Dana had no idea that Jeri was responsible for identifying her to the police. It was not entertaining thoughts of Dana's innocence. Dana had interviewed a private attorney who agreed to accept Norma's now-vacant Canyon Lake condo as payment in full and seemed miffed that Russell had told her that it wouldn't sell. Dana pressed them, stopping short of ordering them to deed it over. "I was under the impression you weren't gonna make any money on it anyway—so I don't understand the problem here. I thought we were *all* family here." Dana made the uneasy link of family ties to the loosening of purse strings by comparing her dislike of Russell's second wife, Yvonne, with her acceptance of Jeri as she would her own mother, "so this issue on money really hurts. Jeri, this is my life we're talking about."

Dana included a list of problems, including a change to a vegetarian diet and a visit from her chiropractor.

Dana hoped to elicit support from employees at her hair salon in Canyon Lake, asking them to "judge me from your hearts and not the news." But she covered herself by saying that if they had already "written me off, well I forgive you. I love you no matter what . . . I can only hope you are behind me."

Dana's letters to Jim took a pleading as well as a challenging tone: "I pray for a chance to rebuild what I have destroyed. Do you have it in your heart to pray for me too? It would help." Dana delighted in hearing that her father "put out an arrest warrant" for Tom. "Tom in jail, YES!! Finally vindicating—for the fuck-wad of my life! Spineless FUCK! Not very Christian I admit, but feels GREAT! I prayed and let God decide what was best and had actually kissed off the Cadi . . ."

Seeking a creative outlet, Dana began drawing on envelopes to Jim and her relatives using paints cobbled together from lipstick, the candy coating from M&M's, Kool-Aid, jail-issue blue eye shadow, pencil lead and baby powder. Her primary subject was clowns, and the way she portrayed their facial expressions usually reflected her own moods. When cheerful, her clowns bore garish smiling faces and when she was upset, the clowns turned grotesque, with jagged teeth and heavy-lidded, bloodshot eyes. Dana's drawings also included clown reptiles, clown snakes and clown fish. For Jason, she drew Batman. Enamored of her own artistic abilities, Dana instructed Russell and Jeri to save her envelopes.

Still without her vegetarian diet and needing a doctor visit for her back, Dana griped to Jim that she felt ignored. The desert heat was pounding on her "concrete condo" and she bemoaned the stifling heat and lack of circulation. Again and again, she begged him to visit.

Jeri, answering Dana's request for money to hire an attorney, typed out a note reminding Dana that Russell had already sold half his stock to finance her wedding and that the Canyon Lake condo wouldn't sell because "no one wants to live in a house where such a horrible event occurred." She asked Dana to cooperate with her lawyer and said they were supporting her by handling her personal affairs, like selling her wedding set, then mentioned that Russell's health had been on a downhill slide since her arrest.

A mere mention of selling a pair of Dana's earrings provoked an angry outburst: "As for my 'things' I want JIM to sell them! I don't want either of you involved other than my wedding ring ... You know the way everyone's so anxious to cash me out makes me feel like I'm already dead! IT FUCKING INSULTS AND HURTS ME! So please honor my wishes till further notice ..."

Dana was unconcerned about hiding her hatred for Norma in response to Jeri's remarks about the inherent difficulty of selling the condo, saying that the "years with Norma Armbrust were a living hell ... I am very sensitive however, as I'm sure you can see."

On April 14, Dana wrote to Jim about getting tossed into lockdown with a twenty-four-hour camera "in the worst cell. No desk or shelves, just a toilet and bed. It's back to meals through a doggie door. ½ hour a day for dayroom time, no rec room. Dayroom time is early, too early to call people.

"I feel so isolated. Not seeing you is hard enough, but not talking to you is a killer. I need you babe in the worst way. *I need to see you more now than ever.*" Out of desperation, Dana called Jim at work, because it was the only time she has access to a phone. In one letter, she wrote, in the early morning, at 1:45 p.m., 3 p.m., & 6 p.m. "Oh great, they just shut my doggie door. Why don't they just shoot me and get it over with?"

Dana said she was placed in lockdown "for my own protection" but added that she didn't believe that explanation and floated a couple of theories. She blamed another inmate who was jealous, but didn't describe the source of the jealousy, and wondered if Bentley arranged it to "make me break down." She enlisted the assistance of another inmate to call her parents so they could call the sergeant who placed her in lockdown. Dana even included a scrap of a note in her letter to Jim with scribbles from her and another inmate commiserating about being in jail and joking about whether the guards got extra pay if they were to attempt suicide.

It is interesting that in her letters, Dana seemed to empty her heart and soul on paper, revealing her inner thoughts and feelings during these difficult weeks of isolation and self-reflection. She appeared completely open but she never came clean to Jim, her friends or family. In reality, Dana's tours of duty in lockdown resulted from standard rules violations and getting into verbal and physical confrontations with guards and other inmates. Dana had often clamped down hard on spin control when it came to her image—as she had when her friends discussed why she was dismissed from the hospital—and no doubt wanted to do the same here. Rather than having her friends and family visualize a raging, combative inmate housed in isolation for fighting, she preferred the forlorn image of herself as a victim of a power-hungry DA and a helpless pawn of media.

Dana partially disclosed why she was placed in lockdown more than a year later, in July 1995, when a psychologist came to evaluate her:

"I was very sick when I first got here—it would be straight line from the bed to use the bathroom. I could drink, but I was very sick when I first got here. I perked up after about two weeks and could look at my dinner tray. Then they put me in PC (protective custody) upstairs. I was aggressive and hostile because people got in my face right off the bat. I was not allowed to mingle and check out what was going on. There was one girl in particular, they slammed me back in lockdown after that. A week after that, I ended up in complete isolation on the 7th floor for five weeks, with a room with a shower, TV." When asked whether that was triggered by any particular incident, Dana answered generally: "I had a real hard time adjusting and didn't understand that I could not talk to them like how I can talk to you. It was a definite role I needed to play and it was hard for me to remember I am in a blue jumpsuit. I was not real cooperative. If I had an opinion, I told them. I don't know if they did it to put me in my place, but I appreciated the time by myself."

In lockdown, confined to her cell 23½ hours a day, Dana wrote letter after letter to stave off loneliness and boredom. Still trying to get support from friends, she penned a second letter to Dave, her realtor friend, complaining about news stories that "twist the truth for a buck," and continued her hobby of smearing Tom, which included "hearing" that he's taken "a big cocaine dive." "That bastard is now trying to get a hold of everything I own for himself." Even after barely a month in custody, Dana's letters started taking on an inevitable institutional hue, in which her status was measured in the number of visits, calls and letters. In this letter, after painting Tom in the worst possible light, Dana colored herself the winner in the support department, receiving more visits, letters and phone calls from friends, co-workers and parents.

One of the more disturbing of Dana's drawings to Jim was christened "Lockdown Monster," perhaps a pun on "Loch Ness Monster," and is a dark, brooding blob with an immense mouth and jagged teeth. Dana attempted to put the best face on her situation by describing an interview with a defense investigator as a cathartic exercise. "It was a relief to unload mental baggage . . . It feels free . . . My life is an open book." She was unnerved by her father's most recent visit, in which they were both sobbing with hands on the glass between them, and she said she felt "like shit" as she tried to soothe her. She asked Jim to be "extra gentle" with her father, saying she feared for his health.

Dana included what was becoming a pro forma attack on Rich Bentley "using the media for his advantage. Know in your heart it's the little prick's only chance. Like a little prick syndrome—all show and no go. It's all ego for the DA, and at my expense . . ."

The longer she was in custody, the more she realized she no longer had control over her former life—"What are you going to do with the stuff Dad can't store?"—and the indignities of being on-camera and incarcerated: "I'm calm considering I just spent 35 mins buck naked on my period . . . in a scratchy wool blanket sitting on the cold cement floor . . ."

Just as Dana felt attacked by people on the outside, she reported that she was becoming a target of "Snakewoman," a nickname for another inmate. Dana claimed to ignore her. "I just clam up and let her make an ass out of herself."

Dana's letters to her father and Jeri reiterated her caring for them, recounted the humiliation of jail life and listed batches of errands. More and more of her news to them and to Jim included snapshots of what her life was like in lock-down.

Like being hauled in front of the sergeant at 4:00 a.m. to plead her case over being in lockdown and vivid descriptions of the chaos and raw emotions that erupt when strangers are thrown together, living day and night in cramped, concrete quarters, peppering her play-by-by accounts with the patois of jail. In one incident an inmate initiated a fist-fight with a trustee, then tried to intimidate a pregnant inmate who was ready to deliver.

"The pregnant woman chased Sophia up the stairs screaming at her . . . As far as I know, she didn't even get a marker and here I sit in lock-down because of that bitch!"

Dana wrote three letters to Jim on April 21 and drew him a tearful half of a clown face. She was melancholy about getting pictures of her growing Queensland Healer puppy, Penny, from Lisa Sloan, tossed around the idea of illustrating a book of poetry from an inmate titled *Lockdown* and struck a combative stance with Tom. "I want transport to divorce court so I can face and fight Tom myself."

She tried to control Jim and wanted her father and Jeri to circle the wagons so he and Jason didn't escape.

She just told Jim that she continued to talk about their relationship with her father, who she said was frustrated because Jim hadn't visited her. "Honey, they want to help us both—you are family to me and that's all that matters." While holding open the loving arms of family life, Dana couldn't help but needle him, charging that Jim simply chose not to accept. Then she went after Jason, who could use some mothering. "Can you let Jeri help fill that void?"

Toward the end of the month, Dana chronicled Jim's conflict: he truly loved Dana, but had been so irreparably hurt that a break-up appeared inevitable. Dana pleaded with Jim to salvage their relationship, even if it was only a friendship, and told him she wouldn't give up on him.

Her days in lockdown consisted of sleeping until noon and peeling the sticky strips from her tea bags to tape up pictures of her dog, Penny. Distraught, she contemplated taking psychotropic medication to cope with the isolation. Finally, on April 24, Jim told her in their nightly phone call that their relationship was over, leaving Dana "absolutely crushed . . . I'm so numb and stunned right now I can't even think."

Even as she tried to salvage crumbs from her relationship with Jim, Dana was cultivating the first of what would eventually become a steady string of jailhouse suitors. She'd penned a letter to Jim expressing emotional anguish on Saturday, but, on the same day, dashed off a cheerful letter to Robert Martinez, "Indio," complete with a questionnaire about his personal history and asking him to detail why he was writing to her.

At the same time, Dana begged Carrie Ann, who visited her in jail, to talk with Jim after revealing that she "got dumped on the phone." Dana complained that she was hurting, but decried Jim's inability to decipher how she was feeling, emotionally and mentally. "I wasn't me! Can't he see that?"

The same theme was repeated in a letter to another longtime friend: "I feel like I slipped through the cracks and nobody noticed. Please notice now." She went a step further in a letter to Russell and Jeri in which she appeared to attribute her criminal conduct to her bad luck with partners.

Dana cast herself as a tragic figure in a relationship with Jim, dramatically questioning why he didn't stop her from "slipping through the cracks," and, in essence, save her from herself. Nobody noticed . . . "Did I make myself yet another bad choice [sic] in men?" Dana, in a letter to another nursing friend, didn't mention Jim's conduct, but instead engaged in another profane rant about Tom obtaining a temporary restraining order against her, which appeared to grind her nose in the fact that she was behind bars and he was not. She seethed over the restraining order: "Does he think I can get out of here soon?" Dana asked if they would pass a message to Tom: "FUCK OFF TOM!!! Leave me alone forever, O.K.?" At the end of the letter, Dana jotted down that she had been reading and painting, and was feeling "a little down" and apologized for "going off on you."

Dana continued to correspond with Jim and Indio, accentuating the transition between her old life and her new life. To Jim, she vacillated between romancing him back into the fold and vilifying him for dropping her at the most vulnerable time in her life. ". . . You certainly made my day by dumping me over the phone. It's not like I'm totally stressing over very much right now. What's one more crisis? Well I hope you don't close the door all the way . . ." To Indio, Dana was animated and flirtatious, and pumped her letters full of jailhouse lingo.

On Wednesday, April 27, Dana was moved to a hospital isolation cell on the seventh floor. Dana now had her own TV, her own shower, a window, a desk and increased phone access—but no contact with inmates other than the trustees who delivered her food trays. She also had rec time in an exercise room but was still alone there. Dana was reduced to asking the guards if they wanted to play Ping-Pong. They declined.

Dana wrote to three other inmates she'd made friends with in protective custody, Linda, Betty and Susan, let them know where she was and offered words of support to them. In contrast to her constant barrage about the poor diet to her father, Jeri, Don, Lisa, Joanie, her personal doctor, and everyone else on the outside, she had a different kind of complaint to her inmate pals: "Their commisary up here is different and doesn't have any women's products or chips & candy! EEK! So I requested the 6th floor comm slips, what will I do without my Fritos and pretzels? And no M & M's? Aren't I a whiner?"

Dana gloated over having her own shower—"No waiting!"—which was modified for handicapped people, allowing her to sit while she shaved her legs, but she was clearly stung from being isolated: "There's a notice on my door that I'm not to have any inmate contact. Makes me feel like I have cooties." If moving to lockdown offered Dana an opportunity to reflect on her actions, the object lesson was lost on her as she busied herself with learning to make jailhouse foundation make-up using talcum powder and hounded the watch sergeant for a mirror because her cell had none.

"[The sergeant] said to me, 'This isn't a hotel!' I know that, but basics are basics and a mirror is a basic. I'd like to be able to put make-up on right and pluck my eyebrows. I made some face base like Sheree' but made it too dark so

I'll have to wait till Mon commissary to get more lotion to thin it out . . ."

Pounding out letters to pass the time, Dana wrote to Indio and Jim, her day room buddies and friends on the outside. To childhood friend Carrie Ann, Dana finger-pointed at both Tom and Jim for ignoring her downward spiral and pleaded with her to act as her ambassador to Jim to convince him to come back to her.

"I have faith in you . . . I know you'll touch his heart somehow. You'll find a way though his ice-maze. I'm preparing myself too for our truthfulness and your saying to forget him . . .

"I have a real talent for choosing men that use me."

CHAPTER SIXTEEN

WEDNESDAY, MAY 25, 1994, 10 A.M

The gardeners were on lunch break, sprawled on a grassy area in the condo complex.

"Excuse me."

Greco had been hoping they'd be there. He walked over to where they lay on the grass with sack lunches and a couple of small coolers between them. They were within eyesight of Norma's condo on Continental Way, in the picnic area next to the guest parking. He couldn't have asked for better timing. He was doing door-knocks in the neighborhood to see if he could find anyone who'd been around and might have seen something on Monday, the day Norma was killed. Greco had wanted to talk to the gardeners who were working in the neighborhood that day. He remembered seeing them curiously looking over at the condo when he got there Wednesday morning, the day the body was discovered.

"I'm Detective Greco with the Perris Police Department," he said, holding out his badge. "I was wondering if you could help me with something. Do you have a minute?"

Greco didn't want to tell them he was investigating a homicide. Sometimes potential witnesses will offer dubious information or shy away from answering questions completely because they are afraid of getting involved with a murder case.

There were five men, most of whom spoke Spanish but very little English. The youngest worker, 17-year-old Gustavo Lopez, was fluent in English and agreed to translate for Greco as he interviewed them individually. Through Gustavo, foreman Concepcion Limon said they were hired by the city of Canyon Lake to keep up the premises and perform sprinkler and pool maintenance. On Mondays, two of them—Jesus Limon and Gustavo Lopez—worked on the sprinklers and pools. First Greco showed each worker a photo of Dana's brown Cadillac, but it didn't register. Then Greco pulled out a photo of Dana with blonde hair.

"Yeah, yeah, I remember this woman," Gustavo said immediately.

Greco was elated but also a little surprised. He hadn't even asked a question but Gustavo was so certain, he was nodding his head emphatically and showing the photo to his father, who also a groundskeeper. Even though they spoke in Spanish, it seemed obvious to Greco that Gustavo was trying to prod his father's memory about seeing the woman, but the older man shook his head.

"What do you remember?" Greco asked Gustavo.

"Well, it was a few months ago. I remember she was walking around over there," Gustavo said, waving his hand. From where they were sitting, Norma's condo was down the U-shaped street to the left.

"What was she doing?" Greco asked.

"She was just wandering around," Gustavo said. "It was like she was in a daze. She had a blank look on her face. It was weird—like she wasn't there. I was looking at her because I thought maybe she was sick or something and because of the funny look on her face. I thought she needed help.

"I went over and asked her if she was OK and if she needed help but she just brushed me off."

"You talked to her?" Greco couldn't believe it.

"Yeah," he said. "She just said, 'No, no, I'm OK.' That was it."

"Did you see where she went?" Greco asked.

"No, I just went back to work," he said. "When I looked up again, she was gone."

Gustavo couldn't fix the time he'd seen her, so it would be impossible to tell whether it was before or after Dana had killed Norma. Greco's mind was racing through the possible scenarios. Was she pumping herself up to go in and murder Norma? Or had she just killed Norma and was looking around to see if anyone could identify her? Greco thought that Dana had parked her car on the street, as opposed to the U-shaped driveway area, which would explain why the workers didn't recognize it. Maybe she had killed Norma, then paced the grounds a bit as she made her way back to her car. Perhaps Dana was looking around to see if she had left anything behind that would identify her, or was hesitating as she contemplated going back inside the condo for some reason.

Gustavo recalled that she had on a flowered print shirt or dress. He also recalled that she "wasn't skinny," but had a sturdy build. When asked if he could narrow down the date he saw the woman in the photo, Gustavo said he was positive it was a Monday because he was working on the sprinklers. The closest he could get to the date was that it was several months ago.

Greco asked Gustavo again if he was sure about the identity of the woman. Did the photo accurately depict the woman he had seen?

"The woman and the picture are one and the same," Gustavo said.

This is going to do it, Greco thought. Although he was ecstatic, he fought to keep a straight face as he collected their contact information and thanked them for their time. He continued knocking on doors in the neighborhood, but found no one who had seen anything. Although Greco didn't mention Norma's murder, several people knew it was his reason for canvassing the neighborhood and invited Greco into their homes so they could question him. Greco obliged them because he knew the neighbors were curious and he wanted to reassure them that the killer was in custody and he was simply wrapping up loose ends. It was dark by the time he finished the interviews and left the quiet Canyon Lake neighborhood.

Greco would call Bentley in the morning. He couldn't wait to let him know that a groundskeeper had placed Dana at the scene. The local DOJ criminalist had compared the dusty shoeprint lifted from Norma's entryway with the Nike shoe taken from Dana's house and come to the conclusion that the same brand of Nike had indeed made the print in the dust—but there were no individual markings, like wear marks or cuts in the sole that could identify that shoe and that shoe alone as the one that made the print in Norma's entryway. In the rush to comply with the statutory forty-eight-hour deadline, Bentley didn't feel comfortable filing the charge for Norma's murder because there were no credit cards or bankbooks connecting Dana to it, and the criminalists, of course, had not yet examined the shoeprint. Placing Dana at the scene with a live witness might give Bentley enough evidence to file the murder count, Greco thought.

So far, the cases were shaping up. Detective Mason Yeo, the sheriff's department detective who was at the Perris station the night Dana was arrested, had been collecting the checks, store receipts, bank records, and other paperwork needed to establish the timelines for the murders and for examining the handwriting. Meanwhile, Ora Brimer, the elderly owner of the antique store where Dorinda was attacked, went to pick up some photos at a Photomat kiosk and was told by the clerk in passing that Dana had left four rolls of film there to be developed. The clerk didn't know what to do with them because Dana had been arrested. Brimer called Detective Rene Rodriguez, who had investigated the attack on Dorinda, and got a search warrant for the photos. The snapshots, taken around Christmas, showed Dana—as a blonde—unpacking Christmas decorations from a big box and decorating a Christmas tree with Jason and his stepsister. They also showed Dana playing on the sofa with Jason and her chocolate lab, Bosco, and bathing Penny, her white and black Queensland Healer puppy, in the bathtub. Rodriguez forwarded copies of the photos to Greco and the other detectives so they could show them to the store clerks to ID Dana.

Evidence taken from Dana's house, as well as from the crime scenes, was routed primarily to the DOJ lab, where it was sorted, catalogued and stored. Some of the evidence remained with either the Perris police or the sheriff's department.

Greco and Antoniadas were getting regular lab reports from the criminalists, but there were no breaks. No blood was found on any of the ropes from Dana's car or house. None of the items collected from the crime scenes had clear, identifiable fingerprints. Although it wasn't surprising, it was disappointing. Greco had been hoping for a palm print or a thumb print from the handle of the glass bottle used to hit June. There were also no palm prints on the iron used on Dora, but since the iron was found in the sink, it was obvious that it had been rinsed off, if not wiped off. Dana was either very careful or had worn gloves. Because of the volume of hair collected at the various crime scenes, the criminalists were continuing to catalog and compare the hairs and fibers collected at the crime scenes with those of the victims, with Dana's and with those of the animals in the various households.

Detective Rodriguez had taken the soft, coiled key ring found hanging from Dana's entertainment center to the antique store, where it unlocked the display case and the cash register. He also showed the collection of ropes from Dana's house and car to Dorinda, but she said that none if them resembled the rope used on her, including the rope separating the framing area from the rest of the store.

Sheriff's detectives searched the empty Canyon Lake house that Dana had shared with Tom on Ketch Avenue, but it stored only a few boxes of cookbooks, cookware and old clothing. Antoniadas thought that Dana might have ducked into that house to change clothing or to stash rope or gloves, but there was nothing with visible blood on it. Another search was made of the boat sold to Dana and Tom by Jeri, which Jeri said she was never paid for anyway. The police confiscated some rope, but nothing else of evidentiary value.

A Riverside detective fluent in Spanish was assigned to interview Gustavo and the other workers to see if he could get any more details. Gustavo again identified Dana from the photograph. The detective asked if he remembered when the body was discovered and Gustavo recalled that it was a Wednesday because on Wednesdays, they worked on lawn maintenance in that area. In relation to the time the body was discovered, the detective asked when he recalled seeing the dazed, blonde woman. This time, Gustavo said it was the Monday prior to the body's discovery. He said he was able to place the time at about 10:30 or 11 a.m., based on the type of work he was doing as well as the fact that they knew that Norma played cards every afternoon, at the time he saw the blonde woman, Norma would have been alone in the house. Later, he recognized the woman who discovered the body, Alice Williams, as someone with whom Norma played cards.

After speaking with Greco, he remembered exactly where the blonde woman was walking. The detective asked if he would show him. Gustavo took the detective over to the U-shaped driveway off Continental Way and walked right up to Norma's condo.

"Here," Gustavo said, standing in front of the postage stamp–sized front lawn. "This is the path she took."

Busted during the weekly cell searches for having a rubber band wrapped around her *People* magazine—"my channel changer"—and a razor blade secreted in the back of her TV, Dana moaned to Indio, "What am I supposed to do with a rubber band? So now if I get another one, do I have to hide it? How stupid!" The television set was mounted so high on the wall, she had to reach up and use a pencil rolled up in a magazine to change the channel. She claimed the razor blade was left there by the previous occupant of the cell. "This is not a good day. I'm going to take a shower to cool off. But what I really need is a hug." Being in isolation with an orange plastic "parakeet band" around her wrist signifying her status in the keep-away ward, Dana demonstrated a masterful array of personas in her letters. She was a saucy flirt with Indio; a remorseful, devoted girlfriend to Jim; demanding and pushy, but full of loving thoughts to her father, and mostly upbeat with touches of wistful loneliness with her friends. A distinction became clear in her letters depending on whether the recipients were in custody or "on the outs." She took advantage of that, particularly in the poem "Contraband Dreams," written and sent to her by Indio. Dana immediately claimed it as her own, knowing that her worlds inside and outside bars would never blend, and that inmates confined to the same institution rarely cross paths.

In solitary confinement, the mail surged in importance for Dana as she wrote up to four and five letters a day and urged her new pen pal, Indio, to write. He, in turn, wrote tender letters 12 pages long and more, caressing with words the woman he was inspired to write to after gazing at her photo in the newspaper. The unspoken rule was to avoid

discussing your case—with anyone—and they held fast to
that. Dana underscored that point to Indio and her other
friends by saying that other inmates who got to know her
for a few days before seeing the news articles would have
been against her if they had read the articles first. Since
Dana was committed to lockdown twice within the first
month, and afterward banished to solitary confinement for,
in Dana's own words, not getting along with her fellow
cellies, one wonders if such exchanges even occurred or if
they were a fiction created to reassure a potential suitor and
friends inside and outside jailhouse doors.

The letters read like diaries that chronicled the monotony,
the spats, the despair and the indignities of life behind bars.
With no work to rush off to, no meals to prepare, no children
to tend and no other distractions, writing letters became an
end unto itself, where time was measured in increments of
waiting for the next sliver of paper to get shoved underneath
the cell door. From souls scarred by street life and violence
and hardened from cycling in and out of jail, heartfelt inti-
macies spilled onto painstakingly handwritten letters, some
in the crookedest scrawls, searching for romance on lined
sheets of college rule. To most, it was an inside joke. Inmate
courtship-by-letter was merely an escape from wasted days
and lonely nights that was shed when they were released or
sent to prison. Dana, pining for release, knew full well that
she would never "kick it" on the outside with a heavily
tattooed, 39-year-old Hispanic drug dealer who had been in
and out of prison his entire adult life. But the exchange was
even. Indio's intention, like that of any other inmate, was
simply to do his time.

Many of Dana's letters included cartoons, articles, Bible
verses and poetry, but they revealed much about Dana when
she not only claimed to have authored Indio's poem "Contraband Dreams," but "dedicated" it to Jim and, on top of
that, tacked on a copyright symbol.

Dana mailed the poem to a half-dozen other people,
mostly on the outside. Being in her cell 23 1/2 hours a day,
Dana had little to occupy her time besides reading, sleeping,
and watching television to drown out the twenty-four-hour
piped-in country western music. She told Jim that watching
an Oprah episode featuring low-fat recipes brought her to

tears because she longed for doing "normal" things like cooking him and Jason dinner. Other times, she said she used TV to escape: "I forget where I am and escape into the program." To inmates she'd left behind on the lower floors, she bragged about niceties, like being able to sit on her bunk and use the phone in peace and quiet and not have to wait to use the communal phones in the day rooms. She wrote to the state unemployment office to appeal the fact that they turned her down for unemployment; to the State Labor Commission for the same appeal; to the Department of Consumer Affairs, Board of Nursing to update her file to include her divorce, changing her name from Gray back to Armbrust, and a request for them to send a list of approved correspondence courses. In response to her request, Dana got Bibles from her friends, and completed a lengthy questionnaire from the prison ministries, signing her name and dating a form to document her conversion as a born-again Christian so she could receive Bible studies through a correspondence course. She continued to coordinate the storage, sale and interminable rearranging of her personal items between Jim and her father. In preparation for her trial, which Dana believed was just around the corner, she directed Jim to take her "nice, hang-up clothing" from his closet as well as from Jason's closet, which apparently she had also used to store her clothing, and requested Polaroids of her shoes so she could select complete outfits to wear to court. She asked Jim to put her "special sunglasses," her clown poster from Sweden and her art portfolio somewhere safe. She successfully "sold" her silk-screening equipment to Jim for $3,000 without money ever changing hands and directed Jeri to auction her antique player piano, which had an appraised worth of $2,500, and her wedding ring, which was valued at $3,700. With the TV as her sole companion, Dana asked for subscriptions to two magazines: *People* and *TV Guide*.

Having heard a tidbit about Social Security Income, Dana implored her father and Jeri to get her an application so she could receive the checks, believing that stating she is an alcoholic qualified her for the program, even though someone else would have to receive the payments. She continued to pester her father to write a letter to the jail requesting a vegetarian diet. "I feel physically ill and need it. I am continuing to throw up on this regular diet they are sending me. Other people here got court orders for veg diets I should be able to also! For example today all I've eaten is: 1 cheese sandwich, 1 apple, mashed potatoes, milk. No salad, no real veges!" Being in isolation prevented her from trading food from her tray with other inmates.

Dana's father and Jeri sent Dana "keep busy" material to amuse her while she was in isolation: a deck of cards and a book, *255 Ways to Play Solitaire*.

As she approached a month and a half behind bars, some of Dana's friends—and old flames—contacted her. Rob Beaudry, her first longtime boyfriend, now married and a commercial pilot living in Northern California, wrote and Dana filled him in with her current propaganda. This time, she explained, she was in isolation because "they feel an inmate headed for state prison may try to make a name for themselves and stab me. All because of the press! I truly despise the media more than ever. Pump the negative. Ignore the truth." She had harsh words for her brother Rick: "My psycho brother Rick wasted no time jumping into the lime light. Someone ought to take him to the vet for a doggie good-nite shot. He makes me sick." Sky-diving friends she had not seen for many years came out of the woodwork to visit, write letters and express sympathy and shock at finding the beautiful, intrepid adventuress and queen of snappy comebacks behind bars. A surprise for Dana was finding another sky-diver also behind bars 250 miles to the north in San Luis Obispo County. When a mutual friend tracked him down, Dana wrote a letter expressing delight that one of their friends was showing support by visiting and writing cheerful letters. Dana cleverly created an atmosphere of kinship when there was none before. "You know, we were never that close. So her love and support is a surprise but very welcome. Gary, we come from such a special era '70s skydiviving' and there are only a handful of us left. I feel the bond is such that no matter what, we should keep the home fires lit." She revealed that in her association with Rob, he'd talked her into ending two pregnancies, for which she never forgave him and chose not to marry him. "I wanted children—he didn't and that would have come between us eventually. Now I regret not keeping one of those babies."

As Dana's relationship with Indio grew, Dana claimed to be perplexed by her break-up with Jim and portrayed herself in the most favorable light: "You know, I'm probably one of the easiest women to get along with. I'm very sporty and adventuresome. I cannot understand this man one bit. If the tables were turned, I'd sure as hell be here seeing him and trying to figure out what happened and how I could help. I love him that much, even as a friend . . ."

When Indio sent her a photo of himself—with tattoo-covered arms and long, straight black hair—Dana supplied him with a flattering verbal self-portrait and dropped hints about creating a relationship. "I'm a 36 yr old little girl wth a broken heart lost in a system that's hell bent to destroy her. I'm vulnerable and I think you know that. I like you alot and you're way sweet to me. Handle me with care, okay? That's all I ask. Mutual respect, and tenderness . . ." In a later letter, Dana ripped into him with a preachy lecture about his lifestyle of drug abuse that had put him behind bars for much of his adult life, a curious turnabout for Dana, who blamed alcohol abuse for her downward spiral and fought a drug habit in the months leading to her dismissal from the hospital. Dana constantly reminded Indio that she was "for real" and was completely open with him, but she apparently decided not to clue him in on her own substance abuse. "I guess I just have to face it—Drugs are your sport . . . There's so much more to life Indio—but if you want to pickle yourself through it—then that's your decision. I'd never be party to it though."

She admitted finding it a relief to vent to him because he was a repeat customer of county jail. "My family and friends do their best to understand—but they don't really have a clue—you do. I must admit, I don't understand how you spent so much time in this system." Dana wrote to her other friends that she enjoyed passing the time by exchanging letters with her friend, and taunted him in the same manner that someone would play with a toy just to see what it can do. "I re-named him 'Kimo' short for 'Kimosabe.' (The Indian of *The Lone Ranger*.) He sent me a photo and I swear he looks like an Indian. Long black hair to his waist, and that Aztec Indian face. He hasn't acknowledged his new name yet so I know it erks him—but he's a man and he'll get over it soon. They usuallly do right? HA HA HA."

When Indio initiated a more intimate form of expression by way of exchanging "fantasies," Dana put her foot down and said she was not into "smut." But it was only a matter of time before Dana succumbed to Indio's advances and she soon became quite skilled at risque exchanges by mail and, later, full-blown sexual fantasies with other inmates.

Dana bemoaned the spotlight as a celebrity defendant, but while she said being in that role wounded her, she clearly took advantage of the intimidation factor inherent in being an accused serial killer. A young woman who'd read about Dana's case in the newspaper wrote to Dana asking rather innocuous questions about her arrest and the placement of her dogs when she was jailed. Dana fired off a quick letter asking her to come for a visit and ask her the same questions to her face. To Carrie Ann, Dana joked about the "dumb" questions and "weird mail" she received, admitting that a letter from this woman had disturbed her. "I refuse to answer strange mail anyway—but this one fried me. So I told her to come see me and ask those same questions to my face. That'll freak her out. Hopefully will shut her up." She sent Carrie Ann a handwritten copy of "Contraband Dreams" in the same letter. To Lisa Sloan, Dana said the same letter made her feel "like a side show. She wrote me a letter that was kind of insulting." Dana wrote out a copy of "Contraband Dreams" to Lisa, too. She complained about getting time in the recreation room at the ungodly hour of 6:30 a.m., but took advantage of the stationary bike and leg machine, then got her first drink of coffee since her confinement which gave her "a buzz. If I had a drink, I'd probably pass out." With a melancholy tone, she told Jim that from her cell window, she had an unobstructed view of the seventh floor and located his house. She gave him a romantic picture of the soft, spring evening with clear skies and "the clouds right on top of the range." Because she was surrounded by buildings downtown, she described watching the sun go down from a reflection in the widepaned glass of the County Administration Center.

When Dana finally got a vegetarian diet, she told Indio

that she was eating too much and needed to lay off the chips so she wouldn't gain weight. "I'm drinking coffee again now that I get a good diet . . . I don't eat much because my metabolism is down from lack of exercise (aerobic) but what I eat is good. My face cleared up and I feel generally good . . . as one can expect here at the County Inn."

Her plan to keep her weight down was temporarily foiled when her next-door neighbor, an inmate by the name of Bill Suff, gave Dana two packages of nutty fudge cookies. A long-time resident of the jail, Bill used his subscriptions to *People* and *TV Guide* to write out a weekly movie schedule for her. She recruited Indio to dig up the story on Bill. "I know his case is serious—but not sure about details and there's no way in hell I'm gonna ask—so try and find out for me. My dad about freaked when I told him who my neighbor was. I told him relax—we rarely ever actually see each other. I've only seen him twice in transport. The creepy thing is, he kind of looks like John Wayne Gacy's California cousin. EEEK!" Dana eventually learned that she and Bill had a lot in common: They were both accused serial killers. Bill had been a resident of the county jail for 2½ years awaiting trial on charges of murdering twelve prostitutes in the Riverside area and mutilating two of them by slicing off their breasts, which were never recovered. Dana found that Bill was also in solitary confinement in the adjoining cell and was so lonely that he was writing two novels and a cookbook. Dana and Bill struck up a friendship formed around their common interest in cooking. Because they could not see one another, Dana summoned Bill by pushing the cigarette lighter button. When the jail was first built in 1990, the cells were outfitted with electrical cigarette lighters similar to those found in cars, except that one had to insert the cigarette in order to light it. It wasn't long before smoking was banned in the jail and the lighters were disabled. Clever inmates found ways to wire the lighters to deliver electrical shocks. The disabled lighters in the cell Dana occupied still made a clicking noise which Bill was able to hear, and he would come to the wicket, the wide, narrow slot in the cell where the food trays slide in. She called the cigarette lighter her call button for Bill.

Dana did not know that Bill had been a county employee

for many years and had traditionally participated in the annual chili cook-off, including the year the serial homicides occurred. That year, as always, sheriff's detectives and DA investigators, along with other employees, attended the event and tasted most of the concoctions in the finals, including Bill's, which was unanimously declared the winner for its tender meat and unusual flavor. It wasn't until weeks after his arrest that some of the detectives began to wonder about the ingredients in his chili, leaving some to wonder whether he had slipped breast tissue from his victims into his blue ribbon chili.

To Dana, Bill was just another person with whom to pass the time. One wonders whether it was mere coincidence that the two were housed smack next to one another or if jail authorities had a macabre sense of humor. Dana reported hearing part of a joking remark from a snickering guard: "I heard one of them say they put us together so we could mate and make . . . I didn't catch the rest—but I'm sure Suff heard it too. What complete assholes! Just goes to prove the mentality we're often spoke of. Most of the deputies are nice up here and polite—but every now and then we get a real weenie patrol."

She and Bill shared a love of horror novels and exchanged Dean Koontz books. Despite their proximity, they were not allowed direct contact, so all of their correspondence went through the mail.

With access to a phone in her cell and no competition from other inmates, Dana patched things with Jim, even though she knew the relationship was doomed. She declared her love for him and hinted about a proposal, coming up with the novel idea that they use this time as a courtship because they hadn't dated before she left Tom for Jim. She told Jim that he had all she had ever wanted in a man, "but I was too fucked up to deal with it." Dana said she realized that she had tossed aside their relationship for "a long road of hell and heartache," but insisted that she would come around and was completely in love with him and wanted to be with him forever. "I'd asked you to marry me if I thought you would." After sending "Contraband Dreams" around to all her friends, Dana finally sent Jim the poem she "dedicated" to him.

The longer Dana was in custody, the more her inmate friends were getting released after serving their time. She wrote a cheerful good-bye to a friend, putting the best face on her situation. "Dig this—they installed a pay phone *in* my room. Now all I need is a mirror and an appointment for a color weave & cut and I'll be stylin. Of course Rec time would be nice. When I told Jim they put a phone in my room, he asked me if they got tired of my shit. (I can nag.)"

After her May 20 appearance in court, her lawyer told her that her preliminary hearing wouldn't come for several weeks and her trial was not likely to occur that year. Dana realized that she wouldn't get any quicker results than from a private attorney and geared up for a longer stay in jail.

The weeks in jail didn't dampen her desire for her beauty treatments. She thought up a cockamamie scheme to somehow convince a top stylist from a nationally prominent, celebrity-studded Beverly Hills salon to drive 60 miles out to the decidedly un-hip county of Riverside to give her a haircut. "I'm gonna write the Jose Eber Salon and try to get someone out to cut my hair—I need it badly." Sponge rollers and styling gel weren't doing much good because she didn't have a mirror to properly curl her hair. Dana also wanted a cut and color. The sergeant had promised to get her a mirror but the least they could do, she wrote, was "let me have a contact visit to get my hair cut."

As time went by, her coterie of outside supporters dwindled and her in-custody cast of characters—and lingo—grew. There was Cha Chi, Killer, Snake Woman, Smokie and Pork Chop, who got into a fight with another inmate. "Hey how's it girl? Heard you and Alicia had a dance? What's up with that? Things are fine up here. No complaints. Just lonely. Write me about your dance and lockdown and I'll write you back . . ." In the meantime, Dana lost another "outside" friend, but tried to buckle down on the ones who remained while blaming it all on her alcoholism. "Can you imagine being *so* damn down that you can't help yourself?" Dana was careful to keep the relationship taut around her, making it clear that a "certain few" would be among the trusted, loyal friends in her inner circle, as if entrée were a privilege, and warned that their bond would be tested. "It is only gonna get uglier, Juli, and I need a certain few to count on—I can see how you will be one of those certain few." Dana noted that her support group should keep in close touch with one another and asked Juli to write or call Jim and her parents and tell them how much they meant to her.

She discussed books, movies and her bad marriage with her outside friends, but with inmates buddies, she was hungry for gossip on the floors below her—who was also in lockdown, who was talking about her case in the day room, how to sweet-talk the guards into sharpening the pencil nubs they left outside their cells and euphoria over scoring a new bra on their weekly clothing exchange. While she was on the seventh floor, Dana bragged about how the male inmates across the pod lined up in their cells to wave and steal a glimpse at their high-profile female neighbor when she went to her cell door to get her daily dose of Motrin.

Inspired by Indio's poetry and Bill Suff's ambitions to write books, Dana also decided to write a book about being in jail from a women's standpoint titled "Beneath Still Waters," inspired by her favorite Emmylou Harris song: "Beneath still waters there's a strong undertow ... the words are perfect, wish I could still remember them all."

THURSDAY, MAY 26, 1994, 10:30 A.M.

Tom nervously fingered the $100 bills in his pocket as he sat waiting for Dana to show up in court. Today they were supposed to settle the divorce. The court attendant told him it would take a little longer for Dana to arrive because the deputies typically transport the vast majority of in-custody defendants to criminal court first. Since very few have to go to civil court, they arrive later. From what he'd been hearing from Russell and Jim, he knew that Dana was not going to be that happy to see him. He'd brought $1,000 in cash with him hoping that it would, in part, help to convince her to settle with him. Dana had completely wiped him out financially with her spending and he had hoped to sell a couple of pieces of equipment to settle things up, but, through Jim, she put her foot down. He was leery of visiting her in jail, so his lawyer volunteered to see her the night before with a proposed property settlement that he thought was fair. But once Dana found out who it was on the other side of the visitors' glass, she stormed off. Tom came by himself to court, bringing only the proposed settlement with him and wondering what he was going to have to do to get her to sign it. He thought a cash-for-equipment deal might work.

Tom had been confused about why they weren't divorced earlier in the year. He had been expecting dissolution paperwork in January but it never came. He got a chill when he thought about his decision to skip their meeting on February 14. That was the day, he later learned from the newspaper, that Norma Davis was murdered. He was supposed to have met Dana that morning. Maybe if he had met her, Norma might not have been killed. But Tom couldn't help but wonder if he was the intended victim. After Dana's arrest, he wondered why their divorce paperwork hadn't gone through in mid-January like it was supposed to. When he looked at their court file for the divorce, he found that Dana had filed two documents. One paper delayed the divorce, extending the marriage by six months. The second paper gave him a chill. It was an insurance policy. When he read it carefully, he found a clause in it stating that if one of them was to die, the policy would completely pay off the Canyon Lake home and it would belong to the surviving spouse.

Tom couldn't believe it. He didn't want to believe that Dana would have killed him. A part of him could not believe that she had done what she was accused of, but another part of him knew that she was capable of violence. There was another strong part of him that still loved Dana. He didn't know if he could ever stop loving the sassy, hippie girl he fell for in seventh grade.

The rattling chains startled him. Looking up, he saw a thinned-down woman with reddish-brown hair in a blue jail jumpsuit being led by two deputies into the courtroom, her hands cuffed to a chain around her waist, her ankles shackled. He saw her eyes harden when she saw him. It was a family law courtroom, commonly referred to as divorce court. It was not set up for criminal cases, so the deputies brought her to the counsel table a few feet from Tom and stood nearby as the judge called the case. Tom felt a lump in his throat. Seeing Dana in her jail clothes brought the reality of the murders and her criminal case right under his nose. He was devastated. He hadn't seen her in months before her arrest. He was trying not to stare, but he couldn't keep his eyes off the inmate who used to be his beautiful, sky-diving, windsurfing, devil-may-care wife, whose smart mouth used to set his pants on fire. How could she have done this to herself? To her family? To him? To her victims?

Before the judge, Dana vehemently protested signing the property settlement that Tom put before her, and demanded the Cadillac and the silk-screening equipment. Tom found it hard to speak. They were at an impasse. The judge calmly addressed them and offered them a counsel table and chairs in her courtroom after she had finished with the rest of her cases so they could sit down and work out an agreement. In remarks directed primarily to Tom, the judge diplomatically suggested that, given the gravity of Dana's case, it would be a very, very long time before the two of them had another opportunity to resolve these issues one-on-one and suggested that they leave court that day with a signed agreement. Tom took the hint and within the hour, when the judge completed her calendar for the day, he was sitting face-to-face with Dana.

Trembling, he felt his anger rise. He was angry for how she'd spent every last dime they had, building a mountain of debt and then blaming him for it. He was angry that she chose to hurt him when she was hurting, instead of talking things out. He was angry that instead of resolving her own pain, she chose to kill, lashing out at innocent victims, just as she had lashed out at him. He was angry that she wouldn't let go of the things they'd bought together—the music and the silk-screening equipment—and wanted to use the material remnants of their life together as a means of striking out at him. He was angry that despite everything, he still loved her.

Tom couldn't get over the fact that he was sitting across the table from her. There was so much that he wanted to say. It would be easier to talk business first. Under the watchful eye of the deputies, they negotiated for a while and finally worked out a settlement in which Tom paid Dana $2,600 in exchange for the music and silk-screening equipment. When the paperwork had been signed, he knew it was time to go, but he couldn't leave without saying something, without finding out if she realized how her actions had affected everyone around her. The hard part was that he couldn't help looking at her. He knew that it might be a very long time before he ever saw her this close, face to face, again.

"Do you realize how many people you've hurt by what you've done?" he finally blurted out.

She looked at him, her ice-blue eyes frosty.

"I didn't kill anybody," Dana said.

"And if I did," she said, dropping her voice to a whisper, "it would have been you."

CHAPTER SEVENTEEN

WEDNESDAY, APRIL 12, 1995, 12 P.M.

"Do you know why I'm here?" the psychiatrist asked.

Dr. Martha Rogers wanted to put her subject at ease. Dana, sitting across the table from the short, stocky psychiatrist, seemed anxious. They sat in an interview room at the jail, separated by a desk. When the psychiatrist arrived, the guard had insisted that a deputy be posted nearby because, the deputy warned, Dana had a history of assaulting staff members, but Dr. Rogers thought the presence of a deputy would inhibit Dana during their session. The deputy finally agreed to a compromise—that a guard could watch them from just outside the interview room through the glass-paneled door.

"To test me to see if I am really crazy, I guess. Nobody has sat down and said, 'This is what we are looking for,' " Dana said, breaking into tears. "It was so hard for me to change my plea. It took me almost a year to decide to change my plea because it took me that long to come to grips to understand a lot of what happened."

On March 10, 1995, Dana went to court, withdrew her "not guilty" plea and pleaded "not guilty by reason of insanity," which means that, under California law, a defendant was "incapable of understanding the nature and quality of their acts" and could not distinguish right from wrong when the crime was committed. The psychiatrist was well aware that the insanity plea was not the sole source of Dana's distress. Most of Dana's anxiety came from the legal notice, filed by prosecutor Rich Bentley several months before, informing the defense that he intended to seek the death penalty. Anything she said to Dr. Rogers would be used in court before jurors who would decide whether she was guilty, whether she was insane and whether she deserved to die.

An insanity plea would add another layer to a criminal trial. The first part of her trial would be staged like any other trial where evidence about the crimes would be presented to a jury, which would render a verdict of guilty or not guilty. If she were to be found guilty, the defense would carry the burden of proving that Dana was insane during the commission of the crimes. The same jury would deliberate a second time to reach a verdict regarding her sanity. If the jury were to find that she was insane, Dana would be sent to a state mental hospital, which would have the authority to release an inmate back into society once they found that the inmate's sanity had been restored.

But if the jury were to find that she was sane, the trial would enter the third phase, where the prosecution would try to convince jurors to recommend the death penalty, and the defense would present more evidence in the hope that jurors would recommend a sentence of life in prison without possibility of parole. In this phase, the prosecution would highlight the egregiousness of her acts, bring relatives of the victims, and introduce her record of misbehavior in jail, illustrating that her violent tendencies continued after her garrest. The defense would undoubtedly describe her productive life helping people as a nurse, and Dana's family and friends could testify in an effort to convince jurors to spare her life.

Dana's lawyer first suggested an insanity defense shortly after her arrest, but Dana resisted. As the months wore on and she reflected on being emotionally whipsawed by an unhappy marriage, alcoholism and drug abuse, multiple miscarriages, bankruptcy and joblessness, an insanity defense made sense to her. Who wouldn't be pushed against the wall by these psychological landmines? In preparation for a possible insanity defense, Stuart Sachs had hired a psychiatrist a few weeks after Dana's arrest to conduct a full psychological examination.

Bentley had been waiting for an insanity defense. He had tried to get a psychiatrist to interview Dana the night she was arrested, but once she invoked, he was legally prevented from having an expert examine her. He knew that Sachs had very little to work with in mounting a defense. Dana was using the victims' credit cards and checks within minutes of the murders, clerks and cashiers identified her and were backed up by handwriting comparison, and all the merchandise from the stores was found at Dana's house. Dorinda also identified Dana, and her eyewitness testimony was backed up by the fact that the antique-store keys were hanging on a hook on Dana's entertainment center. Bentley had wanted to file charges against Dana for the Norma Davis murder, but if he had, it would have slowed the entire case, since she would have had to be separately arraigned on that sole charge, and she would be entitled to a preliminary hearing before it could be consolidated with the other charges. But he was planning to present evidence of Norma's murder under a section of the penal code allowing the introduction of evidence of similar crimes—type of victim, time of day the murders occurred, relationship of the victim to the accused, choice of weapon, etc.—to show continuity in the violent conduct of a defendant. He also intended to use the Davis murder in the penalty phase of the trial.

Insanity cases could be a nightmare for the prosecution, depending on the willingness of a jury to believe the experts. If Dana were to be found insane, she could go to a mental hospital and be released in a matter of months if one of the hospital psychiatrists found her to be sane. Then she would be released back into the community. In the two insanity cases he'd tried, Bentley was prevented by law from warning jurors in his closing argument that if they found a defendant insane, they could look for that person haunting their neighborhoods in a few years. Bentley also knew that Riverside County jurors didn't like the insanity defense—it was very tough to get an insanity verdict—and he figured Sachs knew that as well.

When Dana changed her plea, Bentley hired Dr. Rogers on behalf of the prosecution and Sachs hired another expert, Dr. Lorna Forbes, for the defense, even though Dr. Michael Kania was about to wrap up his report. By the time Dr. Rogers sat down with Dana in April, Dana had already undergone twenty-five separate sessions over nine months with both Kania and Forbes. Even so, Dr. Rogers did her best to soothe Dana's fears about the exam and answer her questions, explaining that she had been hired by both the defense and the prosecution in the past to examine defendants in

various criminal cases and had, in several cases, found inmates to be insane. Dr. Rogers' charge was to perform a
thorough psychological examination of Dana and submit a
report to the judge containing her opinion on whether Dana
could distinguish right from wrong at the time she killed or
assaulted her victims.

Each of the three experts obtained a full written history
from Dana about her childhood, her parents, her brothers,
and major incidents in her upbringing, her marriage, her
education and her career. Each of the experts interviewed
family members, friends and former co-workers. Each
expert administered a full complement of psychological
tests, including the Wechsler Adult Intelligence Scale, the
Rorschach inkblot test, the Minnesota Multiphasic Personality Inventory, the Personality Assessment Inventory, the
Beck Depression Inventory, the Beck Hopelessness Scale,
and the Thematic Apperception Test, in which the subject
looks at black-and-white drawings and suggests scenarios
they might depict. The written tests, like the Millon Clinical
Multi-Axial Inventory III, includes a series of true or false
questions asking the subject to describe themselves, such as,
"I know I'm a superior person, so I don't care what people
think." "People have never given me enough recognition for
the things I've done." "If my family puts pressure on me,
I'm likely to feel angry and resist doing what they want."
"I often criticize people strongly if they annoy me." "I've
had sad thoughts much of my life since I was a child." "I
am often cross and grouchy." Dana seemed to be in an upbeat or perhaps sarcastic mood when she filled out one of
the forms, listing her occupation as "jailbird." Some of the
questions are patently bizarre, like those in the Structured
Interview of Reported Symptoms, designed to root out dis-
orders like paranoia, psychosis, obsessive-compulsive behavior, multiple personalities and schizophrenia. The
questions must be read by the examiner and start off with a
cluster of inquiries bearing the same prefix: "Do you have
any major problems with . . . people reading your mind? . . .
noticing very strange smells? . . . fighting evil forces?"
"When outside, do you become afraid of things like grass
or flowers?" "Do you often have upsetting sexual thoughts
which bother you only on elevators?" "Is the government

trying to keep track of your actions? Are they using military aircraft to do this?" "Can common insects be used for electronic surveillance?" "Do you believe that trees have supernatural powers?" "Do you have any unusual beliefs about automobiles? Do you believe they have their own religion?"

Dana answered "no" for most of these odd questions, but did agree that she sometimes felt as if she were "physically outside of" her body.

"During the crimes, it was like I was watching myself doing the crime, but it wasn't me, it was like watching a movie with the sound off. There was only a little sound in two of them," Dana said. "If that is out of your body, it's the closest I can describe it."

As part of the evaluation, each of the experts interviewed Dana about the murders and the assault on Dorinda. She was not questioned about killing Norma, since Bentley had not filed that charge against her. In each case, Dana said that the victims provoked her by making comments that made her feel ridiculed and rejected, and when they turned their backs on her, Dana slid a rope around their necks.

"Who was number one?" Dr. Rogers asked.

"June Roberts," Dana said.

"Tell me about that morning."

Dana said that June had been raking when she drove up with Jason in the car, and that June had "started right in with my marriage and divorce," which angered her. She characterized the religious, health-conscious widow as being intensely critical of Dana and her marriage. When they went inside for the vitamin book, Dana claimed that June continued to berate her about her marriage.

"She kept on and on and on about Tom, how I did not do enough, and I lost it. She pushed that final button," Dana said.

"Where were you when that happened?" Dr. Rogers asked.

"Right behind her. I choked her with the phone cord."

"Do you remember wrapping it around anything other than her neck?"

"Oh yeah, that chair. I remember a chair but I don't know

where it came from . . . It just all happened at the same time really fast to me.

"It was like I just . . . I don't know how to describe it any other way than I lost it. I was just so consumed, utterly pushed off the edge . . . it must have been quick. As I walked out, she had a little wallet thing. I grabbed it and left. Then I drove us home."

Dana told the psychiatrist that it wasn't planned and that she was so stunned afterward that she took Jason home, despite receipts showing that she was using June's credit cards within the hour. Dana admitted to the psychiatrist that she'd used June's credit cards, but claimed she was shopping primarily for Jason.

"We went out and proceeded to shop up a storm," Dana said. "I felt a need to get a bunch of stuff for Jason. I spent a lot on him."

Dr. Rogers wanted to zero in on the moment when Dana "lost it."

"She was talking to me face-to-face," Dana said, "then she turned her back on me and just kept getting at me . . . without letting me get a word in edgewise. It was just her non-patience, her demeanor that it was my fault, her judg-mentalness, that look on her face. As she turned around, she had a look of . . . big disappointment, disgust," which Dana said triggered thoughts of unworthiness and rejection. "I was real fragile."

In a subsequent interview, Dr. Rogers again asked Dana what she was thinking when she lost control.

"That I was making my mother shut up," she said. "It just built up—the continuing condescending attitude. 'You are worthless. You failed. I told you so,'" Dana said.

"Did you think she was your mother?" Dr. Rogers asked.

"I was so out of it, so consumed, so enraged, I cannot answer that question right."

"What did you see and hear from the past?"

"Her carping at me. I just wanted to shut her up, that is all. That simple—just shut her up."

Dr. Rogers was the third psychiatrist to interview Dana. The first one, Dr. Michael Kania, reported that Dana at first claimed to have found the credit cards in the trash, then said she couldn't recall assaulting June Roberts. Dana finally admitted killing June, focusing on her anger that June had fetched the wrong vitamin book.

To the second psychiatrist, Dr. Lorna Forbes, Dana said that she became incensed after June lectured Dana while she and Jason sat in the Cadillac. "June said that I didn't work hard enough. My responsibility was to make the marriage work. I was really angry. I should have just left. She wouldn't stop berating me. It was all I could do to control my anger." When June brought out the wrong vitamin book, she said she became explosively angry as she followed June into the house. She told this psychologist that June became "a creepy female image" that reminded Dana of her cancer-stricken mother, making her so nauseated, she wanted to vomit. That's when she reached for the phone cord.

To Dr. Rogers, Dana never mentioned the "creepy female image," downplayed the vitamin book and claimed that June had tapped into her poor self-esteem by taunting her about her marriage. She told each psychiatrist that she went home "stunned," and went shopping after sitting at home for several hours, instead of going out shopping immediately, as the restaurant and store receipts indicated.

Dr. Rogers asked her about the sequence of events and Dana candidly described the sequence of the attack.

"I think I hit her after I used the phone cord. I pulled her down so she was on her back and hit her with the wine bottle . . .

"I really don't have any explanation for my actions, I really don't, but I wish I did."

Dana continued her attack on June verbally, twisting the perspective to make herself the victim.

"I was shocked that June came on to me about Tom and I." June was "snippy . . . She was really weird after Duane died. She turned into a different person." Dana said that when she and her parents had run into June at the clubhouse a few weeks before the murder, she'd "snubbed us off." When Dr. Rogers talked to Russ and Jeri later, both of them said that they could not recall June ever being cool to them, although June naturally was somewhat withdrawn as she mourned the death of her husband.

When asked about Dorinda, even Dana seemed pressed to come up with why she had attacked the antique store clerk. She told Dr. Rogers she wasn't sure what it was about Dorinda, "but she really, really got me. She really bothered me. She reminded me of my mother in her alcoholic stages.

"I don't know if she said anything to provoke me or what, I really don't know. But I ended up choking her with yellow propylene rope."

Dana said that they fought, and recalled Dorinda trying to poke her with a broom, but once Dorinda told her about having eight children, she says she let go. She recalls telling Dorinda to "relax" in the same manner she'd told her mother to "let go" the night she died. Dana said she walked out of the antique store feeling nauseous and thinking, "What the hell have I done?" In all of the interviews with all of the psychiatrists, this is the closest Dana ever came to expressing remorse. Dana said she quickly overcame that feeling and visited a beauty salon and a grocery store that afternoon.

Dana minimized her conduct during June's murder with the first psychiatrist, Dr. Kania. But she told him that she "woke up" during a scuffle with Dorinda, something she didn't repeat to the other two psychiatrists. She told Dr. Kania that Dorinda looked like her mother, "like a fat barfly . . . She had a fat barfly look, a pathetic barfly trying to look happy . . . acting like she was real important." Dana said Dorinda "put her down" and made her feel insignificant. Afterward, she said she tried not to think about the attack, but felt depressed and "lashed out in anger" at anything that got in her way.

When she was interviewed by Dr. Forbes, Dana said Dorinda "struck a pose. She gave me a look saying, 'Can I help you?' She comes up and crosses her arms in a condescending manner. I felt sick in my stomach. I wanted to vomit. I wanted her to die." Dana told Dr. Forbes that she saw the "creepy feminine image" in Dorinda's face and after she showed Dana some frames that Dana didn't like, she slipped the rope around Dorinda's neck when her back was turned.

When Dr. Rogers interviewed Dana, she no longer tried to reason that Dorinda's appearance as a "fat barfly" had motivated her to kill.

In answer to specific questions from Dr. Rogers, Dana claimed Dorinda handed her the key to the cash register that was on the plastic coiled ring and that she took nothing else, in conflict with Dorinda's account that Dana had taken the key ring off her wrist and fled with $20 from Dorinda's purse and $25 from the cash register. While discussing this incident, Dana told Dr. Rogers that she put the key ring in her purse, in contrast to reports from officers searching Dana's house, who said the key ring was hanging from a hook on the entertainment center. "They lied about that key being on the side of my entertainment center when it was right there in my purse. There's no reason to lie about a stupid thing like that." She also claimed she had close to $2,700 in her purse. When Julie Bennett went through Dana's purse, she found $1,900 still in the wrapping from Dora's bank and $170 in Dana's wallet.

"They stole cash out of my purse and underreported what they said they found," Dana said. Dana told Dr. Rogers that she got $50 in cash over the total of her purchase every time she used one of Dora's checks, collecting a total of $600 to $700. If that were true, Dana would have had to have visited up to 14 different stores between the time she killed Dora and the time she was arrested, which conflicts with the task force's account of her activities after the murder, the store receipts indicating the additional cash received at the time of purchase, and each of Dora's numbered checks that were recovered, showing the cash received over the amount of purchase at each store. The location of the cash register key ring was noted and photographed when the house was searched. The desire for Dana to sling mud at the police might be explained by Dana's history of striking out at those who hurt her.

Dana told Dr. Rogers that she had been despondent the day Dora was killed and had gone to see her father. When she found he wasn't home, she drove toward Sun City and claims she "blanked out" while driving.

"I turned down a street I never turned down before and got lost," Dana said. "All the houses look the same, they all have gravel in front. I saw one house with the garage door open so I stopped there."

Dana said Dora invited her in when she told her that she was lost. Dana claimed that the church-going widow sighed and said, "I don't have time for this," but walked to the back of the house to fetch a Thomas Guide map book.

"So, she turned her back on me, continuing to bitch [while we were] somewhere in the back of the house. I choked her with the phone cord," Dana said, adding that Dora made her feel the same way her mother did when she was yelling at her.

"I had that overwhelming, like, detached feeling," she said. "Stupid as it sounds, I felt hurt and rejected. Actually, all of them were kind of like that, but when I look at them, that is so stupid, but that is how I felt."

"Then what?" Dr. Rogers asked.

"I hit her in the head with an iron."

"And then?"

"That was it. Her purse was on the right next to where we were. I took her wallet, the checkbook and passbook in it and I left."

"Then what happened?"

"I had this overwhelming need to shop. I went to every grocery store in town, filled up my whole car with stuff, stuff I didn't even need, cake decorations, Baxter's soup."

"What was going on when you used the iron?"

"I don't know," Dana said. "Why did I grab the wine bottle? The same thing, I don't know why."

"Was she facing you when you used the iron?"

"She was already down on the ground."

"I would have to assume they were giving you a little fight," said Dr. Rogers, who knew from examining the police reports and crime-scene photos that her victims desperately fought for their lives.

"No," Dana said. "As I remember, it was not much of a fight."

Dana told the psychiatrist that she put the iron in the sink and rinsed off her hands with a towel and water. By the time Dr. Rogers asked her about where she'd shopped that afternoon, Dana had forgotten her accusation the police about taking $600 to $700 in cash from her purse. Dana recounted her visits to the bank, grocery stores, the stationery store and the health food store, which accurately accounted for the cash found in Dana's purse and corresponded with the receipts and the the checks belonging to Dora that Dana used.

With Dr. Kania, Dana's story of killing Dora had huge

gaps. She said she was "in a haze" after leaving her father's house, got lost and felt "pulled to" Dora's house. She told him that she didn't recall exactly what happened, except that she stopped to ask for directions. When Dora told her that she was "in a hurry" and "didn't have time for this," Dana told her that she recalls seeing the back of the victim's head as they walked down the hallway and next recalls seeing Dora on the ground and seeing an iron on an open shelf in the hallway. She told Dr. Kania that she recalled picking up the iron, but didn't remember hitting Dora with it, saying she "woke up" after the murder. Her next memory was seeing the bloody iron in the sink, but she didn't look at Dora's lifeless body on the floor. At the time, Dana said, she'd thought, "There is nothing you can do with this person . . . she's beyond help."

Despite being "spaced out, like it was surrealistic," and feeling grief and tremendous sickness, Dana managed to find Dora's bankbook, checkbook, and other credit cards, which Dana said were conveniently sticking out of Dora's purse, got back into her car, and somehow found her way to the local shopping center. Within minutes of killing Dora, Dana's alleged confusion didn't prevent her from finding Dora's bank and signing Dora's name to her checks. She told Dr. Kania that she'd had an overwhelming need to "stock up" because she sensed doom.

In her interview with Dr. Forbes, Dana said the "creepy female image" was superimposed on Dora's face after Dora allegedly said that she "didn't have time" to help her. When Dora turned her back, Dana said she became enraged and used the phone cord and threw Dora to the floor. In this version, Dana remembered reaching for the iron and bludgeoning Dora with it. She told Dr. Forbes that she bought a briefcase because she recalled that her mother wore a uniform and carried a briefcase to a Scientology meeting, something she didn't tell the other psychiatrists.

Dana told Dr. Rogers that after the attack on Dora, she realized she had a "major problem" and wanted to get some counseling.

"I needed help, but no one was willing to listen to me."

When Dr. Rogers asked Dana whether she'd considered confiding in Jim or her parents, Dana reversed herself and said she was "petrified" about talking to anyone and said that she didn't trust Jim. "I didn't want to talk to him. I was very evasive." She said she couldn't unload "something like this" on her parents.

"You realized there was a problem?" Dr. Rogers asked.

"Yeah, all of it was a big cry for help in a sick way," Dana said. "Yeah, I have this problem; I don't know exactly what it is. I sure would like to fix it; I would like to feel it is fixable.

"I'm not quite sure what it will take, but I really want to get through this. It's killing me."

DECEMBER 29, 1996

Your Honor,

My mother, Dora Beebe, was killed March 16, 1994. The after-effects of that death have plagued our family, wreaking hardship, illnesses, sleeplessness and horror-haunted mental images of how she must have suffered. We all, after nearly three years of living with an unfinished tragedy, need closure. We need to put it behind us.

The trial of Dana Gray, accused of my mother's murder, has been postponed again and again. The defense has obtained many continuances, and we feel that the time has come to put an end to them.

Please do what you can to see that further continuances are minimized and give the survivors (who are also victims) a chance to resume our lives.

Sincerely yours,
Julia Whitcombe

It's hard to explain years of delay to witnesses and relatives of victims as the judicial system lumbers along at a glacial cadence. As the years passed, Rich Bentley periodically received calls from relatives of the victims asking when the trial would start. Trial dates were set and continued at the request of defense, and to the dismay of the victims' relatives who found the process never-ending, emotionally exhausting, and nightmarish. Judges, defense lawyers and prosecutors understand why this is so. It's the nature of the defense, in most cases and particularly in death penalty cases, to delay as long as you can in hope that the passage of time will dull the memory of witnesses and increase the chances that evidence will be misplaced or lost. A defense attorney would rather not risk having jurors see a tearful, frightened Dorinda Hawkins pointing a trembling finger at her attacker just a few months after she was left for dead at the back of an antique store. Why not let time heal the victim's psyche, so when Dorinda finally faces her assailant years later, she is composed, unafraid, and perhaps unable to remember each detail of the attack? Trying a heinous, sensational case shortly after a highly publicized crime spree—particularly when fear of the killings is still fresh in the minds of potential jurors—fairly guarantees a conviction and the harshest possible sentence. In Dana's case, each new murder and attack was well publicized, and with the publicity came a steady increase in public fear and pressure on authorities and law enforcement to catch the killer. It was the same group of individuals from whom jurors would be selected to sit in judgment of Dana. It is to the defense's benefit to allow a generous cushion of time to soften the public's memory and to blunt the emotional impact should they be called as jurors.

Once Bentley indicated that he would seek to send Dana to Death Row, he knew the case would automatically slow to a crawl. A defendant facing capital punishment is automatically allowed to have two defense attorneys—at taxpayer expense—to share the increase in work inherent in death cases. Another reason for delays was a series of requests for discovery, i.e., that the prosecution turn over to the defense all of the police and lab reports, evidence logs and every piece of evidence and paperwork the prosecution intends to use against a defendant. Stu Sachs often sought delays in order to obtain and review the materials turned over by the prosecution. After Dana's insanity plea there was another delay as each side appointed experts to examine Dana and render their opinions. As more time went by, the second defense attorney left the practice of law to became a court commissioner, a position similar to a judge. Another attorney had to be appointed to assist Stu and needed months to become familiar with the case. There were more delays when the defense attorneys had to try other cases, including another death penalty case that had been scheduled before Dana's trial. Then the defense filed motions to cease the photocopying of Dana's mail and the taping of her visits. Dana's case was then assigned to a different judge in another courtroom.

Bentley was ready to try the case and was prepared to deal with an insanity defense. It had been no surprise that Dr. Forbes and Dr. Kania had found that Dana was legally insane at the time of her actions. In his 23-page report, Dr. Kania concluded that Dana was suffering from severe, psychotic depression tinged with alcoholism, though he hedged his opinion as to whether she was aware of her criminal acts. "There is indication that at times she was aware of what she had done, but at other times she experienced a sense of unreality and estrangement from her actions . . . She took the wallets of two of these women in an action reminiscent of her actions as a child when she took money from her own mother's wallet when she had been mistreated by her mother." Dr. Forbes wrote a 29-page report finding that Dana had an "unspecified disassociative disorder" coupled by depression and alcoholism and a series of "severe losses." "She had absolutely no awareness of the enormity of her offense as she acted on bizarre distortions of the identity of older women, all the result of earlier maternal abuse."

Bentley had tried two insanity cases to completion, and in both cases, the defense attorneys had hired Dr. Kania, who concluded that the defendants were insane. Bentley cross-examined Dr. Kania both times and found that he wasn't even using the latest forensic definition of legal insanity, but was quoting outdated case law. He was aware that Dr. Kania was often the expert of choice among defense attorneys and that he usually found that defendants were insane. Bentley was not familiar with Dr. Forbes, but he disputed both experts' opinions. If Dana had no awareness that her actions were wrong, why would she wash off the blood after the killings? If she didn't know what she was doing, how did she find banks, stores and restaurants so quickly after the killings? How did she know that she needed to sign the victims' names on the receipts? If Dana had no awareness of her actions, why did she cease her attack on Dorinda after Dorinda's pleas to spare her life because she had eight children?

Bentley found more satisfying answers in Dr. Rogers' hefty and comprehensive report. At 163 pages, it not only offered a thorough examination of Dana's mental state, but discussed and dissected the other experts' diagnoses and compared the consistency of Dana's answers to their questions and psychological tests with answers Dana gave to her, as well as follow-up questions to Dana and a comparison of Dana's behavior with what others observed during her childhood, at work, and at home. Dr. Rogers found that while Dana was most certainly a disturbed individual who suffered from depression and abused alcohol, she was sane.

One of the biggest hurdles in reaching a diagnosis was evaluating the veracity of a defendant who clearly had a stake in the findings and who had been first evaluated by "friendly" defense experts before an expert examined her at the behest of the prosecution. Dr. Rogers said she sympathized with Dana's dilemma.

"I think this lady has really struggled with how much to be honest because obviously her life is on the line," Dr. Rogers wrote. "Overall, I think she has done about as well or better than many individuals facing the death penalty—a lot more open than many, since some defendants, of course, never even acknowledge their crimes. But she was a lot more unreliable, distorting or selective in her reporting than I have seen in cases which were ultimately adjudicated as insanity."

She noted that Dana's alleged loss of memory of the murders when discussing them with Dr. Kania seemed to have disappeared by the time Dr. Rogers interviewed her. "This most likely reflected some kind of systematic and self-serving withholding of information rather than actual loss of and return of memory . . . I think she started out feigning some memory lapses which, to her credit, she later thought better of doing and gave up."

Dr. Rogers was also suspect of Dana's statements that she'd felt hurt, insulted and rejected by the victims just prior to the attacks. They conflicted with Dana's own answers on tests and interviews with people familiar with Dana's inclination to strike back with "castrating zingers," to never let people take advantage of her and to project blame when in conflict with others. The psychiatrist questioned Dana's reliability regarding the severity of the abuse she'd suffered from her mother, reports of suicide and suicidal thoughts, the history of her symptoms and her mental state. "The noted fluctuations [about her history of symptoms and mental state] appeared to be situational and/or a result of attempting to deny or exaggerate to herself and others about the severity of her disturbance at various times, perhaps in part to make herself feel better, or to obtain empathy from others, or to find an explanation that would make it easier to live with what has happened, or to build a rationalization for her offenses."

She noted that Dr. Kania's diagnosis treated seriously Dana's claim that she was suffering from hallucinations, particularly hearing voices. Dr. Rogers found that this was not noted by either of the two psychiatrists who saw Dana prior to the offenses in 1993 and early 1994, was not noted or mentioned by Dana during her multiple mental health screenings after her incarceration, and was not even noted by Dr. Kania until after he had been seeing Dana for five months. After Dana complained of hallucinations and delusions in October 1995, she was examined by a jail psychiatrist with negative results. She also denied having auditory hallucinations to Dr. Rogers, who said Dana's answers on exhaustive psychological testing were not consistent with hallucinations or delusional thinking. The "voices" Dana reported hearing, Dr. Rogers said, "were a product of her own mind and were internal conversations and did not reflect a major loss of reality."

The most curious aspect of Dana's crimes—her choice of elderly women as victims—was explored by Dr. Rogers. Dana admitted that she'd never linked her crimes with any maternal issues until after Dr. Kania "really, really dug" and encouraged her to consider that possibility.

"While she saw the victims as similar to her mother in various ways, and they 'reminded' her of her mother, she didn't believe they were her mother. There was not the precipitous loss of reality testing of a delusional person. Most crimes perpetrated as a product of hallucinations are in reaction to fear of being harmed . . . which was not the case

in these crimes, nor had she suffered any 'command hallucinations' telling her to perform the crimes."

The maternal trigger seemed suspect to Dr. Rogers after
looking at how Dana first chose victims with clear family
ties. When Dana thought that might focus attention on her,
Dr. Rogers suggested, she switched to strangers.

Dana had told each of the examiners about voices telling
her to stock up, in reference to what she claimed were food
shortages as a child, but neither her brothers nor the boarder
Michael Carpenter recalled a lack of food. Dr. Rogers said
Dana later admitted that they were not actually voices, but
an "inner need." She added that luxury items like fancy
foods, clothing, perfume and toys "hardly constitute things
one would be stocking up for the holocaust. Rather, the
procured items were consistent with her past reported shopping patterns . . . She made hair appointments, went to restaurants, and had a massage. The alleged nihilistic delusions
about needing to shop because of some feelings that the end
was near or the holocaust was coming and she needed to
prepare for it simply have little credence . . ." In interviews,
her family and friends reported her preoccupation with
money, her propensity to buy what she wanted when she
wanted it and her persistent and manipulative pursuit of a
great aunt to change her will. Court records indicated that
she'd been having financial problems since 1988, which
points to Dana's focus "on her own wants and lack of concern about the needs and feelings of others to the point of
ruthlessness," Dr. Rogers wrote.

The question of whether Dana knew what she was doing
at the time of the murders was answered by Dr. Rogers'
examination of the crimes. The use of multiple means to kill
a person, she wrote, "is more indicative of a greater degree
of sustained intentionality, deliberation and malice in killing
than crimes where one method only was used. The repeated
efforts to choke Hawkins, where she reported that she nearly
passed out or did pass out several times is also indicative
of a sustained intention to deliberately kill." Dana said she
had at one point calmed down from an earlier insult before
entering June's house, but got angry again, which Dr. Rogers said suggested deliberation rather than a build-up of anger and loss of control. When she took June's credit cards,

she selected those within a close geographic radius and left behind those from JCPenney and the Broadway department stores, showing that she consciously sorted through the cards rather than just grabbing them, as she claimed.

In the attack on Dorinda, the limited conversation between her and Dana was enough to suggest that Dana never lost awareness of what was going on during the attack. Even when she entered the store, Dana asked if Dorinda was "alone again," which suggests premeditation and an awareness of what she was about to do. Dana's awareness of her crimes was also apparent in the fact that she left no fingerprints, cleaned blood from herself, threw away June's credit card when she was done with it, hid credit cards of Dora Beebe's in a drawer at home and knew that she had to sign the victims' names on the credit card receipts and checks. Dana had expressed to the psychiatrist her surprise at the time that the bank teller didn't ask for ID when she withdrew $2,000 from Dora's account, a clear acknowledgment of wrong-doing. Shortly after the murders, Dana had the presence of mind to lie to a cashier who recognized the name and asked if Dora was all right. Dana had replied that Dora wasn't feeling well.

Dr. Rogers had trouble determining the degree to which Dana's drinking affected her when the offenses were committed because Dana gave contradictory accounts, sometimes grossly exaggerating and sometimes minimizing her alcohol intake. Dr. Rogers suggested that Dana could have consumed alcohol when the offenses were committed, which would have heightened her impulsiveness, irritability and inclination to project blame. Dr. Rogers also had difficulty sorting out the conflicting and contradictory information Dana gave about her suicidal thoughts in her personal history to her and the other psychiatrists, and also to jail psychologists. None of Dana's friends—including her best friend—and no family members recalled any suicide attempts or threats.

Dr. Rogers concluded by saying that her pattern of crimes was consistent with a serial killer, albeit a very unusual one with three clear psychological triggers: a desire for money, a desire for power and domination, and displaced family anger.

Simple maternal hatred didn't fully explain Dana's homicidal rage. She suggested taking a longer look at Dana's childhood pattern of hurting people when she felt humiliated or didn't get the attention she felt she deserved. Cutting holes in her mother's dress, wetting her half-brother's bed and trashing her teacher's classroom involved "violence" toward inanimate objects, and reflected choices she made as a child.

"These childhood 'crimes' parallel her adult crimes to a greater degree than the thefts [of money] from her mother . . . These incidents of acting out include similar psychological elements as these crimes, of feeling put down and enraged over loss of face, of feeling humiliated . . ." Dr. Rogers noted that individuals who face far more severe childhood deprivations and abuse also become enraged, but do not kill people. In addition, the vast majority of truly mentally ill people do not kill.

Rather than looking at problems with her mother, Dr. Rogers suggests looking at Dana's bank balance at the times of the murders. "Spending money was one of the ways Dana Gray habitually dealt with the void of her unmet emotional deficits and narcissistic need to fulfill herself through possessions. She reported a childhood of both being spoiled and also financial deprivation. As an adult, she had become used to buying what she wanted." Even after she became unemployed, she purchased golf lessons, bought a $1,000 mountain bike, redecorated her home, placed Jason in a private preschool and continued with her hair and manicuring appointments.

Ultimately, it wasn't money or unresolved maternal issues that motivated Dana to kill. Although Dana hit the stores within minutes of her crimes, shopping wasn't the sole or even the primary goal in each crime. Dana's satisfaction, Dr. Rogers found, came from domination, power, and control over her victims.

It makes sense, Rich Bentley thought after reading Dr. Rogers' report.

Given the multiple modes of death and the prolonged struggles with the victims, Dana was a classic power killer who enjoyed watching her victims suffer as she extinguished them, like a child making a bug squirm under a magnifying glass. After years as a nurse, Dana had become desensitized to the sight of blood and had no doubt seen patients die. What Bentley couldn't fathom was how she left these very bloody, very messy crime scenes and went shopping for hours without so much as a speck of blood on her, or at least none that people noticed.

As the months rolled by, he had watched the pile of letters to and from Dana pile up in his office. He had read through a few of them and had discerned a few that might be useful in showing that Dana was not insane. Now he was accumulating letters from the victims' families. They wanted Dana brought to justice. Bentley sympathized with them. He hoped that the fusillade of letters to the judge would do some good. When he had gotten another call from the Beebe family weeks before, they'd suggested writing a letter and he agreed, thinking it could help move things along if the judge knew that they, too, were waiting for their day in court.

Bentley picked up the bundle of letters from the Beebes, thinking it was tragic that Dana was so wrapped up in herself that she chose to hurt truly innocent victims that were so cherished by their families.

"I was always glad to bring my friends home, when I was a child, because I was so proud of my mother," wrote Julia Whitcombe:

> She was pretty and funny and warm, and a better cook than anyone else's mother. One of my friends recently told me how my mother was the only person who made her feel pretty as a child. She made our clothes, and sometimes fashioned the patterns as well.
>
> Her family was my mother's principal preoccupation . . . but she had other interests. She could make anything grow in her garden, she knew who'd won the latest golf tournament, the football, baseball or basketball game. She was up to date on the news and informed about local and national concerns. Nobody made a better pie. Her quilts were lovely. Music and friendship with Lou Dormand filled much of her

life in recent times, as did caring for the most pampered cat this side of the Mississippi.

Our entertainment consisted almost entirely of family visits to all the sisters and grandmothers on both sides of the family. In the American Legion Hall and the Church, we had pot luck dinners, went to the dances and sang, sang, sang. Mother's voice, a sweet soprano, sings on in my memory. She always sang to us—silly songs, old songs. I sing them now to my grandchildren.

As my sister and I went through the house after Mother was killed, we encountered little pieces of paper, in her handwriting, of quotes or maxims that had been meaningful to her. I liked this one, "They say 'don't look back when you get old' but I spend a lot of time doing it anyway. Maybe if I'd known that when I was young, I'd done a lot of exciting things so I'd have better old lady dreams."

I wish her old lady dreams had not ended in a nightmare.

WEDNESDAY, SEPTEMBER 9, 1998 10:30 A.M.

"Miss Gray, I'm going go over the charges. If you have any questions, please ask."

Judge Dennis Myers looked down from the bench at the accused killer in the blue jumpsuit, huddled with her lawyer. During her stay in jail, Dana's weight had ballooned upwards of fifty pounds. Her brown hair was now completely gray, the curls just brushing her shoulders. The gallery was half-filled with weeping family members holding hands in the front row. Behind them were an assortment of reporters and photographers.

"Your attorney has indicated that you wish to withdraw your plea of not guilty by reason of insanity and enter a plea of guilty to each of the charges in accordance with a plea agreement. In exchange for your plea of guilty, the district attorney will recommend a sentence of life in prison without possibility of parole. Is that your understanding?"

Dana nodded her head and said, "Yes." It was barely audible.

"In count one, you are charged with Penal Code Section 187, the willful, deliberate and premeditated murder of a human being, to wit, June Roberts. To count one, how do you plead?"

The courtroom was pin-drop silent.

"Guilty."

The relatives of June Roberts let out a sigh. Their hands were now clasped in a human chain across the front row, their heads bowed. Van Owen, his knuckles white from grasping his wife's hand, lifted his tear-stained face heavenward. As the judge carefully read each count, the victims sobbed silently, releasing emotions they had been holding back for years.

Dana's trial had been scheduled to begin September 8. But one week before, Stuart Sachs had called Rich Bentley and told him that Dana wanted to plead guilty to everything in exchange for life in prison without parole. The prosecution would be spared the expense and the victims the emotional trauma of a trial. Dana would avoid rolling the dice before a jury, which could send her to Death Row. Each side threw in a sweetener. Bentley agreed that he would not file the Norma Davis homicide against Dana. Sachs agreed that Dana would waive her appellate rights, meaning that she would forfeit her right to appeal any aspect of the case. That meant the case would be over for good. Bentley suspected the defense might have been motivated to take a plea by the Dora Buenrostro trial. That August, Riverside County jurors convicted the 39-year-old woman of killing her own children, rejected an insanity defense and sent her to Death Row. She was the first woman sentenced to die from Riverside County. Bentley didn't know how much of an effect it had on a decision to offer a plea agreement, but he was looking at ending the case on the eve of trial.

Bentley had called the relatives and told them about the offer in order to get some feedback, and found them grateful that Dana would finally admit her crimes. For them, it would be a relief to end the case. In a meeting with District Attorney Grover Trask, Bentley and Sachs, they weighed the support from the relatives' families with the question of whether Riverside County jurors would recommend a death verdict for Dana, who had lived a crime-free life until the murders. Trask had agreed to accept Sachs' plea bargain.

Just a few feet away, Dana sat at the counsel table with her back to the grieving relatives, the hard, metal chain wrapped around her hips and binding her ankles as three deputies stood watch. As the victims' families silently sobbed, Dana used her little girl voice, saying the same word over and over again:

"Guilty."

"Hey, Joe, we had your girl in here today," the bailiff squawked over the police radio.

"What're you talking about?" said Greco, cruising in his patrol car.

"Didn't you handle the Dana Gray case?"

"Yeah, that was my case."

"She pleaded guilty this morning. Good job."

Greco was silent for a moment. Now working for the Riverside Sheriff's Department, he was on routine patrol in Moreno Valley, a suburb of Riverside County. Greco used to work patrol with Dave Kirkendall until he was transferred and became a bailiff in Judge Myers' courtroom. When Kirkendall saw Dana pleading guilty, he had the dispatcher patch him through to Greco in his patrol car. Greco couldn't believe that no one had told him that Dana was going to take a plea. He would have wanted to be there.

"OK," Greco said. "Thanks."

It was over. No fanfare, no trial, no testimony, no tense moments waiting for the jury's verdict. On one hand, it was anti-climactic, but on the other, it felt satisfying that the case was over. Greco slid the radio mic into its slot and drove to the nearest satellite police station, where he used a land line to call Bentley, who filled him in on the plea. Bentley told him about Sachs' offer to plead to everything in exchange for LWOP. The DA's office gave up charges for Norma's murder and the defense gave up the right to appeal. Bentley said it all happened pretty quick. Greco was so excited, he had to go tell someone. He felt like celebrating. He drove back to his station and told his sergeant and they talked about the case and some of the difficulties he had had with the investigation. Greco left after a few minutes to go back to work. While he felt happy and satisfied, a part of him felt hollow.

Greco got back into his patrol car to think. Over the years, bits and pieces of the case had always been in the back of his mind. What nagged him the most was Dora's death. Could he have arrested Dana any sooner? If they had arrested Dana sooner, would Dora still be alive? Could he have moved any faster? He had been haunted by Dora's murder and felt partially responsible for her death, replaying the events of that day over and over again in his mind, starting with Jeri's phone call and ending with Dana's arrest, trying to see if he could have done anything differently. But after looking at the timelines, he realized that by the time he got off the phone with Jeri, Dana was gone. Even if he had left his office at the Perris station and driven straight to Dana's house, she would not have been there anyway. He knew it was no comfort to Dora's relatives, but at least Dana did not kill anyone else and would never have the opportunity to hurt anyone again.

Then there was Norma's murder. Greco never understood why Bentley didn't file murder charges against Dana. There was never any question about who killed Norma. It wasn't a whodunit. But since the case was never filed, Dana was never formally held to answer for that charge, leaving Norma's death in a void. Greco considered Dana's acceptance of the plea agreement a tacit acceptance of the killing. Besides, if Dana wasn't responsible for Norma's murder, why was it made a condition of the plea bargain? Agreeing not to file charges for Norma's murder was the prosecution's only concession in the plea bargain, and by Greco's reasoning, Dana had admitted it.

Greco's thoughts wound toward the victims and the domino effect the case had had on everyone associated with it. When Norma died, it sent Jeri's daughter, Susie, over the edge. Dana could never legally be held responsible for Susie's death, but even Jeri thought that the person who killed Norma also killed Susie. He heard that Alice Williams, Norma's friend, had passed away several months after Norma's death. Greco knew that she had been terribly shaken by Norma's death. It didn't seem fair that any of the victims, from Norma to Dora to Alice to Susie, had to die like that. Greco wondered about Dora's beau, Louis Dormand. How many others were there? Was Dorinda ever able to put this behind her? What about the grief-stricken, sleepless nights that relatives and friends of the victims had to endure for the rest of their lives? Dana's plea was one small comfort, but it could never replace what she took from them forever. Profound, prolonged suffering doesn't grab headlines like a quick murder.

Now it was over. Dana was not going to walk away from this and she would never get out to hurt anyone else. Greco felt satisfied that he was able to be part of it, but he knew he would never stop wondering if he could have done more or solved the case sooner.

A few months later, Greco paid a visit to Russell and Jeri to see how they were doing. Russell looked much better. The last time Greco had seen him, he was tense, tired and weak. Now he was cordial and calm and seemed optimistic, and offered Greco a drink. Dana's plea was well behind them and she was already in prison serving her life sentence. Even though Russell still cursed Bentley, he seemed happy about the plea bargain and understood that Dana would be behind bars forever.

"Her life's all screwed up anyway," Russell told Greco, sitting on the same couch he had when he used to visit Jeri during the investigation. "She threw her life away. I don't know what happened. I don't know where I went wrong and how she got so—bad.

"I wish there was something I could have done to help her."

Greco didn't know what to say, so he just let Russell talk.

"I'm not angry with you," Russell said. "You were just doing your job.

"I know she's not innocent. I just don't want her to die."

Hate the sin, love the sinner. Greco knew that Russ loved his daughter unconditionally no matter what she'd done. Greco personally thought Dana deserved the death penalty. But he knew that if Dana had been sentenced to die, it would have killed Russell. Russell was happy because he could still see her and talk to her on the phone and tell her that he loved her, a gift Dana had stripped from the victims' relatives.

As he was getting ready to leave, Greco glanced up and saw the same clown drawing he'd seen hanging for years in their living room. It was a dark drawing and the clown seemed oddly ominous. Greco had heard that Dana was pretty good at drawing clowns while she was in jail and wondered if it was one that Dana had drawn or had given to them. Greco said his good-byes to Russ and Jeri as he headed out the door.

He knew there was a reason he always hated clowns.

EPILOGUE

Several years after the conclusion of this case, the City Council of Perris, facing a budget crisis, disbanded its police department. Detective Joseph Greco is now working for the Riverside County Sheriff's Department.

Detective Chris Antoniadas took a medical retirement, started his own private detective firm and quickly attracted a number of high-profile corporate clients.

Deputy District Attorney Rich Bentley is currently trying high-profile cases with the Riverside District Attorney's Office.

Detective James McElvain is working for the Riverside Sheriff's Department, and Officer Wyatt McElvain is employed as a community service officer.

In accordance with her plea agreement, Dana Sue Gray is currently serving a life sentence at the California Women's Prison in Chowchilla, California. She is not, and never will be, eligible for parole.

NEXT STOP, MURDER...

THE RAILROAD KILLER

The Shocking True Story of Eight Gruesome
Murders and the Man Suspected of
Committing Them

WENSLEY CLARKSON

Angel Maturino Resendez is described by most who know him as
a quiet, polite, soft-spoken man, a loving husband and father to a
baby daughter. But law enforcement officials suspect that he
might be responsible for upwards of eight grisly and random
killings in a span of two years, all of which occurred near the
southwest railroad line that the killer is believed to have ridden on
his twisted murder spree. In each case, the same mode of attack—
and the same slow and painful death—appears to have been used,
pointing to the methodical slayings of a serial killer. Is Angel
Maturino Resendez the ruthless Railroad Killer—a sadistic slayer
who led police on one of the longest manhunts in history?
Bestselling true crime author Wensley Clarkson digs deep into the
heart of a horrifying murder case to uncover some stunning
answers.

AVAILABLE FROM ST. MARTIN'S PAPERBACKS
WHEREVER BOOKS ARE SOLD